GUILTY BUT

INSANE

J. C. BOWEN-COLTHURST: VILLAIN OR VICTIM?

JAMES W. TAYLOR

MERCIER PRESS

IRISH PUBLISHER – IRISH STORY

MERCIER PRESS
Cork
www.mercierpress.ie

© James W. Taylor, 2016

ISBN: 978 1 78117 421 0

10 9 8 7 6 5 4 3 2 1

A CIP record for this title is available from the British Library

Printed and bound in the EU.

CONTENTS

John Colthurst Bowen-Colthurst.

This bookplate shows the badge of the Royal Irish Rifles above the family arms of Captain Bowen-Colthurst – an amalgamation of the Bowen and Colthurst coats of arms. The Latin motto translates as 'Just and Resolute' and comes from Horace, *Carmina* (III, 3.1): 'The just man who is resolute will not be turned from his purpose, either by the misdirected rage of his fellow citizens, or by the threats of an imperious tyrant.' Colthurst loosely translated this as 'The Triumph of Right'.

ACKNOWLEDGEMENTS

Special thanks and appreciation must first be conveyed to Georgiana Bowen-Colthurst Sutherlin of Spokane, Washington State, USA, for details furnished about her parents, for access to their papers, for trusting me with them and for answering the many questions I put to her. Her co-operation was vital and on no occasion did she attempt to influence my conclusions. Her husband, Douglas Sutherlin, told some wonderful anecdotes about his father-in-law. Dr Francis Sheehy Skeffington, of Cambridge, England, made many constructive comments and suggestions in teasing out the truth. Dr Paul W. Miller, MD, BCH, BAO, DMH, MRCPsych, a consultant psychiatrist in Belfast, gave very generously of his time in reading the manuscript, meeting me to discuss the case and providing a professional opinion of the character and mental condition of Captain Bowen-Colthurst. My thanks to the Irish Military Archives for the use of their resources. Extracts from the Sheehy Skeffington papers, the property of the National Library of Ireland, have been reproduced with the kind permission of the Library and the Sheehy Skeffington family. Thanks also to Mary Feehan, Wendy Logue, Elaine Towns and all at Mercier Press.

Séamus Moriarty extracted much of the information held at the National Library of Ireland, reviewed earlier drafts of the manuscript and made several constructive suggestions. Dr Donal Hall and Kevin Myers were invaluable advisers. Dan Malloy carried out the tedious task of proofreading several versions of the story and offered many useful ideas. My good friend Gerry Murphy very kindly put the maps into a presentable format and improved the quality of the photographs. The late John Fitzwalter Butler, 29th Lord Dunboyne, was most obliging in furnishing information about his family.

Mention must also be made of the assistance given by: (*in Ireland*) Charles Callan, John Culleton, Liam Dodd, Jim Doyle, Commandant Ultan P. Edge (Press Officer, 2nd Eastern Brigade), Carol and Cormac Egan, Larry Gittens, Jim Herlihy, Moira Hodge, Jim Hoey, Commandant Victor Laing (Irish Military Archives), Patrick Hugh Lynch, Noel McDonnell (Cathal Brugha Barracks), Dominic McGinley, Bryan Mac-Mahon, Major General P. F. Nowlan, Major General The O'Morchoe, CBE, CB, MBE, Colonel John J. O'Reilly (Executive Officer, 2nd Eastern Brigade), Michael Pegum, Lieutenant Colonel Brian Reade (Officer Commanding 2nd Infantry Battalion and Cathal Brugha Barracks), Neil Richardson, Liam Riordan, Angela Ryan, Richie Ryan, Alan Sheehy-Skeffington, Micheline Sheehy Skeffington, Tricia Sheehy Skeffington, Adam Taylor, Emma Taylor, Aoife Torpey (OPW), the staff of the Gilbert Library, the National Library of Ireland and the Wexford County Library; (*in Northern Ireland*) Colonel W. M. Campbell, OBE (Royal Irish Regiment), Colonel W. R. H. Charley, OBE, DL, Richard Doherty, Keith Haines, Captain Jaki Knox, MBE (Royal Ulster Rifles [RUR] Regimental Museum), Tommy McClimonds, Amanda Moreno (Head of Collections, Museums of the Royal Irish Regiment), Terence Nelson (RUR Museum), Deaglán Ó Mocháin, Bobby Rainey, Derek Smyth, OBE, David Truesdale and Major Roy Walker, MBE (RUR Association); (*in Great Britain*) David Ball (Leinster Regiment Association), Colonel David Benest, OBE (Defence Academy), Skeena Bowen-Colthurst, James P. Kelleher (Royal Fusiliers Regimental Museum), Major Denis P. Lucy,

Professor Thomas McAlinden (Hull University), Captain James McNeish, Alastair Massie (National Army Museum), Hugh Pitfield, Major General Corran Purdon, CBE, MC, CPM, Eileen Sheehy Skeffington, Alex Shooter, Colin Smythe, Mr L. A. Spring (Surrey History Centre) and Tom Tulloch-Marshall; (*in Canada*) Annette and Matthew Bowen-Colthurst, Michael Bowen-Colthurst, Jean Eiers-Page (Prince Rupert City and Regional Archives), John Gilinsky, Jim Hume (*Times Colonist*), Rod Link (Editor, *Terrace Standard*), Joyce Linell and Elida Peers (Sooke Region Museum and Visitor Centre), Ruth Manning and Fern Berg Webber; (*in the USA*) Edward John 'E. J.' Sutherlin; (*in France*) Eddie Brittain and John Calder; (*in Sweden*) Martin Hugh Morris.

And finally, to my wife, Maura Ryan, who was wonderfully patient while I spent so much time on this project.

To all of these I am very grateful.

INTRODUCTION

Some years ago, when I was writing a history of the 2nd Royal Irish Rifles, I attempted to supply biographical details of the officers who served with that battalion during the Great War. It very soon became clear that one man in particular, Captain John C. Bowen-Colthurst, had had such a varied and controversial life that I would have to omit much of his story to avoid his dominating the narrative. Most of the information I found in the public domain, and especially on the Internet, reduced Captain Bowen-Colthurst to an evil or deranged British officer who murdered, or caused to be killed, at least six people during the 1916 Easter Rising, including Francis Sheehy Skeffington, Thomas Dickson, Patrick McIntyre and J. J. Coade. Conspiracy theories abound, and it is commonly believed that the British government perverted the course of justice, initially by attempting to cover up the murders he committed and then by arranging a verdict of insanity in order to avoid a death sentence.

My own earliest recollection of the name of Captain Bowen-Colthurst dates to a few months after his death, when the Irish broadcaster Telefís Éireann transmitted *Insurrection* in 1966 as part of their celebration of the fiftieth anniversary of the Rising. As a youth of twelve I was highly influenced by this television series, which glorified the heroes of the Irish Volunteers and the Irish Citizen Army. I clearly remember the representation of Bowen-Colthurst as a crazed man summarily shooting an innocent civilian in the street. Being a proud nationalist I had no reason to doubt this negative interpretation, and over the years the portrayal of Bowen-Colthurst scarcely changed. In

1981 the BBC transmitted a television docudrama entitled *The Crime of Captain Colthurst,* which was by no means a fair or accurate representation of the facts, and implied, without any of the military, political or medical files being available, that there had been a deliberate cover-up by the army and that many of the witnesses at Bowen-Colthurst's trial had committed perjury. The main sources used, apart from the transcript of the court martial and the report of the Royal Commission of Inquiry, were the accounts left by Francis Sheehy Skeffington's wife, Hanna, Sir Francis Vane and Monk Gibbon, all of which are far from impartial. In particular, Hanna Sheehy Skeffington was writing propaganda, which was quite understandable at the time, but it means that her account must be approached with some caution in terms of it being an accurate historical source. Despite this, these three sources have become the accepted foundation on which most accounts of Bowen-Colthurst's actions in Dublin have been based to date. But they are flawed in many ways, as I shall show in the following pages.

As recently as 2011, RTÉ One transmitted a television programme entitled *Réabhlóid*, about the murders, but failed to provide a balanced report, preferring instead to recycle the earlier, inaccurate accounts. Over time, by comparison, relatively little attention has been focused on the indefensible murder of at least fifteen innocent civilians in North King Street by the 2/6th South Staffordshire Regiment.

Based on the conflicting evidence uncovered during my research, I came to realise that the vilification of Bowen-Colthurst was one of the many myths surrounding the 1916 Rising, one that historians over the years had made little or no effort to critically examine. For example, descriptions in books by Max Caulfield (*The Easter Rebellion*) and Peter de Rosa

(*Rebels: The Irish Rising of 1916*) of Bowen-Colthurst's activities are taken almost verbatim from the accounts of Hanna Sheehy Skeffington, Vane and Gibbon. The Wikipedia entry for Francis Sheehy Skeffington (accessed in January 2016) includes remarks such as 'this event resulted in a Westminster-ordered cover-up' and 'a telegram was sent to Sir John Maxwell ... ordering the arrest of Bowen-Colthurst, but Maxwell refused to arrest him'.[1]

I decided that the case of Captain Bowen-Colthurst deserved deeper and more critical examination than it had received to date. Much new material emerged during my research that was fascinating and previously unknown. Accordingly, I set out to bring the true facts of the matter to the public attention. This book is not an apologia for Bowen-Colthurst's actions in Dublin; rather it is a presentation of the available evidence and allows the reader to come to his or her own informed conclusions. I freely admit that, at times, the more information I uncovered, the more perplexed I became. He was clearly a man of high intelligence and courage, impulsive and charming, yet flawed, easily influenced, vindictive and eccentric, with a mental weakness when extreme exhaustion or excitement set in. He was also a loving father and proud to be Irish, aspects of his personality that are often overlooked.

In my attempts to gain a balanced view, I was able to trace a grandson of Bowen-Colthurst living in British Columbia, Canada – Michael Bowen-Colthurst. He very kindly put me in touch with Georgiana Sutherlin, a daughter of Captain Bowen-Colthurst by his second marriage. I sent her the material I had accumulated and was not surprised that she considered it all to be very negative. However, after several exchanges of correspondence, I was able to convince her of my genuine interest in presenting a balanced view of her father. Before long

I learned that she was planning her first visit to Ireland and we arranged to meet in Belfast during autumn 2004. I was relieved to find that Gee, as she is known, is a very warm person without any airs or graces. She brought some wonderful photographs and documents from the records her father had kept. It was clear from our discussions that Gee is also a victim in this story. She vividly remembers, as a teenager, being taken out of school and placed under police protection while a search went on for an assassin who was targeting her father. Yet she adored her father, though she considered him more like a grandfather because of their age difference. Many of the anecdotes in this book originated in my conversations with her.

As our contact continued, Gee provided me with more photographs and papers, including the autobiographical notes of her mother and recollections of her cousin, Peggy Scott. Later she sent some scrapbooks and miscellaneous documents for eventual donation to the Royal Ulster Rifles Museum. The scrapbooks, about Tibet and South Africa, are predominantly newspaper cuttings and pictures from illustrated magazines, but interspersed with these are occasional gems of personal information. I must point out that Gee emphasised that I should write the story as I see it: 'Don't worry about trying to please me – there are many facts that are unpleasant but I came to grips with them many years ago. You are the first author to do any research into the facts. My father was his own worst enemy many times.'[2]

During the preparation of this book, I was asked to give a lecture on the subject in Dublin in the autumn of 2011. Needless to say, reactions were mixed. After the lecture one person introduced himself as Dr Francis Sheehy Skeffington, a grandson of Frank and Hanna. He, with his wife, Eileen, asked to see my research and, on reading it, later observed: 'I have to say that your talk and the manuscript have stimulated Eileen and me ... to look again and more critically at the history of my Sheehy Skeffington grandparents. Some of the family received wisdom has to be called into question, but I find it takes time to do that and modify long-held views without going over the top and rejecting them entirely.'[3] In subsequent correspondence he and I amicably teased out several disputed points, and where agreement could not be reached on a couple of occasions, I have included both versions of events within the narrative.

John Bowen-Colthurst is an important yet relatively un-known figure in the story of the Rising. His actions, their con-sequences, and the perceived attitude of the British authori-ties towards the murders, caused widespread disaffection in the country and were partly instrumental in shifting Irish public opinion towards independence. This is his story.

Note regarding Chapter 4

To understand the Great War chapter clearly it is necessary to know how the British Army was organised in 1914. In simple terms, the basic unit was a section; four of these made up a platoon of about fifty men; and there were four platoons in a company (which also included a company headquarters), giving a total strength of roughly 230. Four companies, designated A, B, C and D, jointly formed a battalion – the four companies were divided into platoons, numbered 1 to 16. Bowen-Colthurst was in command of C Company, 2nd Battalion, Royal Irish Rifles. The strength of a battalion was approximately 1,000 men when headquarters, transport, supplies, signallers and cooks are included. There were four battalions in a brigade and three brigades in a division. The usual ranks, from the lowest, were:

rifleman (a private); lance corporal; corporal; lance sergeant; sergeant; company sergeant major (CSM, warrant officer, 2nd Class); regimental sergeant major (warrant officer, 1st Class); second lieutenant; lieutenant; captain; major; lieutenant colonel (the commanding officer of a battalion); brigadier general (commanding a brigade); and major general (commanding a division).

Note regarding the forms of names

There is potential for confusion among the various forms of names used for individuals mentioned in the book. I have attempted to reduce this by using the surname Bowen-Colthurst in the Introduction and elsewhere if the name is used in a direct quotation, but shortening it to Colthurst throughout the rest of the narrative. Colthurst is the form generally used in original quoted matter. For Major Sir Francis Fletcher Vane, either Major Francis Vane, or simply Major Vane is the form generally adopted throughout the book. Francis and Hanna Sheehy Skeffington generally, but not always, used the non-hyphenated version of their surname. I have employed this version, which is how Francis signed the 1911 Census.

1

THE BACKGROUND AND EARLY LIFE OF JOHN BOWEN-COLTHURST

'Life', Captain John Bowen-Colthurst will remind you, 'has a big IF in the middle of it.' If things had been different, if he had never laid eyes on an Irishman named Francis Sheehy Skeffington, his life would have followed a different course ... and with mug of tea in hand he will ignore airliners overhead and cars whizzing by outside, to recall his youth in the days of good Queen Victoria.[1]

This story is set in a different era, when Ireland was an integral part of the British Empire with a society divided by religion, culture, class, property, political aspirations and wealth. The old ascendancy class was endangered by an increasingly powerful Irish middle class, which was campaigning to establish Home Rule and a Dublin parliament. This change was feared by the ruling minority, the Protestant landed elite, who could not hope to retain their power under such a regime. The Great Famine of the 1840s was within living memory and agitation for land reform was well under way through the Land League. Into this society, John Colthurst Bowen (known within the family as 'Jack') was born at 13 Morrison's Quay, Cork city, on 12 August 1880 and was baptised in the old Anglican parish church at Aghinagh. He was the eldest son of Robert Walter Travers Bowen, JP, and Georgina de Bellasis Greer, of Oakgrove, Coolalta, Killinardrish, County Cork. The Bowens were descended from Colonel Henry Bowen, a Welsh officer in Oliver Cromwell's army, who settled in Ireland in the seventeenth century. Robert was the second son of Captain John and Mary Bowen *née* Honner, of Oakgrove. Georgina was the only daughter of Alfred Greer, JP, of nearby Dripsey House. Her mother, Peggy, was the only daughter of Major John Bowen Colthurst, 97th (The Earl of Ulster's) Regiment of Foot, Dripsey Castle, Coachford, County Cork. The Bowen family name was changed to Bowen-Colthurst in 1882 under the terms of the will of Georgina's uncle, Joseph Colthurst, whereby Georgina inherited the estate of Dripsey Castle. The old MacCarthy Castle of Carrigadrohid, destroyed in 1650 by the Cromwellian army, was part of the estate and stands on a rocky island in the river beside the road bridge to Killinardrish.

In this close-knit, religious family, John's siblings were Mary Beatrice Clothilde 'Pixie', born in 1879; Peggy de Billinghurst Frieda, born in 1882; and Robert 'Robbie' MacGregor, born in 1883. Because of his height (as an adult he stood at 6 feet 3½ inches), John escaped the usual childhood bullying and from his youth took up the typical sporting pursuits of the privileged landed elite. He had a warm relationship with his father, who died in 1896 at the relatively young age of fifty-six. They would hunt, fish and shoot together as the opportunity arose.

Educated privately, including for a short period in Germany, John went on to attend public school from 1894 in the Army Class at Le Bas House, Haileybury College, Hertfordshire, learning the basics of military life and command. He always planned to pursue a military career, something that was quite common and traditional among the ascendancy class, though more commonly they took up less onerous commissions in the part-time militia battalions rather than actually joining the regular army. In 1898 he entered the Royal Military College, Sandhurst, with the aim of becoming an officer, and passed straight into the middle school, which reduced his time there from eighteen months to one year. His intermediate examination results for December 1898, in which he came second, were:

Subject	Maximum	Achieved
Military administration	300	236
Military law	300	230
Tactics	300	259
Fortification	300	218
Military topography	300	278
Languages – German	300	253
Total	**1,800**	**1,474**

Having passed out second, with honours, in June 1899, he was commissioned into the 1st Royal Irish Rifles on his nineteenth birthday, 12 August 1899. This was no mean feat: out of the 113 successful cadets only eight qualified with honours, so he would have had great expectations of an eminent career.

2

WAR IN SOUTH AFRICA

From as far back as the seventeenth century, frequent battles had raged over possession of land in South Africa. By the late nineteenth century, the British were attempting to gain the economic power of the gold mines in the Dutch Boer republics of the Orange Free State and Transvaal for their Empire. They also wanted to take over these areas so they would control a zone ranging the entire length of Africa, from Cairo to the Cape. The first Anglo-Boer clash happened between December 1880 and March 1881, and the Boers, under provocation, subsequently invaded the British areas of Natal and the Cape Province on 10 October 1899, thus initiating the Second Boer War.

At that time, the 1st Royal Irish Rifles were based at Fort William, Calcutta, the largest fortress in British India. Recently arrived Second Lieutenant Bowen-Colthurst was assigned to take 150 men from there to South Africa to reinforce the 2nd Battalion, which had suffered heavy losses at Stormberg in December, when British forces were defeated by the Boers. The draft left on 22 January 1900 for embarkation at Bombay and, on arrival in South Africa, began a short period of training with the restructured 2nd Royal Irish Rifles. The battalion then travelled northward by train to the Orange River, arriving there on 13 February. It was there that Colthurst got his first taste of action in the skirmishing at Bethulie Bridge, before the British forces continued on to Springfontein. By this time the southern part of the Orange Free State was settling down and, on 20 February, the Rifles marched eastwards to Smithfield, where they were assigned to accept surrenders and collect arms from the Boers who had returned to their farms.

------ Route taken by Bowen-Colthurst

Orders were received from headquarters on 28 March to position one company – about 120 men including Colthurst – together with twenty-five men of the mounted infantry at Helvetia for proclamation duty, outlining the terms of surrender to the local population, and to send a further three companies to Dewetsdorp. Before leaving Helvetia, Captain William J. McWhinnie, the officer in charge, heard that there was a small party of Boers in the area of Dewetsdorp and so took the precaution of bringing the small mounted infantry group under Lieutenant Charles R. W. Spedding with him. Having reached Dewetsdorp on 1 April, orders were received by telegram to move immediately to Reddersburg and await further instructions, so the main column headed off early on the morning of 2 April, in heavy rain, which slowed progress.

The move had been ordered because a Boer commander, Commandant Christiaan De Wet, had fought a successful engagement at Sannah's Post on 31 March, destroying the waterworks that supplied Bloemfontein. Lord Roberts, the British commander-in-chief, was anxious about the two Rifles detachments, especially the one at Dewetsdorp, which was only forty miles south-east of Sannah's Post, so General Sir William Gatacre, who was in Springfontein, was ordered to move the detachments back towards the line. Unfortunately, Gatacre did not mention anything about De Wet in his telegram, nor did he place much emphasis on the need for haste. Captain McWhinnie therefore knew nothing of his troops' precarious situation, but had sent the mounted infantry back to Helvetia on 1 April to ensure that those there had received their orders.

The column regrouped in the afternoon and moved off again. After stopping for the night, the Rifles set out on 3 April and marched until 10 a.m., when a cloud of dust was reported to the west. A defensive position was taken up on a horseshoe-shaped ridge called Mostert's Hoek, about four miles north-east of Reddersburg. The area was too large for the British force to defend indefinitely: the mounted infantry held the western side, and the infantry companies the remainder. Without being detected, De Wet had been shadowing them with a small force of 110 men since the previous day, but had been joined that morning by reinforcements, bringing his numbers up to some 500 men. He saw that the British force was not strong enough to occupy the whole ridge, so immediately gave orders to General De Villiers to advance and seize the western end of the ridge. De Wet then divided his remaining troops into small companies, with orders to occupy small hills that were between 600 and 700 paces to the east, leaving to himself and Commandant Nel the task of seizing a small ridge that lay south-east of the British lines. Before making his attack he sent a note to McWhinnie: 'Sir, I am here with five hundred men, and am every moment expecting reinforcements with three Krupps, against which you will not be able to hold out. I therefore advise you, in order to prevent bloodshed, to surrender.'[1]

The offer was declined, so De Wet immediately began his attack, inflicting several casualties, but his Krupp guns did not arrive until late in the afternoon and only a few shells were fired before darkness set in. McWhinnie sent a dispatch rider eighteen miles west to Bethany, seeking assistance, and divided the whole position into four sections. De Wet now had over 800 men at his disposal and restarted his attack at dawn, his artillery playing havoc with the Rifles' positions. He was sure that reinforcements would come to the aid of the British, and attempted to force a surrender before that happened. The regimental history of the Royal Irish Rifles recounted:

At 8 a.m. the enemy were firing on the mounted infantry at a range of thirty yards from one of their sentries, and the British could see nothing to fire at in return. Shortly afterwards the western half of the horse-shoe was rushed from the northern side, where the enemy had assembled in large numbers unperceived, and the mounted infantry then capitulated, some time before 9 a.m. The enemy then proceeded to creep up closer and closer to the localities held by H and A Companies, and at the same time the position was also being assaulted from the west and south. D Company's position was now taken. The enemy's tactics were to bring a very heavy and accurate fire to bear on the British from a distance, whilst they kept pushing in their spare troops to fifty yards from the hostile infantry … A Company was then captured, and the assault was continued as before, and also from the east.[2]

The Boers were now descending on the British in large numbers and the defenders were broken up into small groups, so, to avoid the risk of a disaster, McWhinnie decided to surrender. Total casualties were three officers and about twenty men killed, twenty-four men wounded, six officers and 452 men taken prisoner.[3]

In the overall story of the war, this was a minor incident. General Gatacre arrived too late to help and did not pursue the withdrawing Boers; as a result of this affair and other failures, he was relieved of his command and sent back to Britain. The propaganda machine in Britain made the best of things, as shown by this piece of jingoism from the illustrated weekly magazine *Black & White Budget* of 21 April: 'Surrounded by overwhelming odds and exposed to severe tropical storms, our gallant fellows fought like tigers for four-and-twenty hours on end, until their ammunition gave out. When the last cartridge had been fired they were forced to surrender to avoid utter annihilation.'[4] However, De Wet saw things differently:

> I ordered the gunners to keep up a continuous fire with our three Krupps. This they did from half-past five until eleven o'clock, and then the enemy hoisted the white flag. My men and I galloped towards the English ... But before we reached them, they again began to shoot, killing Veldtcornet Du Plessis, of Kroonstad. This treacherous act enraged our burghers, who at once commenced to fire with deadly effect. Soon the white flag appeared above almost every stone behind which an Englishman lay, but our men did not at once cease firing. Indeed! I had the greatest difficulty in calming them, and in inducing them to stop, for they were, as may well be imagined, furious at the misuse of the white flag.[5]

Apart from Du Plessis, the Boer losses were only six wounded.

The Earl of Rosslyn, a special correspondent with the *Daily Mail* who had been captured elsewhere, was part of a group of prisoners that included Colthurst and which was sent to Pretoria:

> Officers and men had to trudge for some hours over the veldt, carrying their coats and other articles ... Next morning we marched till ten o'clock and stopped at a farmhouse about four miles from Dewetsdorp, where sixteen sheep and plenty of bread were served out. It was interesting to note the difference in Tommy Atkins. From the draggled, morose, bitter, and saddened soldier, he changed at once into the forgetful, cheerful, well-filled man. Such is the effect of a good meal and a dirty pond in which we all bathed.

The officers underwent no such transformation. Poor chaps, I was sorry for them. They had but one topic. They argued and debated for a long time whether they could be blamed for the disaster … We were lucky in having fine weather, as we camped on the veldt every night … We were not allowed to enter Winburg the night of our arrival, but Commandant Grobler drove out and paid me a visit, bringing a bottle of whiskey with him. There was a sudden rush for pannikins, and the forbidden liquor soon disappeared much to the amusement of our kind donor.

Next morning we started early through the town. The officers were taken to the Winburg Hotel for breakfast, where, after a wash and an excellent meal, under the supervision of a German guard, they were told they might go to a store and buy what they wanted before the train left … The officers had a first-class corridor carriage reserved for them, and a compartment adjoining for their servants.[6]

Colthurst spent six weeks in the 'Bird Cage', the officers' prison on the outskirts of Pretoria comprising a large shed of corrugated iron with a mud floor. It stood in the middle of a bare compound surrounded by a triple fence of barbed wire. Inside were lines of small iron beds for about 120 occupants. The treatment of the officers was reasonable during their captivity, the major problems being boredom and the cold at night. As the main British force approached, the prisoners went through a period of extreme anxiety as their captors fed them a diet of misinformation as to their future prospects. An early indication of the vindictive side of Colthurst's nature manifested itself at that time, as he explained in a letter to his mother:

We were released on the glorious 'fifth of June' the day that the

British flag floated over the capital of the Transvaal. Previous to our release we had been having a fairly exciting time and had a narrow escape of being carted off to Lydenburg. Having seen our former gaolers, about 50 villainous looking Hollanders, safely *inside* the barbed wire, with a few loaded rifles outside, I started for the town and saw Lord Roberts triumphal entry on the afternoon of the fifth, the march past was a splendid sight, and many of us would have given a lot to be in it. All officer prisoners of war had a personal interview with Lord Roberts on the 6th while the remainder of my time in Pretoria was spent wandering round the town knocking old Burghers down. I am afraid the Sunday school lessons of my youth were forgotten in the desire for retaliation, which, however, was only partially gratified.[7]

The British initially considered the campaign to be over, but a protracted guerrilla war was pursued by the 'bitter-enders'. Colthurst was placed on duty protecting the lines of communication from being disrupted. The main Boer unit in the area was under the command of Commandant Danie Theron, whose Scouting Corps gained a reputation for destroying railway bridges and trains during this period. In a letter dated 1 July 1900, Colthurst summarised his impressions of the Boers:

The job we have now on hand is not very exciting but means a good deal of hard work. Captain Spencer and myself with three other officers and 300 men are at Klip River, half way between Johannesburg and Vereeniging. There is a fine bridge here and a pumping station. Ever since we came here we have been hard at work digging trenches, redoubts, etc. ... We have a good many Boers in the hills round, about 700 I think, they are however a cowardly lot of devils and content themselves with sniping the pickets occasionally at long range ... It is very cold here now, hard frost every night but everyone is in the best of health. I wish Robbie [his brother] would come out and we would start on some farm of 50,000 acres with a private gold mine, the soil is very fertile and would grow anything, but the Boers don't try to cultivate it. They graze a few cows and a few horses and grow a few mealies or potatoes, a little tobacco, and a tree at each side of the doorway.

In spite of my hatred and contempt of the Boers ... I have been trying to pick up the 'Taal'. I can read Dutch quite easily, but can only speak sufficient for commandeering purposes ... When I was captured the whole of my kit was taken by the Boers, or rather all I had with me except the clothes I stood in. I took the lens off the telescope and it, I suppose, is still hidden under a boulder on the field of battle. They got my rifle, field glasses, and revolver, but by judicious commandeering I am gradually replacing them.[8]

Having been promoted to lieutenant on 20 August, Colthurst began home leave and was back in Cork by the end of October. On 7 November 1900 the conservative *Cork Constitution* reported that he 'was received with great rejoicings by his tenantry ... and the heartiness of his welcome bore ample testimony to the popularity of his family in county Cork, and the good feeling which exists between landlord and tenant on the property which he owns'.

On 7 February 1901 Colthurst left London to rejoin the 1st Royal Irish Rifles in India and arrived in Bombay on 2 March. His twenty-first birthday did not go unnoticed at home – the *Cork Constitution* of 15 August reported that 'the tenantry of the Oakgrove and Dripsey Castle estates had bonfires lighted at various points of vantage, and rejoicings at the coming of age of Mr John Bowen-Colthurst were very general … [he] succeeds to estates at Carrigadrohid, Killinardrish, and Dripsey'. The Rifles moved from Calcutta to Fyzabad in the Punjab on 3 February 1902, while Colthurst was sent back to South Africa to collect 149 men. He returned to Bombay with them on 24 March and rejoined his unit in early April. During this time, Colthurst engaged in womanising to some degree, a weakness that continued throughout most of his life, but he turned against alcohol and gambling at an early stage. He also developed an obsessive passion for religion that was to dominate his life.

3

SERVICE IN TIBET

In 1903 Colthurst gained a musketry certificate, passing second out of the School of Musketry for India. In languages he passed the higher standard of Urdu, lower standard Persian and elementary standard Pashto. He wrote to his sister Pixie from Mankapur on 6 April 1904:

> I am out for a week's shooting in the jungles north of the Gogra River, staying on a Rajah's property. Forbes of my Regiment is with me. We have been having quite good sport and have shot a good many Cheetal. Forbes has, I think, shot five – one a very good head of 33 inches. My best head measures 31½ inches and is also a good one. We also got a good deal of other sort of game – pig and small game. One boar I shot had particularly fine tusks. Cheetal are … the spotted or Axis deer of India … I go back to Fyzabad on the 10th, to Lucknow on the 15th, and leave for home on 1 June.[1]

His leave was cancelled, however, and he was soon to embark on a new adventure, as events in Tibet were coming to a head because of British fears of the expansion of Russian influence into that country. In 1901 Lord Curzon, viceroy of India, sent a letter to the Dalai Lama complaining about continued incursions over the border by groups of Tibetans and the restrictions imposed on Indian trade. He threatened to resort to more practical measures to enforce the observance of an existing treaty, but his letter was returned unopened. Instead, the Dalai Lama sent a mission to Russia carrying presents for Tsar Nicholas II.

In 1903 it was announced that Colonel Francis Young-husband would lead a mission to Lhasa to negotiate with the Dalai Lama and establish a commission there. Younghusband, whose escort consisted of three native Indian regiments – the 8th Ghurkhas, and 23rd and 32nd Pioneers – crossed the Tibetan border in summer 1903, but their progress was stalled by the onset of winter. Then, on 30 March 1904, 2,000 soldiers of the Tibetan army blocked their way at Guru. The Tibetan general fired the first shot and within ten minutes his army had suffered about 700 casualties from the British counter-attack. Younghusband's mission advanced to Gyantse, where he was opposed by another Tibetan force and severe fighting ensued. Reinforcements were ordered in from India, including a machine-gun detachment from the 1st Royal Irish Rifles.

Colthurst was chosen to lead this detachment, which consisted of Sergeant James Lyle, six riflemen and two Maxim machine guns. They left Fyzabad on 18 May and arrived by train at Siliguri on the evening of 20 May. The subsequent march of fifty miles to Darjeeling was performed in twenty-eight hours. There they were attached to the 1st Royal Fusiliers under Lieutenant Colonel Edward J. Cooper, DSO. The rest of the Tibet Field Force was composed of the 7th British Mountain Battery (with four ten-pounder guns), the Muree Mountain Battery (with two ten-pounders), the 40th Pathans and two field hospitals.

They set off on 24 May and the first phase of the journey was through Sikkim to Chumbi, 110 miles away. Initially the march brought them down a rough track to the cable bridge over the

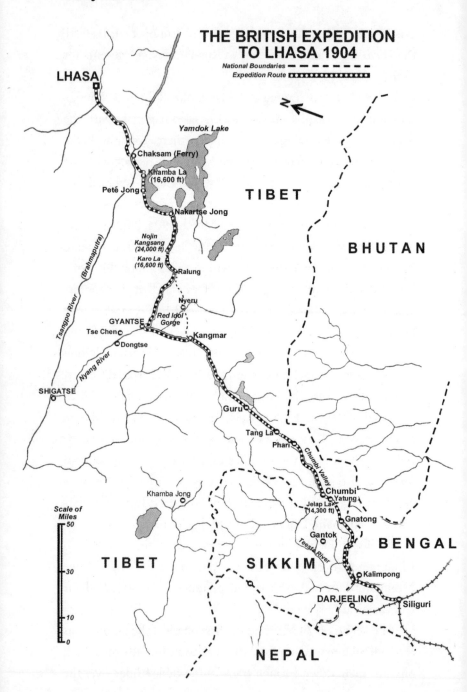

THE BRITISH EXPEDITION
TO LHASA 1904

National Boundaries ▬ ▬ ▬ ▬
Expedition Route ▣▣▣▣▣▣▣▣▣▣

LHASA

Yamdok Lake

Chaksam (Ferry)
Khamba La (16,600 ft)
Peté Jong

TIBET

Nakartse Jong

BHUTAN

Nojin Kangsang (24,000 ft)
Karo La (16,600 ft)
Ralung

Nyeru

GYANTSE
Tse Chen
Red Idol Gorge
Kangmar

Dongtse

SHIGATSE

Guru

Tang La
Phari

Chumbi Valley

Khamba Jong

Chumbi
Yatung

Tsangpo River (Brahmaputra)

Nyang River

Jelap La (14,300 ft)
Gnatong

Gantok

BENGAL

TIBET

SIKKIM

Teesta River

Kalimpong

DARJEELING
Siliguri

Scale of Miles
50
30
10
0

NEPAL

Teesta River, then up through thick jungle in oppressive heat. The weather soon turned to torrential rain that soaked the men to the skin, with leeches adding to their difficulties. Colthurst sent a letter to Pixie on 31 May from Gnatong:

> By a strange fatality, on the very day on which I would in the ordinary course of events have embarked on the *Circassia* at Bombay, I find myself in the opposite corner of India in an out of the way spot five miles from the Tibetan frontier ... Of course it's as much a disappointment to me but you would not have your brother refusing to go on active service.
>
> I got your letter yesterday and was very sorry to see about Mother being unwell – tell her not to worry about me or anything: what does it matter whether both ends meet or not – put your trust in God and push for yourself ... I am very well and will bring you home a few knick-knacks from Lhasa. I sent home some heads last fortnight from Lucknow. The leopard-skin is for you – it looks best on the wall – please have the other heads put up somewhere in the house. This place is over 12,000 feet up – we marched across snow yesterday – and cross the Jelap Pass ... tomorrow.[2]

Having been issued with winter kit, the soldiers crossed through the mountain pass of Jelap La (14,300 feet) on 1 June in a snowstorm, with the altitude causing them to stop every hundred paces. The next day they descended to the outskirts of the base depot of the Tibet Mission at New Chumbi. There they were visited by Colonel Younghusband, who explained that there was much fighting going on in the region of the fortress-town of Gyantse.

On 12 June they set off again and marched thirty miles to

Phari Jong. On 17 June the force crossed the Tang La (15,200 feet) on the arduous 136-mile journey to Gyantse.[3] Initially the days were hot, but later they became windy and dusty. The nights were very cold and it was almost impossible to sleep. Gyantse was reached on 26 June after the Pathans, Ghurkhas and Sikhs had engaged in a skirmish with the enemy at Naini, where over 300 Tibetans were killed. Colthurst reported on these events in a letter he sent to the commanding officer of the 1st Royal Irish Rifles, dated 29 June 1904:

> The Tibetans were absolutely surrounded. I got as far to the front as I could but never loosed off, as most of the fighting was house to house and done by the 40th Pathans and Pioneers; although the Gyantse garrison did a lot of shooting at Tibetans trying to get away up the big valley on the left ... The 40th Pathans enjoyed themselves immensely and slew about 150, the Pioneers accounted for another 100 ... The Gyantse Garrison also accounted for a good many Tibetans; the fight was over about 5 p.m., the Tibetans fought with great pluck, a lot of them were left hiding in cellars, it being impossible to get at them. We got into camp that night about a mile from the Mission and about two miles from the Jong, after a fairly stiff day, 17 mile march wading across rivers, etc.[4]

They then prepared for the forthcoming assault on Gyantse fort, which had been holding up the mission's advance:

> We commenced operations by moving down the left bank of the Nyang River to clear villages and a large town and monastery. The Royal Fusiliers were in front and advanced through the villages on the left bank very slowly, which we found to be deserted; they got as far as a large monastery where they stopped, but managed

to secure some cattle, sheep, chickens, etc. I happened to be on the right flank and more or less on my own ... I started by managing to upset the gun mule in a river and nearly drowned him – we had to cross several pretty deep rivers and canals. Sergeant Lyle did some pretty shooting at 1,100 yards and I pushed on to about six hundred yards from the nearest houses; the fight that followed was the prettiest you can possibly imagine. The town [Tse Chen] was built on the side of a pretty steep hill and appeared to be full of Tibetans and on top of the hill was a line of sangars and big stone forts; when the Fusiliers were ordered to stop, the Ghurkhas and Pathans pushed up, the Ghurkhas had a good start and climbed up the left edge of the hill (the batteries shelling the sangars), until they got to a large round fort on the very top of the hill, into which they could not climb and the Tibetans inside were shelling them with rocks (this part of the fight was alone worth coming to Tibet to see). However, the Ghurkhas stuck to it and eventually we saw them climb over the edge and bayonet all the Tibetans inside; meanwhile the 40th Pathans had gone straight for the town absolutely regardless of the enemy's fire and had some pretty stiff fighting there too. I turned the Maxim on whenever I saw anybody move and expect we hit one or two (I actually only saw one man fall as Sergeant Lyle got him in the open). I hear the Tibetans lost over 400 killed.[5]

Colthurst would appear to have been under some stress in his excited and fatigued condition. A copy of the above letter was pasted into one of his Tibet scrapbooks and below it is a revealing note in his own handwriting, dated 1905 at Dripsey: 'I regret writing such a cold-blooded letter', demonstrating that he was aware of his callousness and lack of discretion, and that he was capable of remorse.[6]

An armistice was called on 30 June and peace negotiations were started but broke down on 5 July. The assault on Gyantse began. In all there were four Maxim guns supporting the attack: their function was to seek out targets wherever the defenders seemed to be most concentrated. Colthurst recorded in his diary:

> Guns fire at Jong at 1 p.m. Parade at 3.30 p.m. and march out to attack Palkor Chode [a monastic complex near the fort] from the west. Do not press attack as intend to make real attack from the east at 4 a.m. Got back from attack on Palkor Chode at 9.30 p.m. and parade again at 11.30 p.m. March all night by a circuitous route to reach Palla about 3.30 a.m. Attack on Jong commenced about 4 a.m. At it all day. Fire 1,492 rounds from gun and got hit by a spent bullet. Jong captured by a fine assault by 8th Ghurkhas at 5 p.m. Over 700 Tibetans killed. A hard day's work.[7]

Having occupied the fort and cleared the outlying areas, the mission then camped on the left bank of the Nyang River until 14 July, when the decision was made to move towards Lhasa, 147 miles away. Heading off in monsoon rain, the column of over 3,000 men stretched for eight miles. By 17 July they had camped at the foot of a glacier on Nojin Kangsang, with the Tibetans being reported four miles away. The next day they went through the Karo La (16,600 feet) and, two miles beyond this, the enemy was engaged. The Royal Fusiliers led the uphill attack supported by the mountain guns and Maxims. Colthurst clinically recorded: 'Fire 185 rounds from gun. They do not stand. Seventy Tibetans killed.'[8] At the time this was the highest altitude at which a military engagement had ever taken place. On 19 July undefended Nakartse Jong was reached and a

Tibetan delegation came out to hold talks with Younghusband. Much to their dismay, however, he insisted on carrying out full negotiations at Lhasa.

The march continued on 21 July along the edge of Yamdok Lake, in cold rain and hail, and moved through the Khamba La (16,600 feet) to the ferry at Chaksam on the Tsangpo (Brahmaputra) River, where they halted on 25 July. The crossing of the river took several days, but the expedition was now only forty-one miles from Lhasa. The advance resumed on 31 July and the force finally encamped one mile south-east of the Potala, the Dalai Lama's palace at Lhasa, on 3 August. The next day the Rifles detachment formed part of Younghusband's guard of honour as he rode into the Forbidden City through the western gate to the Chinese Residency.

Younghusband began tedious peace negotiations with the acting regent, the National Assembly and other Tibetan representatives. The young Dalai Lama had fled before the British entered the city. In the meantime, Brigadier General James Macdonald, the person responsible for the security and safety of the mission, was busy procuring food supplies. As the long discussions continued, Colthurst spent his spare time fishing and buying souvenirs at the bazaar that the locals had set up just outside the camp. He wrote to Pixie on 7 August:

> We are camped within two miles of the Potala and no one is allowed to enter the town. Negotiations, however, do not appear to be getting much 'forwarder'. One thing is we cannot winter here and may have to burn a monastery next week to make them hurry up … My only amusement is fishing, which is fairly successful, up to about five pounds. I do not know the brand of fish. Having got here we are now principally thinking of getting

back. It is roughly 400 miles march to Siliguri, so will take about six weeks.[9]

Fortunately no such drastic action as burning a monastery was required because progress towards a settlement was finally being made. Another letter followed to his elderly spinster aunt, Eliza Travers Bowen, of Coolalta House, Carrigadrohid, on 20 August:

> Life here is not exciting – a good deal of rain and very cold at night (down to 34°). I hope, however, that negotiations will shortly reach something definite, and in any case we cannot stay here after 15 September at the latest, so will be back in India by November. We are more or less confined to camp but Lhasa City is dirty and uninteresting. The Potala and the monasteries of Sera Depan and Goden would of course be worth visiting … The Tibetans here appear to be a harmless lot of people. The country is very hilly but the valleys are very fertile. They grow a lot of wheat, barley, mustard and bean crops and keep pigs, chickens, Yaks, cattle, goats and sheep. There is also good shooting, lots of partridge and pigeon and on the hills several species of deer, wild sheep, etc. The rivers also are full of many different kinds of fish … I hope to get a year's leave next year, so you will see enough of me and will, probably, be rather tired of me by the time my leave is up … I am very glad that mother has got over her illness so well. I was really anxious.[10]

Colthurst wrote to his mother on 26 August:

> I intend having a month's shoot in the Central Province and leaving India for home about May 1905 … I don't think I shall require any money for some time. In fact I shall probably have

saved about £100 by the time I get back to India. I was extremely glad to hear of your having got over your illness so well … I wish I was at home and am looking forward to the prospect of seeing you all again next year.[11]

The negotiations finally concluded and the Treaty of Lhasa was signed on 7 September in the Potala Palace. For this event, the Field Force lined the road from the bottom of the hill right up to the entrance of the massive structure. The Royal Fusiliers and Colthurst's squad were closest to the top, being the bulk of the non-native troops with the expedition. From a British perspective, the most important item of the treaty involved an agreement that no foreign power, without the consent of Great Britain, could concern itself in any way with Tibetan administration, be allowed to construct roads, railways or telegraphs, or open mines, nor could any portion of Tibet be sold, leased or mortgaged to any foreign power.

As tensions eased, the troops were finally allowed into Lhasa to see the sights and do some shopping. The delayed return journey began on 23 September, with the expedition divided into three columns. Winter was moving in and snow had already settled on the high ground. Although there was frost at night, it was hot and dusty during the early stages of the march. By 30 September they were across the Tsangpo and spent the day crossing the Nabsa La (16,800 feet) to the fort of Peté Jong; breathing was very difficult at that altitude and there was a heavy frost. Within days their feet became very sore, the wind was bitterly cold, and by 4 October their milk supplies had frozen. The weather became clearer as they passed groups of Tibetans harvesting their crops, and the sight of a few trees, after all the barren land that had been traversed, raised their spirits. Gyantse was reached on 6 October, and for many days after that the march was not too difficult as the road had been improved since their outward journey, though the cold wind and their painful feet continued to cause problems. Having crossed the Tang La with the first column, Colthurst recorded on 16 October that there was 26 degrees of frost. He had just reached camp at Chumbi the next day when a thick blizzard descended while the remaining two columns were still in the open. Colthurst was lucky to avoid the worst of the weather that beset the others and it took two days for the force to reunite.

On 20 October they set off again and encountered frozen snow, fallen trees and telegraph wires that seriously hindered their progress. The next day they came back across the frontier at the Jelap La in snow that was feet deep and, by then, most of the detachment was more or less snow blind. But the worst was over as they descended again towards the plains of India. Colthurst noted in his diary: 'Bad road but rejoice in seeing woods ... Admire tree ferns and butterflies.'[12] The heat and leeches now became the dominant problems and many of the pack mules collapsed. Darjeeling was finally reached on 28 October, where they received a heroes' welcome with cheering crowds and bands. The following day the Irish Rifles separated from the Royal Fusiliers at Kurseong. On 30 October they continued twenty-two miles into a very hot Siliguri, completing a trek of forty-five miles in twenty-six hours. It was 155 miles from Chumbi, and they had marched a total of 440 miles from Lhasa in thirty-two days.

On 1 November the detachment left Siliguri by train and arrived at Fyzabad on 3 November, where they made a triumphant entry headed by a bugler. Colthurst received the Tibet Medal and a clasp for his service at and around Gyantse, being mentioned in the 1st Royal Irish Rifles Battalion Orders on 4 November: 'The excellent work done in the field and the good character and discipline of this party throughout the recent operations reflect the greatest credit on all concerned and also on the battalion to which they belong.'[13] Colonel Cooper wrote to the Rifles' commanding officer to say how well the detachment had performed: 'In Lieutenant Colthurst they had a keen, dashing leader who took great trouble with his work. In the men they had a steady, keen and smart lot. Throughout the expedition ... they were always cheerful and their marching and conduct were splendid. It was quite a pleasure to have such a lot under one's command.'[14]

Colthurst was given command of either G or H Company, one of the eight companies (A to H) that made up a battalion at that time. On 28 March 1905 G and H Companies, including Colthurst, were sent to Chakrata. That year he qualified as a German Interpreter, First Class. While at Chakrata he spent time with a Bible-study group at the local Miss Sandes Soldiers' Home, and began to develop an intense interest in fundamentalist Christianity. Elise Sandes had set up many of these religion-based homes to provide a wholesome retreat for British soldiers, with the aim of providing a facility to which the men could go instead of bars, opium dens or brothels. Colthurst was then finally granted his long-delayed home leave.

4

HOME SERVICE

During the summer of 1905 Colthurst attended a Christian temperance convention at the Lake Hotel, Killarney, County Kerry. At these kinds of gatherings he met and befriended several like-minded and influential people who would guide and help him in the years to come, including Reverend J. Stuart Holden and Captain Robert Wade Thompson.[1] When his leave finished, he returned to India.

Also in 1905 his brother, Robbie, had conspired with Horace de Vere Cole in the Zanzibar Hoax when, with a small group of undergraduates, they successfully pretended to be a retinue of the Sultan of Zanzibar and made a visit to Cambridge, where they received an official reception from the mayor at the Guildhall and were shown around the university. Later in the year Robbie joined the staff of the Earl of Aberdeen, lord lieutenant of Ireland, as assistant private secretary, and was later appointed vice-chamberlain. His connections in that position proved most useful to the family in their time of need in the future.

While Colthurst was in India, back in Ireland unrest was growing amongst his family's tenants. On 1 September 1907 a meeting was held near Dripsey, under the auspices of the United Irish League and the Land and Labour Association. The speakers included two local members of parliament, Daniel D. Sheehan and Eugene Crean. The object was ostensibly an anti-landlord campaign, but in reality it focused on the Bowen-Colthurst estate, where tenants were negotiating the purchase of their holdings. During the meeting Colthurst's sister, Peggy, stepped onto the platform but was refused permission to address the crowd. Near the end of the meeting the platform was pulled down; Peggy jumped off and luckily was unhurt, and 'while not molested, Miss Colthurst displayed a calmness and courage that were remarkable'.[2] To ease some of the general agitation, the Irish Land Act 1909, introduced by Chief Secretary for Ireland Augustine Birrell, was drafted with the aim of reducing land congestion and forcing landlords to sell to tenants where more than three-quarters of the tenantry on their estates wished to buy their holdings.

Most of Colthurst's free time in India was spent at game shooting, and he recorded that 'Hunting in the Kadir or vast jungle between the Ganges and the Jumna Rivers, with head-quarters at Meerut, was a truly wonderful experience. In the winter there were vast quantities of duck (of 30 different species), teal, snipe, quail, partridges, peafowl, pigeon, hares, antelope, hog-deer, boar, jackal and the occasional leopard.' During one such hunting trip, on 29–31 October 1907, he shot '41 partridges, 27 ducks, 21 teal, 11 pigeons, 7 quail, 7 hares, and 3 peacocks: a total of 134'.[3] On another occasion he was with Captain Henry R. Goodman, who remembered:

I was on a shooting expedition with Captain Colthurst in India and we put up for the night in a bungalow. Terrier dogs were barking all night and we did not sleep. At breakfast the following morning I said I wished that dog was shot that kept us awake. Captain Colthurst got up from the breakfast table without saying a word to anyone and went out. I next heard a shot, a rifle shot fired, and it was followed by the piteous howls from a dog. Captain Colthurst came back and said he had shot the dog. I asked if he had killed the dog, and he said, 'No' adding 'the dog is sufficiently wounded to die'. I mention that as an eccentric act. It was so entirely against the nature of Captain Colthurst to do a thing like that.[4]

Although his action was considered by Goodman to be out of character, it was later presented as proof that Colthurst was capable of irrational and extreme behaviour.

Colthurst was promoted to captain on 21 December 1907. He returned to England from India on 29 July 1908, being stationed at Aldershot for two months with the 2nd Royal Irish Rifles. For the next three years he served with the 5th Royal Irish Rifles, a militia unit, in Downpatrick, County Down. Colonel R. H. 'Bob' Wallace was his commanding officer and one of the Orange Order's most esteemed leaders, being, at that time, grand president of the Grand Orange Council of the World.

It was in Downpatrick that Colthurst came to own a book entitled *A Collection of Orange and Protestant Songs* compiled by William Peake (published under the authority of the Grand Lodge of Ireland and the Grand Black Chapter of Ireland in Belfast in 1907). He was seemingly so annoyed by the apparent sectarian nature of its contents that he wrote to Colonel Sir Frederick W. Shaw, DSO, JP, DL, commanding officer of the 5th Royal Dublin Fusiliers, who had some influence in the Order. A reply to this letter, dated 22 March 1909, is pasted in Colthurst's copy of the book:

> I got that book of songs ... whoever compiled it ought to be set upon, but gently. Remember I told you that there are many extremists in the Orange Society whose style and views I never

did approve of. But it is the same in all secret societies. Please do not imagine that the tone of these songs, with their willingness to swagger, reflects the views of the Orangemen in general. I'm glad that you called my attention to it as I may be able to do something to check such effusions.[5]

It is to his credit that Colthurst made an effort to confront perceived bigotry and it must be noted that the Royal Irish Rifles consisted of men from all faiths and regions of Ireland; sectarianism was not tolerated or practised within the regular battalions of the regiment. Having said that, Colthurst was strongly against the Roman Catholic Church as an organisation, and would rave about the Jesuits and the Pope, but this attitude did not extend to individuals and their choice of religion.[6]

Having been passed suitable for promotion to major, Colthurst's military career was on the rise, with every hope of reaching high rank. At this time he became friendly with Fred Crawford, who later gained notoriety as the principal gunrunner for the Ulster Volunteer Force (UVF), and this friendship may have played a role in Colthurst's later opposition to action against the unionists in the north of Ireland. Crawford wrote in a later letter that he considered Colthurst 'a young friend of mine ... a very nice fellow'.[7]

In October 1909 Colthurst's engagement to The Honourable Rosalinda Laetitia Butler was announced. Linda, as she was known, was born at Sevenoaks, Kent, in 1881, the youngest daughter of Robert St John Fitzwalter Butler, 16th/26th Baron Dunboyne, and Caroline Maude Blanche Butler *née* Probyn, Lady Dunboyne, of Knappogue Castle, County Clare. It appears that Colthurst and Linda met through hunting circles. Her father worked as a lawyer in London and had inherited the title from his brother, though the bulk of the family wealth had gone to the only daughter of his predecessor. The couple married at Quin, County Clare, on 2 April 1910. The *Limerick Chronicle* of 5 April reported this society event: 'As the bride, who looked very charming, entered on the arm of her father, who gave her away, the Hymn *Thine for Ever, God of Love* was sung by all present ... With the bridegroom was, as best man, Captain H. R. Charley, Royal Irish Rifles ...'.

Among numerous valuable wedding gifts, a present of the title deeds of a stretch of land on Vancouver Island was given to the bride by her brother, the Hon. Robert Butler.

The reception was held at Knappogue Castle:

> When the bride and groom reached Knappogue for the ... reception, all the staff and tenants were lined up in the courtyard to meet them as they arrived in a coach drawn by four horses. A banner was hung from the walls which read, 'Long live Captain Colthurst and his beautiful bride' ... A number of Catholics, who attended the wedding ceremony in the Church of Ireland Church in Quin, contrary to the instructions of their parish priest, had to seek pardon from the Catholic Bishop Michael Fogarty of Killaloe, as the offences were considered 'reserved sins' which ... could only be absolved by a bishop.[8]

Having spent their honeymoon at Oakgrove, the newlyweds moved to Ballymote House near Downpatrick. Fred Crawford wrote to Colthurst on 31 March 1911, referring to the imminent arrival of Colthurst's first-born: 'I do not think it would be fair to either you or your wife to allow you to come on a day's fishing with me under the circumstances; better put off our day's fishing till after the little event. We would then be happier as there would be no anxiety. With first events dates are very uncertain.'⁹ Robert St John Bowen-Colthurst was born on 18 April 1911.

Colthurst was posted back to the 2nd Royal Irish Rifles at Dover in late 1911. He was attached to the staff of Brigadier General Francis S. Inglefield, CB, DSO, 12th Infantry Brigade, during manoeuvres in 1912, and was camp adjutant for six months at Lydd in Kent for the Rifles' musketry training that year. In September the battalion moved to Bhurtpore Barracks at Tidworth, where his daughter, Dorinda Katherine, was born on 15 November. For several years in succession he held a lectureship in musketry in Birmingham.

Ever ambitious and anxious to enhance his prospects, he sat the examination for entry to the staff college at Camberley in 1912. The college course was intended to train future commanding and staff officers. Although he failed the examination in 1912 because of the short time he had available for preparation, he did pass in 1913. Only selected officers were permitted to sit the exam and they had to be supported by confidential reports from three senior officers of their battalion and from three general officers commanding brigades, divisions and commands, who in the case of Colthurst were Brigadier General Inglefield, Sir Horace Smith-Dorrien, KCB, DSO, Southern Command, and Sir Arthur Henry Paget, GCB, GCVO, Eastern Command. While he waited for a place in the college, Colthurst served at Dover as acting brigade major (the executive officer to a brigadier general), 12th Infantry Brigade, January and February 1913, and passed the preliminary examination in French in 1914.

A new commanding officer of the 2nd Royal Irish Rifles, Lieutenant Colonel Wilkinson Dent Bird, DSO, of the Royal

West Surrey Regiment, was appointed on 24 September 1913. Resentment at the imposition of an outsider, and the consequential loss of promotion prospects within the regiment, grated on Colthurst. He adopted a negative attitude towards Bird from the start and failed to accept that his new commanding officer was a very capable and experienced leader. 'The first command Lieutenant-Colonel Bird issued when he arrived at Tidworth was to clear the billiard room as he desired to use it as a lecture room. He was informed by the Mess President that the billiard room was for the use of the officers to play billiards and not for his maps, diagrams and lectures.'[10]

By this time Ireland was in the depths of a political crisis as a result of government attempts to introduce Home Rule. Ulster unionists had vowed to oppose this, by force if necessary, and formed the UVF. It was feared that army and police barracks in the north of Ireland would be raided by the UVF in a bid to procure arms. Then, in March 1914, many officers stationed at the Curragh in County Kildare proffered their resignations rather than move against the UVF. Bird issued orders for the battalion to be mobilised and was thought by Colthurst to have offered the services of the 2nd Royal Irish Rifles for active operations in Ulster. Being heavily influenced by the Curragh incident, and perhaps swayed by his friendship with Fred Crawford and Bob Wallace, Colthurst displayed the impulsive nature that was ultimately to end his military career: he railed at Bird, accusing him of not understanding Irishmen and saying that he never would. Colthurst would not obey orders to undertake military operations in Belfast, the home of the regiment, and said that whoever appointed Bird to command an Irish battalion was capable of appointing a Brahmin to command a regiment of Pathans![11]

Colthurst was extremely lucky that such immature and

insulting behaviour towards his superior officer did not lead to his being court-martialled and dismissed from the army. Bird made a disciplinary report on the episode, but was overruled by Colthurst's powerful connections through his brother, Robbie.[12] Colthurst apologised and the matter seemed to be settled, but it clearly confirms his impulsiveness and that he could be given to extremes of behaviour when under stress. He also demonstrated a narcissistic personality disorder in his character, manifested mainly by a grandiose sense of self-importance, a lack of empathy and an unwillingness to recognise or identify with the feelings and needs of others.[13]

Colonel Bird continued to have doubts as to Colthurst's stability. In the summer of 1914 he told Colthurst that he was going to give him an unfavourable report about his personal manner:

> I think he was not a very good company commander. Certainly, on one occasion I had that in mind. As far as I remember I checked Captain Colthurst for something with reference to his company. He went to the door and shut it and, opposite me, bellowed out in a loud voice 'Do you mean to say anything against my company?' ... I think he was very fond of his company. He attached himself very much to it. He thought it was the best company in the regiment. He, I think, completely lost his head and, when I reprimanded him, I don't think he realised it as a matter of fact at all.[14]

Colthurst then told Bird that he would prefer not to serve under his command on active service but was informed that it was too late to make a change. The Great War had begun.

5

THE GREAT WAR

The 2nd Royal Irish Rifles were ordered to mobilise on 4 August 1914 and formed part of the 7th Infantry Brigade in the 3rd Division. On 13 August they left for France and by 22 August their brigade had reached the Belgian village of Ciply, south of the town of Mons. Early on the morning of Sunday 23 August, the men were advised that contact with the enemy was imminent: the battle of Mons was about to begin. Having marched to Harmignies, they were sent forward to reinforce the Royal Scots on high ground north of Harmignies railway station. The Rifles had begun to entrench on the right flank of the British defences when the enemy's artillery opened fire at about 3.45 p.m. They were soon out on a limb as the Germans had crossed the Condé Canal. The bulk of the 3rd Division had withdrawn to a new defensive line south of Mons and the Rifles were separated from their brigade. Lieutenant Gerald Lowry, of Colthurst's C Company, recalled:

> From here we were able to look down the valley below, and saw, to our great amazement, as far as the eye could see, a teeming mass of German soldiers, advancing with parade-ground efficiency. It was a thrilling introduction to an enemy we were destined to fight for four years; but we had little time for reflection, and opened fire at 800 yards range ... into the advancing horde, who literally shivered with the shock and melted away ... All the afternoon the German infantry came on, line after line as far as the eye

could see, with a superb courage until, with our rifles almost red hot and our men tired with ceaseless firing, they succeeded in approaching to within 200 yards of our line ... All this while the German artillery had been gradually finding our position, and, just before darkness came, it became thoroughly unpleasant.[1]

The Battle of Mons

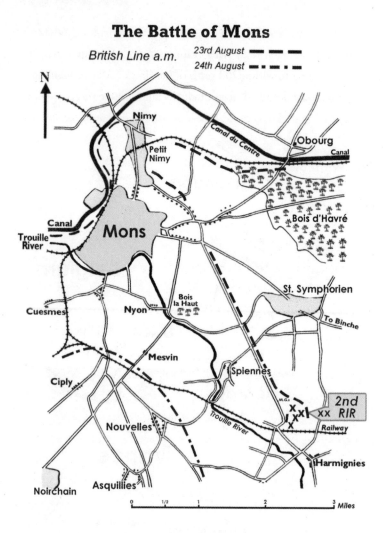

British Line a.m. 23rd August ━━ ━━ ━━ 24th August ━■━ ■━ ■━

As night fell the Germans brought up six machine guns and started to advance again but had to pull back in the face of further murderous rifle fire. The battalion held the line until ordered to withdraw at 2 a.m. the following morning. They moved off across country in the direction of Bavai, where they finally linked up again that evening with the rest of the brigade. Colonel Bird described the great retreat:

One got so little sleep during the retreat and advance, when at best orders came in at midnight or a little earlier, and reveille was at 4 a.m., and physically one was so tired with marching … So little time, also, was available for entrenchment when we did stand to fight, that, as a rule, villages which seemed to afford some cover were selected as our 'localities'. As a result the enemy's artillery was afforded a series of good targets on which fire could be and was concentrated, and our men, who perhaps were somewhat crowded in the villages, suffered accordingly.[2]

The battalion formed the rearguard of the 7th Brigade when, on 25 August, they retired thirty miles to Maurois with the Germans hot on their heels. The Rifles had marched forty-five miles in forty-eight hours. At 7.30 a.m. orders were received to march to Bertry and, on arrival, a guide brought them to a line south of Caudry where they proceeded to entrench. This line was to be held in case the Germans broke through the main body of the British forces, which had turned about and made a stand at Le Cateau in an effort to stall the German advance. According to Rifleman Joseph Goss, a nineteen-year-old from Belfast:

Some time later (about 2 p.m.) severe fighting flared up again and under very heavy pressure the 7th Brigade fell back from the village of Caudry. The survivors of A and B Companies, RIR, had joined the Battalion and directions were then received apparently for the Rifles (assisted by units of the R[oyal] F[ield] Artillery) to cover the withdrawal of the Brigade from the vicinity of the village.[3]

The retreat resumed for eighteen miles to Beaurevoir, which the battalion reached in pouring rain at midnight. Many men tried to fall out and pick up biscuits and meat left in the bivouacs

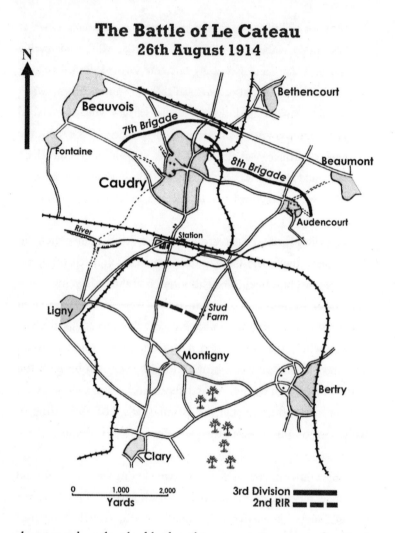

The Battle of Le Cateau
26th August 1914

N

Beauvois

Bethencourt

7th Brigade

Fontaine

8th Brigade

Beaumont

Caudry

River

Station

Audencourt

Ligny

Stud
Farm

Montigny

Bertry

Clary

0   1,000   2,000
Yards

3rd Division ▬▬▬
2nd RIR ▬ ▬ ▬

they passed, as they had had nothing to eat since some food had reached them during the action at Le Cateau. Corporal John Lucy observed a shell-shocked Colthurst:

> The officers at last began to feel the strain. One captain turns his whole company about and marches back towards the Germans. The commanding officer gallops after him, and the captain tells

him he is tired of retreating. It is bad for the morale of the troops, so he prefers to fight and perish if necessary. The un-nerved captain is relieved of his command, and his gallantly docile company comes back to us under a junior, and joins the tail of the column.[4]

By now Bird was biding his time, waiting for a suitable opportunity to rid himself of Colthurst. He recalled:

I was trying to find the brigade but, whenever I rode away from the battalion, the battalion moved off. I asked him [Colthurst] why that was done, and his reply and demeanour were such as to convince me that he was quite incapable of leading men and I suspended him from duties for a time.[5]

Proceeding as brigade rearguard, the battalion headed off at 2 a.m. on 27 August to Ham. Arriving there at 4 a.m. on 28 August in very thick fog, it crossed the Somme, then continued to Tarlefesse, a suburb of Noyon, a total march of twenty-six miles. The men rested there until noon on 29 August, after which they took up a line of outposts in the dense woods of Bois d'Autrecourt, north of Salency. This was the day that Colthurst's son Theobald George was born, and it was also around this time that Colthurst was restored to command of C Company because of the depleted number of officers available. The paths in the wood were extremely difficult and, as night fell, it became very dark, so much so that the men could not see their own hands before their faces. The Rifles had to remain in position until 2 a.m., when they set off with two guides in single file, each holding on to the man in front as if blind. By dawn they had cleared the wood and acted as a rearguard to the division marching to Vic-sur-Aisne. Lieutenant Lowry remembered:

So the retreat continued day after day, deploying at intervals, getting such good cover with the aid of our entrenching tools that the Germans suffered heavily from our rifle fire and never knew where it came from. Except for the exhaustion, it was really splendid fighting, combining as it did rapidity of movement with the maximum effect on the enemy.[6]

By 5 September the battalion had almost reached Châtres. The long retreat was now over and it was time to go on the offensive: the Battle of the Marne had begun and the German advance was being checked. The following morning Lieutenant Lowry's mood changed to joy as the Rifles advanced towards the enemy: 'It had been very difficult to deal with the men, as for some time, like the officers – though we did not say so – they felt enraged at always being ordered to retire, as since Le Cateau we had not been permitted to have a really good biff at "Jerry".'[7] The battalion moved as part of the reserve, with the weather changing dramatically on 11 September when the temperatures dropped and heavy rain fell. Battling the elements, they marched onward until 14 September, when they reached the railway bridge over the Aisne near Ecluse. This bridge had been destroyed, so the river was crossed by means of an improvised footbridge made from a barge with planks alongside. The crossing was made in single file, which took a considerable time, and the Germans opened fire as soon as the head of the column approached the bridge. Corporal Lucy described the situation:

We had hardly cleared the shelled area near the bridge when bullets began whistling about us. We must have been within a couple of hundred yards of enemy riflemen but though we looked hard through the undergrowth we could not see them. We cursed them, and relying on the luck of soldiers, we bowed our heads a little, shut our jaws, and went stubbornly on … Our own shells were now bursting a short distance ahead, just beyond a crest line clearly visible to us. This line marked the near edge of a large plateau, and as we made it in a last rush we found this plateau edge forming a small continuous cliff of chalk varying from two to four feet high, giving good protection from bullets, and fair cover from shell-fire.[8]

According to Lowry:

We had a splendid fight that day, taking the hill and the wood on its summit before evening … Our flank here swung round into a wood, and we lined a bank fronting a stubble field which led upward at a gentle slope to the village of Condé, which both commanded the hill we occupied and the river below.[9]

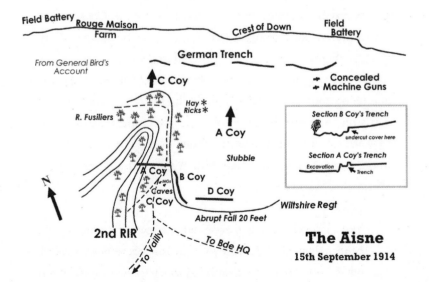

D Company was sent to occupy high ground at La Fosse Margnet; A Company followed and took up a position further to the left. Two platoons of D Company moved forward and began to entrench but had to move back again to avoid being fired on by their own artillery. Bird described subsequent events:

> The German position on the Aisne was good. Their artillery commanded the flat marshy valley, all bridges were broken so that our guns could not cross and, as a result, when our infantry occupied the southern edges of the bluffs on the north of the valley, they found themselves without artillery support, close to entrenched infantry who could not be reached by our guns, and exposed to the full force of hostile artillery fire. The Germans, then, gained the time they required to bring up reinforcements, and when they arrived were able to attack in advantageous circumstances.[10]

By nightfall the 3rd Division held high ground in a semi-circle about Vailly, the 7th Brigade being on the left, and the 2nd Royal Irish Rifles were due south of Rouge Maison. The division's war diary reported that 'the weather from the 13th to the 21st September was wet and cold and the infantry in the trenches, being unable to take off their wet boots or to cook and being constantly under shell fire had a trying experience'.[11] Early on 15 September a patrol from D Company was ordered forward to ascertain the whereabouts of the enemy and came under heavy fire. Lowry, then with A Company, described the events that followed:

> The ... colonel, wishing to make sure whether we were up against the main body of the enemy and whether they were entrenched, ordered two companies to attack, including my own. There was

practically no cover, and the ground was hard and bare, so we proceeded by short rushes ... The Germans were, however, waiting for us, and when we got to within a few hundred yards of their line they opened a perfect hail of machine-gun and rifle fire and shrapnel – a veritable tornado of flying, shrieking metal, well directed. Part of the company on our left got into the first line of German trenches, but were ultimately compelled to retire, as it was obvious that not only were the Germans dug in, but were in full force. Captain Bowen-Colthurst, who commanded this reconnaissance, was badly wounded in the assault, whilst two officers were killed and half the men killed or wounded; the machine-gun and shrapnel played havoc among us as we were getting back across the open valley.[12]

Bird, who rejoined the battalion at daybreak, had a different perspective:

On arrival at the hill crest I found the officers and men of A and D Companies standing about, and on asking what they were doing I was told that they thought the Germans had retired. I at once ordered two officer's patrols to be sent out to clear up the situation. I then went a little north and found Major Spedding who pointed out the enemy's trenches in a hollow 700 yards from us and told me he had sent C Company to occupy the edge of a wood some 300 yards from the enemy.

I agreed that this was sound but demurred in regard to the officer selected for this duty [Colthurst] as I had no confidence in his judgement and feared he might make a rash attack. Major Spedding, however, assured me that strict orders had been given to him not to proceed beyond the wood. I then asked how long ago C Company had been sent off and he replied 20 minutes.

As the distance to the edge of the wood was not more than a quarter of a mile and as no firing had been heard, I concluded that probably the Germans had retired, and ordered A Company to move forward east of the wood in support of C Company.

I now saw what I took to be a few Germans running away and, as this seemed to show that their trenches were still held, signalled to A Company to halt. No firing, however, took place, and I therefore sent my adjutant to the commander of A Company to tell him to advance but to proceed with the greatest possible caution. Major Spedding now joined A Company, and with the Machine Gun section the company moved forward. Almost immediately it began to attack by rushes and was met by heavy rifle, machine gun and artillery fire. The movements of the other company were hidden by the wood. About now the officer's patrols returned and reported one officer wounded and the enemy in force. As it was obvious that our partial attack could not succeed I sent my adjutant for B Company … and placed it in position to cover the retirement of the two other companies.

Meanwhile C Company had succeeded in rushing a trench and taking a few prisoners, but being met with heavy artillery fire and counterattacked was driven into the wood where A Company and the machine guns had been forced to take shelter. Those companies now streamed in disorder out of the wood and I rallied them 200 or 300 yards further back behind the crest. The Germans dropped several percussion shells among us as the men were rallying … I understand that the OC C Company, who was wounded, subsequently stated that he was under the impression that he had been sent forward to attack the Germans. I asked the OC A Company, who was also wounded, when I met him at Home [UK], why he had attacked, and he said that he had a faint recollection of having been told to advance with caution, but seeing the other company attacking he did so too.[13]

Lucy described Colthurst that day as he urged A Company to support him:

> … a tall gaunt captain with the light of battle in his eye. A very religious man he was too, always talking about duty, and a great Bible reader. Tall, sinewy, with pale face and pale-blue eyes, colourless hair, and a large, untidy, colourless moustache, he came at us looking for blood. He reminded me of a grisly Don Quixote. 'They have gone,' he cried jubilantly and with certainty, in a cracked voice, 'all the Germans have gone away, except about one platoon, which I have located in that wood to our left front. I intend to capture that enemy platoon with my company, but I want volunteers from A Company to move across the open to support me, while I work forward through the wood, which enters the left of my company line. Now, who will volunteer?' … [After the attack] the warlike commander of the left company, bleeding from several wounds in various parts of his body, and looking more fanatical than ever, would not have any of his hurts dressed until he had interrogated his prisoners. He questioned them in German, and was removed from them with difficulty, and made to lie on a stretcher.[14]

Colthurst, in an excited and agitated state, came close to shooting some of the prisoners before being restrained – in my judgement, this shows he was clearly not suitable for wartime leadership. In the opinion of Dr Paul Miller:

> Again, this indicates that at times of extreme stress he acted

in extreme ways and that he lacked self-control or an entirely balanced state of mind. His apparent lack of awareness of his wounds at this time indicates a significant level of dissociation … whereby an intolerable emotional conflict is so cut off from the person's consciousness that he becomes unaware of it.[15]

Colthurst had been hit three times. One bullet made a non-penetrating wound about four inches long and two inches wide to the left side of his chest; the extent of this wound prevented it from healing for a long time. Another bullet fractured the radius of his right forearm, near the elbow, and a third pierced the upper part of the same arm, removing some of the biceps muscle. As there were many wounded during the attack and insufficient medical help was available, Colthurst refused to take up the time of the doctor and was attended by an unskilled Belgian nun. He spent four days being transported in a cattle truck, without even a proper sling to support his arm and the broken bones grating against each other all this time. Having embarked at Rouen aboard the hospital ship *St David* on 19 September, he arrived at Southampton and was admitted to the Royal Herbert Hospital at Woolwich.

A medical board at Tidworth on 5 October granted him sick leave and he returned to his home in Cork. An examination at Cork Military Hospital on 18 November noted that the wounds were healed but movement in his right arm was limited. From there he seems to have been sent to Dublin, as on 21 November Dr Alfred R. Parsons, FRCP, at the Royal City of Dublin Hospital, observed that Colthurst had a loss of power in his right arm and that he was in a condition of marked nervous exhaustion and was quite unequal to any strain, stress or excitement, which would probably bring about a nervous breakdown.

He was rated as unfit for duty and granted sick leave for two months, being fit only for light duty thereafter. He was unable to sleep, suffered from headaches, and also had trouble with his ears. The next day Colthurst sent a letter home to his wife, Linda, from Wellington Barracks, Dublin, revealing just how delicate his physical and mental condition was:

My own heart and life,

Your sweetest letters reached me today and yesterday. It is good to be able to write fairly easily again and so I can write to you. My little one, I find I have made a mistake in coming here – I am not yet up to any exertion of any sort – and so I am applying for another Medical Board. I will let you know the results later on, but it is quite possible that they will grant me an extension of sick leave and, if so, I will return to Coolalta, especially as I can get no massage here. It is too stupid to be so weak still.

You little one, I know you will be glad if I come back to you, but I wouldn't return if it wasn't necessary. Not that I don't love you above all the words in the world. I am, however, really a 'crock' still, I'm afraid, and get 'cooked' very easily. However, I'll let you know if I return. You best of wives.

I saw Dr Parsons yesterday and he said I was to take two months complete rest and go to bed *very* early, so I am sending on his report and asking for a Medical Board. It's very stupid of me as I thought I was all right … I saw the Thompsons of Clonskeagh last night. They all asked for you and asked me out there to stay, and it's possible I may go out there as I cannot get any sleep in barracks. My nerves are weak or something and the trams keep me awake. I'm going to a Christian soldiers meeting tonight, here in Dublin. God bless you and much much love, you nicest wife.

Ever yours, Jonathan.[16]

In correspondence with his wife he liked to use the pet name 'Jonathan Jones'.

It is likely that Colthurst was suffering from post-traumatic stress resulting from the attack in which he was wounded. This would usually result in nightmares and daytime intrusive thoughts about the experiences.[17] A medical board at King George V Hospital, Infirmary Road, Dublin, reported on 1 December: 'he is suffering from nervous exhaustion, the result of active service'.[18]

Another letter was sent home on 22 December:

> Dearest ... If you write to mother please say I have everything I need, blankets, etc., also that I am not tiring myself as I am not doing any duty, also that I shall probably return home on an extension of sick leave ... Please send me the War Office letter on my desk telling me to apply for a Medical Board ... Take great care of yourself and take your tonic and go to bed early. Much much love, Jonathan.[19]

A medical board on 5 February 1915 found him 'still somewhat debilitated' and unfit for home service. On 5 March, while staying at Oakgrove, Colthurst bade farewell to his brother, Robbie, who was heading off to join the 1st Leinster Regiment in France. Ten days later a devastating tragedy struck when the 6 foot 4 inch Robbie was shot through the head over the parapet of a trench at St Eloi. An obituary appeared in *The Irish Times* on 23 March: 'Always an optimist with regard to the future of Ireland, he had devoted his life to the service of his country, and the forwarding of Irish interests. His loss to the whole country is great.'

Colthurst's period of convalescence was prolonged by attacks of nervous depression as he felt guilty for surviving when many, especially Robbie, had not. On 24 March, hoping to receive clearance to return to the Front, Colthurst had a consultation with Dr Parsons, who reported:

> I have today made a detailed examination of Captain Bowen-Colthurst and find him organically sound, with the following exceptions:
>
> Impaired range of movement and power in right arm due to a wound.
>
> A slight haze of albumen in the urine.
>
> Exaggeration of the knee reflexes which can readily be obtained above the patella.
>
> In my opinion Captain Bowen-Colthurst's nervous system has not yet become quite normal, and in my opinion also I do not think he is quite fit to bear any great strain without a definite risk of his breaking down.[20]

This confirms that Colthurst was suffering from a nervous debility because of his war action.[21]

On 25 March 1915 he received a telegram from the War Office commanding him to rejoin his regiment at the Front, but a medical board that day found him unfit for service. This was a considerable setback as he was one of the most senior members left in his regiment and would have expected that his chance to command a battalion could not be far off. It was also a serious blow to his already vulnerable mental state. He then applied for a position in the United Kingdom and was appointed brigade major under Brigadier General Reginald W.

R. Barnes, DSO, taking up his duties on 10 April at Ludgershall. A medical board at Tidworth, Wiltshire, certified him fit for general service on 5 May, noting that 'there is still slight impairment in the movements of the right forearm, otherwise he has recovered'. This determination may have had more to do with the need for officers rather than a true improvement in Colthurst's condition. He was replaced as brigade major on 10 July and prepared to return to France.

6

A CAREER RUINED

Just as things had started to improve, a ticking time bomb exploded following a damning complaint made by Colonel Bird on 11 April 1915 that had finally worked its way through the system:

Captain J. C. Bowen-Colthurst showed, during the first few weeks of the campaign of 1914, that his military capacity and judgement were of so low a standard and his mind so lacking in balance that in my opinion he is not fit to be entrusted with the leadership of a company in the field. This officer so far broke down on the morning after the action at Mons, and his actions and demeanours exercised so dispiriting an effect on his men, that I was obliged to suspend him from the command of his company. Three or four days later, when the pressure of the enemy's pursuit had somewhat relaxed ... I reinstated him in command of his company pending a decision by the Brigadier as to his future. I also verbally informed the Brigade-Major of the action that had been taken. Unfortunately an opportunity of thrashing out the matter did not occur before Captain Bowen-Colthurst was disabled.

On this occasion Captain Bowen-Colthurst showed great want of judgement, although displaying, I believe, high personal courage. The circumstances were as follows: during the forcing of the passage of the Aisne, I was placed in command of the Wiltshire Regiment and my own Battalion, the two forming the advanced-guard of the 7th Infantry Brigade. On the afternoon of 14 September, the advanced-guard crossed the river and occupied the heights of the right bank near Vailly. Next morning soon after daybreak, the remainder of the 7th Infantry Brigade passed the Aisne, when I rejoined my Battalion. On reaching the heights I found that Major Spedding, the Second-in-Command (now missing), had shortly before my arrival sent Captain Bowen-Colthurst's company forward to a distance of between 400–500 yards in front of the line held by the Battalion, for the purpose of occupying the northern edge of a copse which seemed to extend to a locality favourable for outflanking a German trench visible at about 750 yards from us.

When I demurred to the despatch of this Officer on such a mission – for throughout the campaign he had shown himself the least efficient and reliable of the company commanders – Major Spedding assured me that Captain Bowen-Colthurst had received definite orders not to proceed beyond the wood. It seems, however, that on reaching the edge of the wood Captain Bowen-Colthurst saw a portion of the enemy's trenches, which were invisible from the line held by the Royal Irish Rifles, lying about 250 yards to the front.

Without communicating with the Battalion headquarters Captain Bowen-Colthurst promptly led his company forward and captured this portion of trench. The enemy at once delivered a vigorous counter-attack supported by heavy Artillery fire, with the result that Captain Bowen-Colthurst's company was driven back with heavy loss, the whole of the officers (four) and about 75 NCOs and men being killed or wounded.[1]

Bird's statement shows that the stress of Colthurst's military service had affected his ability to function in the field. However, taking into account his statement below in his own defence, it may be that there was not as much dysfunction as believed, and that the behaviour was simply an expression of his personality traits. But that does not rule out the strong likelihood that he was suffering from significant mental health problems.[2] The battalion war diary for the attack had recorded: 'A and C Companies ordered forward to attack; came under heavy fire, artillery, machine guns and rifle and were compelled to fall back, a good many casualties'. This appears to contradict Bird as to what the orders actually were, but he was wounded on 19 September and neither he nor Spedding was available to assist the diarist.

On 21 July Colthurst received a telegram to proceed at once to the Front and rejoin his regiment. He believed that, having held a staff appointment, he was being given command as the senior available officer. However, on arrival at Folkestone he was summoned to the War Office and, without any explanation, was told to join a reserve battalion, the 3rd Royal Irish Rifles, at Portobello Barracks in Dublin. Only then was he made aware of Bird's report. The complaint was so contrary to his own recollections that he bizarrely instituted his own sworn enquiry before two lawyers, Justin McCarthy and Henry C. Bowen, the latter a relation of Colthurst's. Six non-commissioned officers (NCOs), all present at the Aisne, gave evidence that more or less supported his point of view, but this was a futile and immature method of contradicting a superior officer and one for which there was no provision in military regulations. The fact that Colthurst was unable to get his case investigated further by the War Office, and that he thought he had redeemed his reputation at the Aisne before he was seriously wounded, preyed greatly on his mind, creating a considerable sense of frustration at this perceived injustice.

While at Portobello Barracks he made a statement for the War Office on 31 July, pointing out that Bird did not know him very well as, out of his sixteen years of service, he had only served under Bird for a few months. Being sure of himself and confident in his abilities, he requested that the opinions of other commanding officers who knew him better be obtained regarding his fitness for leadership in the field. He also requested that the two generals on whose staff he had served be consulted. 'I have been on the Staff College list of my Regiment since 1906 and I would ask that the recorded opinion of the three senior officers of my Battalion, on my application to enter for the Staff College Examinations … be examined.' He then proceeded to address the issues arising:

> I received verbal orders from Major Spedding (now missing) to advance through the wood with my Company – and to clear up the situation. In the absence of Colonel Bird, Major Spedding was commanding the Battalion at that time. Outposts had reported that the sound of wheels had been heard at night and it was believed that the enemy were retiring. Major Spedding and I both knew from the report of our Scouts on the previous evening that the nearest Germans were entrenched about 200 yards outside the wood. I had a piquet close to the front edge of the wood watching the Germans. I asked Major Spedding specially if he wished me to attack, and he replied 'Certainly!' On reaching the front edge of the wood I directed No. 9 Platoon to hold the edge of the wood and to open fire on the Germans in front. This was done with considerable effect and several Germans were seen to fall.
>
> I was then reinforced by the Battalion Machine Guns, and I directed No. 9 Platoon and the Battalion Machine Guns to keep up the fire from the edge of the wood, No. 10 Platoon to work

up the valley in the left and to attack the German right. Nos. 11 and 12 Platoons to remain in reserve in the wood under CSM Harte. The attack made by No. 10 Platoon was successful, and the whole of the occupants of the trench, some 20 Germans, were put out of action, [and] six unwounded prisoners of the Prussian 64th Regiment were taken. A strong German 2nd line, some 300 yards away, was discovered behind the captured trench, and I directed No. 10 Platoon to fall back to the wood with their prisoners. Only two of my Platoons (about 80 men) were engaged in this attack, and of these only one Platoon advanced beyond the cover of the wood. The Platoon Commander of No. 10 (2nd Lieutenant Magenis) and the Battalion Scout Officer (2nd Lieutenant Swaine) who volunteered to go with him were both killed close to the captured trench. Lieutenant Peebles, Commanding No. 9 Platoon was subsequently wounded when the wood was shelled – but I have been unable to ascertain that there were more than 15 casualties, including officers, in the two Platoons during this attack and the firing and shelling which followed.

While this attack, which I was directing, was in progress, Major Spedding was himself directing another attack on the trenches to my right. This second attack was being carried out by A Company – Major Spedding came up to Nos. 11 and 12 Platoons ordering them to advance through the wood and attack in conjunction with A Company the German trench on my right. This attack was unable to reach the German trench and suffered heavily. Although Major Spedding is now missing, the fact that these two platoons of mine were led forward by Major Spedding himself, goes to prove that my attack on the left portion of the German trenches was in accordance with his orders.

The Germans then opened a very heavy shell fire on the wood and on our lines and the Company continued to suffer further casualties from shell fire throughout the day. The trench which had been captured by No. 10 Platoon was not re-occupied by the Germans until some five hours later. I would very especially ask if Lieutenant-Colonel R. A. C. Daunt, DSO, at present Commanding 1st Royal Irish Rifles, be asked if he has any objection to my serving under him in command of a Company.[3]

Lieutenant Colonel Daunt, from a County Cork family, was one of Colthurst's large circle of influential contacts.

Colthurst absolutely denied that he had broken down after the action at Mons or that he had caused any of his men to become dispirited, though this was clearly not the case. In conclusion, he complained that the incidents referred to in the report occurred in the autumn of 1914 and there had been an inordinate delay in the report being made and processed; it was not written until April 1915 and he did not receive it until July.

Colthurst's statement was forwarded to the War Office by Major General Sir Lovick Friend, general officer commanding-in-chief of the forces in Ireland, with these comments:

> Forwarded and strongly recommended for favourable considera-tion. It is difficult to understand why Colonel Bird's report has been so long delayed – it is dated 8 April 1915 – although the in-cidents referred to occurred in August and September 1914, and there does not appear to be any strong reason for the report to be made after such a long delay. As to the incident on 15 September on the Aisne, I would point out that the Officer Commanding the Battalion (Major Spedding) evidently acquiesced in Captain Colthurst's action as he co-operated with him and supported his attack as much as he could. This action itself bears evidence of Captain Colthurst's great personal bravery and dash and resulted

in the capture of a portion of the enemy's trenches, and if anything can be said against such action – it can only be to say that
it was an excusable error of judgement.[4]

The truth appears to be that Colthurst made an attack with one
platoon while Bird and Spedding thought the whole company
was attacking. In consequence, Spedding committed further
troops to an assault that was already being reversed. As well as the
officers, an additional nineteen men were killed that day because
of the attack by the two companies and the subsequent shelling
of the wood – these figures are favourable to Colthurst's version
of events. The delay in Bird making a report can be attributed
to the fact that he had lost a leg in action four days after the
attack, with Spedding being reported missing on the same day.
Moreover, Bird would readily be amenable to forming the worst
opinion of Colthurst's actions based on previous experiences.

Even with his powerful connections, Colthurst could not win
in these circumstances: as he had persuaded non-commissioned
officers to testify on his behalf and contradicted a high-ranking
officer, this effort was doomed from the start. Having gone
through many channels, the matter was finally settled in a letter
from Major General Frederick W. N. McCracken, formerly of
the 7th Infantry Brigade, who by then (5 September 1915)
was commanding the 15th (Scottish) Division. He stated
that he was fully aware of all the circumstances dealt with in
Bird's report and that he entirely concurred with the opinions
expressed. He added that, before the war, it had come to his
notice that Colthurst was below average compared to the
efficiency of company commanders in the battalion: 'Under
all the circumstances I do not consider this officer is qualified
in all respects for promotion.'[5] This seems to demonstrate that

when those higher up the chain of command balanced all of the information about Colthurst they clearly felt that he was not capable of command at a senior level. Alternatively, of course, they could be seen to be protecting one of their own.

A confidential War Office memo of 17 September stated that Colthurst was not to be promoted or to rejoin the British Expeditionary Force, and should be so informed. A copy of McCracken's report was shown to Colthurst, though he appeared to have forgotten this when he revisited the issue many years later. He was rated unfit for promotion and told that he would not serve with the army at the Front again. To compound his misery, on the domestic front it was about this time that he was also distressed by the death of a newborn daughter.

Colthurst's duties in Dublin were to drill raw recruits and address meetings as a recruiting agent – a difficult task, as military bands were sent in advance to the various districts. The bands having thus given timely warning of his imminent arrival, when Colthurst followed some hours later he would find that the younger men were nowhere to be seen. His mother, Georgina, recalled:

> From these recruiting expeditions I have often seen my son return absolutely worn out and in a state of extreme physical exhaustion after long and fatiguing marches. I urged upon him the necessity of consulting a doctor about himself, but his own idea was to carry on, faithfully carrying out whatever duty was allotted to him. The condition then prevailing in Dublin made this recruiting work especially trying and disheartening ... The death of his little daughter and his wife's very serious illness just before the outbreak of the rebellion further disturbed and depressed his mental condition.[6]

Clearly there must be questions over his mental state coming up to the time of the Easter Rising. Michael Slater, a soldier serving under Colthurst, recalled that he was greatly feared but respected by the troops since his return to Ireland, though his behaviour became more and more erratic – he kept himself aloof, stalking about, repeating phrases to himself. His orderly was often drunk and the talk was that Colthurst had specifically requested this man so that he might convert him, reading out long passages from and beating him over the head with a Bible.[7] 'It is easy to understand how, at the onset of the 1916 Easter Rising, Bowen-Colthurst was a mental powder-keg just ready to blow up.'[8] Obviously, he had serious mental health issues, which in particular circumstances could lead to a crisis with far-reaching consequences.

Captain John M. Regan, a district inspector of the Royal Irish Constabulary (RIC) who had recently been seconded into the army, recalled his time in Dublin when he joined the 3rd Royal Irish Rifles and was posted as second in command of a company under Colthurst:

I had heard of him years before in Clare, where he had married a lady in hunting circles and, even in those days, he was regarded as somewhat eccentric. He was a first-class soldier. Brave as a lion, he had a personality more suitable, perhaps for an army commander than for a captain. Whatever might have happened in a regular battalion, no one could stand up to him in the 3rd Battalion, a militia unit. He was definitely not normal, and was sincerely religious, but, unfortunately, religion with him amounted almost to a mania. His bravery was without question. A sergeant … told me that the captain had charged a German army corps with a platoon. He seemed intent on reforming the officers of the

battalion by getting them to attend prayer meetings. More unlikely subjects to work upon it would have been difficult to find.
In each officer's pigeon hole in the mess would appear, from time
to time, a notice to the effect that a meeting, with prayer, would
be held at a certain place on a particular afternoon and that free
teas would be provided. I well remember the second in command
[of the barracks, Major James Rosborough], a very long service
regular officer, looking at his invitation (he was it appears known
as the 'quart pot' in India on account of the amount of drink he
could hold without ill effects) and saying, 'If he offered us free
whiskies and sodas, Regan, he might get some of us to attend.' I
greatly doubted it myself.

I had only been a week or two in the company when he
informed me that he wanted to see me in the battalion orderly
room the following morning. I feared that as a temporary officer
working with a regular company commander and all regular
NCOs I was not regarded as fitting the bill and so attended the
orderly room with some slight trepidation. I was therefore more
than surprised when he informed the CO that from what he had
seen of me as second in command of his company, I was fitted to
command D Company which was then vacant …

I was exceedingly sorry for him in the serious trouble which
he got afterwards into during the rebellion, and I thought the
awful act committed by him in shooting prisoners without trial
showed in itself his state of mind at the time.[9]

Through his recruiting work, Colthurst was aware of one of
Dublin's best-loved characters, the eccentric County Cavan-
born Francis Sheehy Skeffington, a thirty-seven-year-old journalist and pacifist who dressed in knickerbockers, supported
votes for women and vigorously opposed recruitment and

the war effort. Sheehy Skeffington had championed the Irish Labour leader Jim Larkin during the Dublin Lockout of 1913 and, in a speech made at a meeting at Beresford Place on 23 May 1915, blamed the Allies for causing the war, declaring that if any power should be crushed it should be England:

> If you die here at home you have died defending your opinion as an individual and as an Irishman. If you go to the front and die, you have died doing the dirty work of England and strengthening the power of England. Stay at home and take the consequences even if the consequences be death, and if you died for it you die the same as Robert Emmet and Wolfe Tone.[10]

This speech resulted in Sheehy Skeffington being tried and imprisoned on 9 June 1915 for making a statement likely to prejudice recruitment, but he was soon released on licence under the Prisoners (Temporary Discharge for Ill-Health) Act 1913, having gone on a short hunger strike. After that he went on a tour of the USA, disseminating anti-British propaganda. He was an embarrassment to his father-in-law, David Sheehy, MP, who had several meetings with the chief secretary in an attempt to alleviate some of the retribution Frank was bringing down on himself. A Dublin Castle police file shows how he was regarded by the powers of the time. Phrases used included 'a very mischievous character', 'a contemptible creature' and 'a great nuisance'. Even the exasperated chief secretary added, 'He can't keep quiet if out of bed. To bargain with him or his helpless relatives is impossible.'[11]

At times called a crank, Sheehy Skeffington proudly pointed out that 'a crank is a small instrument that makes revolutions'. Despite this pronouncement it was an anxious man who wrote to his father on 26 March 1916: 'Anything may happen in the next months. A safety valve militant, but not militarism, is needed, and will be still more needed if, and when, the inevitable disillusionment comes to the physical force people.'[12] He also told Captain Jack White, a founding member and drill instructor of the Irish Citizen Army, on 5 April: 'Things are very grave here. The military authorities are determined to provoke bloodshed – to cause another '98 and get an excuse for a machine-gun massacre.'[13] In a letter to the *New Statesman*, dated 7 April, Sheehy Skeffington wrote:

> The situation in Ireland is extremely grave. Thanks to the silence of the daily Press, the military authorities are pursuing their Prussian plans in Ireland unobserved by the British public; and when the explosion which they have provoked occurs, they will endeavour to delude the British public as to where the responsibility lies.

On Wednesday 19 April 1916 Alderman Tom Kelly, a member of Sinn Féin, read out a document entitled *Secret Orders Issued to the Military* at a Dublin Corporation meeting; this was said to have originated in the chief secretary's office at Dublin Castle. It had been delivered to him by Sheehy Skeffington, who had been asked to do so by Patrick J. Little, a solicitor and editor of the nationalist *New Ireland*, who was unable to publish it because of military censorship.[14] The contents outlined a plan by General Friend to intern all known nationalists belonging to Sinn Féin, the Irish Volunteers and other groups; it later became known as the Castle Document. The document has generally been considered a forgery drawn up and distributed by the Military Council of the Irish Republican Brotherhood, who had infiltrated the leadership of the Irish Volunteers. Although the authorities vigorously denied the document's authenticity, it was enough to persuade Eoin MacNeill, chief of staff of the Volunteers, to back the Rising, which the Military Council had been planning for some time. Ireland was now moving inexorably towards rebellion.

7

THE 1916 RISING

Colthurst was out fishing on Easter Monday morning, 24 April, when the rebellion broke out in Dublin, but he quickly made his way back to Portobello Barracks. Urban warfare against their own civilians was not something for which Colthurst, or indeed the British Army as a whole, had any real experience or training. He was the wrong man in the wrong place and totally unsuited to the situation in which he found himself. The army must bear some responsibility for subsequent events because Colthurst was already considered unfit for active service, although, in fairness, a rebellion had not been anticipated, and he was supposed to be employed only at training and recruitment. To him it was intolerable to have Irishmen killing soldiers who had been and were defending Ireland. The very thing that had caused his initial problem with Colonel Bird – the thought of being on active service against his own countrymen – was now happening and the thought of it devastated him, sending his frail mental balance into free-fall.

Unfortunately, Lieutenant Colonel Walter E. C. McCammond, Colthurst's commanding officer, was in hospital with pleurisy, and that led to a certain element of indiscipline. Portobello Barracks (later renamed Cathal Brugha Barracks), lies on the south side of the city below the Grand Canal and just off Rathmines Road. It covers an area of forty acres and was built to accommodate about 2,000 men, but at that time only quartered some 600 men, half of whom would have been

Dublin 1916

Scale

1 km

Richmond Barracks
Kilmainham
Islandbridge Barracks
South Circular Road
Kingsbridge Railway Station
Royal Barracks
Arbour Hill
South Circular Road
Royal Hospital
Steven's Hospital
Rialto
South Dublin Union
James's St.
Guinness's Brewery
Thomas St.
Christchurch
Dolphin's Barn
Cork Street
The Coombe
Jacob's Factory
Bishop Street
Dublin Castle
Four Courts
River Liffey
Carlisle Bridge
Grand Canal
Wellington Barracks
South Circular Road
Camden St. Lr.
Grantham St.
Byrnn's
Camden St. Upr.
Aungier Street
Grafton Street
Mount Jerome Cemetery
Harold's Cross
Portobello Barracks
Grove Road
Portobello Bridge
Delahunt's
Kelly's Corner
St. Stephen's Green
Trinity College
Grosvenor Place
Rathmines
Rathmines Road Lr.
South Circular Road
Davy's Public House
Adelaide Rd.

79

on duty elsewhere. Throughout the early days of the rebellion wild rumours abounded regarding an imminent attack on the barracks and of alleged successes of the rebel forces. Naturally enough, the troops were jittery and the consensus among them was that strong measures needed to be taken. Many soldiers who were home on leave reported for duty and these reinforced the garrison, most of whom were raw recruits undergoing training. The remainder consisted of old soldiers fit only for home service or troops recuperating from wounds or illness. Colthurst may also have considered the rebellion as an opportunity to restore his military standing, much as he had attempted to do with his attack at the Aisne in September 1914.

An early warning sign of how Colthurst's attitude was developing involved William Boland, an ex-soldier of the Royal Irish Regiment, who had been arrested in the early afternoon of Easter Monday. The next morning Colthurst asked him if he had any complaints and Boland stated that soldiers had assaulted him. Colthurst shortened the grip on his swagger stick as if about to strike Boland and said, 'the less complaints you make about the military the better'. Boland was then placed in handcuffs and put into solitary confinement.[1]

Lieutenant Max C. Morris of the 11th East Surrey Regiment was attached to the Irish Rifles at the start of the rebellion, and from 6 p.m. on the Tuesday evening commanded a picket of thirty men in the vicinity of the nearby Davy's public house, located just on the other side of Portobello Bridge. Some distance ahead of them on the city side was Jacob's biscuit factory, a rebel strong point, from where shots were being fired. Morris's orders were to defend Davy's from being occupied by the rebels before an anticipated attack on the barracks and to keep the streets clear, but also to avoid conflict if possible.

At about 7 p.m. a large crowd was observed, approaching on both footpaths behind Francis Sheehy Skeffington, who was alone in the centre of the road handing out anti-looting leaflets and was in fact heading towards his nearby home at 11 Grosvenor Place.[2] The crowd was calling out his name and Morris, recognising the distinctive Sheehy Skeffington from a photograph and description he had been given, ordered two men to arrest him and take him to the barracks while the crowd was gradually persuaded to disperse. Part of the reason Morris ordered the arrest was because Sheehy Skeffington was thought to be causing a crowd to gather.[3] Shortly afterwards, Sergeant John A. Maxwell, Regimental Provost-Sergeant of the 3rd Royal Irish Rifles, took Sheehy Skeffington from the east gate

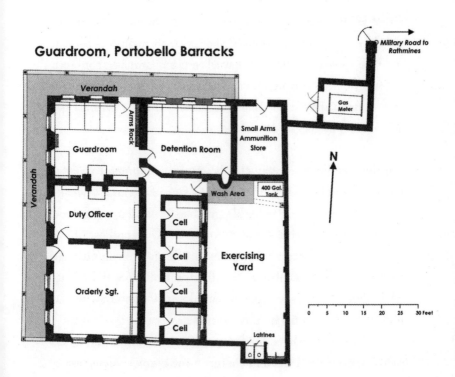

Guardroom, Portobello Barracks

guardroom to the Orderly Room of the adjutant, Lieutenant Samuel V. Morgan. Sheehy Skeffington explained that he was not a Sinn Féiner and, though in sympathy with them, was opposed to militarism and in favour of passive resistance. He was then returned to the guardroom while Morgan sought advice, as no charge had been made against the prisoner. The garrison adjutant, Captain G. Stratford Burton, told him by telephone to detain the prisoner pending further enquiries. It was then that Colthurst searched Sheehy Skeffington and handed over some documents to the adjutant, none of which was incriminating and in fact proved that Sheehy Skeffington had been focusing his efforts on trying to form a committee to stop looting in the city. One leaflet read:

> When there are no regular police on the streets it becomes the duty of the citizens to police the streets themselves to prevent such spasmodic looting as has taken place. Civilians (both men and women) who are willing to co-operate to this end are asked to attend at Westmoreland Chambers (over Eden Bros.) at five o'clock this Tuesday afternoon.[4]

Sheehy Skeffington was actually returning home from that meeting, which had failed because of a lack of attendees. Meanwhile, his formidable wife, Hanna, had been delivering food during the day to rebel strong points at the General Post Office and the Royal College of Surgeons, in addition to volunteering to carry dispatches. Sheehy Skeffington himself was friendly with some of the leaders, particularly James Connolly, who had nominated him as his literary executor.

According to Major Sir Francis Vane, who, on offering his services, had been placed in charge of the barracks' defences:

It seems to have been a well-known fact that Colthurst was an hysterical officer and fanatical, a fact which I can to an extent confirm. On the second day of the Rebellion, I went into the Mess room to get a sandwich and found him alone there. He was sitting with his elbows on the table and his head between his hands, and on my appearance, he turned to me saying: 'Is it not dreadful, Sir Francis, to have to shoot Irishmen' – a sentiment in which I heartily agreed.[5]

When a report was received that rebels were in Alderman Kelly's house, Major James Rosborough, the acting commanding officer at the barracks, having consulted the general officer commanding, ordered Colthurst to occupy the tobacco shop owned by Alderman James J. Kelly at Kelly's Corner, 35–36 Upper Camden Street, at the junction with Harcourt Road, about 300 yards beyond Portobello Bridge. This was the first of a series of errors: the correct address should have been the home of Sinn Féin Alderman Tom Kelly, Sheehy Skeffington's associate, at nearby Longwood Avenue, South Circular Road.

By now Colthurst had succumbed to the pressures of the confused military scenario he faced and, without any authority, made the extraordinary and questionable decision to take Sheehy Skeffington along as a hostage, his hands tied behind his back, which was contrary to every rule of warfare as understood in the British Army at the time. With them were about forty men and Second Lieutenant Leslie Wilson, 5th Royal Irish Fusiliers, who noticed that the captain was in a highly excited condition. Before they left the barracks the unfortunate prisoner was told to say his prayers, which he refused to do. Colthurst then ordered his men to take off their hats and said:

'Oh Lord God, if it shall please Thee to take away the life of this man forgive him for Christ's sake.'

Just as they moved out onto Rathmines Road, at about 11 p.m., they encountered three young men, J. J. Coade, Laurence Byrne and Dermot Keogh. Colthurst demanded to know what they were doing on the street when martial law was in force. He was told that they were returning home having just been to a Sodality meeting in the nearby Roman Catholic church. Under orders, a soldier then struck one of them – Coade, a nineteen-year-old – on the left side of his head with a rifle butt. Distracted by two other civilians who happened on the scene, William Devine and John Hughes, Colthurst pointed his revolver at them while they explained who they were. On turning round again, Colthurst noticed Coade and his friends moving away. At once he shot Coade, mortally wounding him in the abdomen. Lieutenant Wilson later testified at the Royal Commission of Inquiry into Colthurst's killings that Coade used offensive language and called Colthurst a 'bloody fool'. Wilson was not very forthcoming with his evidence (even though he was then taking Holy Orders) and was contradicted by the two civilian witnesses, Devine and Hughes, who stated that Coade gave no offence. However, the Sodality meeting had ended at 8.30 p.m., over two hours before the incident, so it is possible that Coade and his companions were observed loitering in the vicinity of the barracks during that interval.[6]

The soldiers then proceeded towards Portobello Bridge, with the captain shooting a rifle in the air. Circumstantial evidence indicates that Colthurst shot at least one other civilian en route, as some witnesses stated that they saw him kill with a rifle, whereas Coade was shot with a revolver. At the bridge they met up with Morris's picket and Colthurst divided his own group in two, leaving Lieutenant Wilson at the bridge with Sheehy Skeffington, under orders to shoot the hostage if the advancing group was 'knocked out', while he proceeded to Kelly's with the rest of the men. Morris thought Colthurst 'did not seem to be right in the head at the moment – he seemed to be labouring under tremendous excitement', while Wilson later admitted that he would have carried out the order.[7] Private Walter J. Farrell, 3rd Royal Irish Regiment, was with Wilson's group and overheard him saying to Sheehy Skeffington: 'I am going to leave you here in front and I want you to say your prayers now, for if we are fired on you shall not get the time.'[8]

Over at Kelly's Corner, Alderman Kelly had been dining with his sister and Patrick James McIntyre, editor of *The Searchlight*, an anti-trade union and anti-German nationalist publication. He was interviewing Kelly for an article about Indian students. Also present was a 'well-known gentleman, a Conservative', a Mr Lyons, whose full name was not disclosed at the later inquiry. McIntyre, aged thirty-eight, was a self-serving and unscrupulous character, who was expelled from the Socialist Party of Ireland in 1904 and had become notorious for his blackleg activities. He was for a time the Dublin branch secretary of the Workers' Union. Kelly, a justice of the peace and former high sheriff of Dublin, left the premises for a short time at about 11 p.m. and crossed the street to a shop to buy some fruit for McIntyre's supper. At that time, Thomas Dickson, aged thirty-one, a diminutive Scotsman of Irish parentage, a 'deformed' invalid and editor of the loyalist weekly *Eye Opener*, was making his way to his home in the adjoining Harrington Street when he heard shots being fired by the approaching troops and rushed into Kelly's for shelter.

Republican sources from this time show that neither

McIntyre nor Dickson were popular individuals amongst those
who were part of the rebellion:

> What may not be known is that the two men ... were two of the
> tools previously used by the Dublin Employers' Federation in the
> attempt to 'smash Larkinism'. McIntyre published a scurrilous
> weekly called 'The Toiler', which had no other purpose than to
> slander Larkin. Arthur Griffith was not above making use of him
> for the same purpose. He got space in 'Sinn Féin' for some of his
> abuse and replies to his attacks were more often suppressed than
> published.[9]

Michael Noyk, a solicitor with republican sympathies, claimed
that McIntyre was 'a very unattractive character' and Dickson
was 'a very unsavoury gentleman ... who wrote a blackmailing
paper ... Dickson was purely occupied with blackmailing'.[10]

When Colthurst arrived at Kelly's shop he ordered one of
his men to throw a grenade through the stockroom window
to the side of the premises. This caused considerable damage
and injured a shop assistant.[11] Kelly's sister recalled the captain
ordering them to put their hands up and saying, 'Remember, I
could shoot you like dogs. Martial Law is proclaimed. I am an
Irishman myself. We have shot persons in the street before we
came in.' When the names of those present were being taken,
McIntyre introduced himself as a loyal subject, but one of the
soldiers said that his publication was a rebel paper, confusing
it with *The Spark*, which fitted that description. The captain
grabbed him by the collar and ordered: 'Take that man, and
if he resists shoot him like a dog.' Dickson was also arrested.
After twenty minutes the patrol rejoined the detachment at the
bridge and Colthurst's whole group returned to the barracks

about midnight. Sheehy Skeffington was kept alone in a cell while the two others who had been arrested were put in the detention room.[12]

Colthurst went to bed at 3 a.m. but, being unable to sleep, spent time reading his Bible. He came across a passage in Luke 19:27 that appears to have impacted on his fragile mental faculties: 'But those mine enemies, which would not that I should reign over them, bring hither, and slay them before me.' No amount of evidence or explanation had been able to convince him that Sheehy Skeffington, McIntyre and Dickson were not dangerous subversives. He had set himself on a course that both ruined his life and ended the lives of others.[13]

Second Lieutenant W. Monk Gibbon, Reserve Hired Transport Depot, Army Service Corps, a Dubliner, aged nineteen, who had reported to the barracks at the start of the rebellion, recalled Wednesday morning, 26 April:

> The Rising had gone to Colthurst's head. It had made him fighting mad; or rather it had released, as too much whiskey can release in another man, whole areas of unsuspected and often highly unpleasant aspects of personality, a hidden sadist and fanatic … In certain respects one seemed to be participating in a chaotic dream rather than in real life … By this time I knew Colthurst by sight; a tall officer with a slight stoop of the shoulders and a very grave expression. Even if I had not already known him and heard nothing of his behaviour the night before, I would have been struck by his appearance when I saw him now early on Wednesday morning. Around his eyes were two huge black circles, almost as though they had been blacked in to allow him to take part in some circus turn … He looked as though he were carrying the whole weight of the insurrection upon his shoulders.

Striding about near the entrance to the orderly room he was just one more fantastic element in the general uncertainty.[14]

Out of curiosity, and having heard from a soldier about how brave Sheehy Skeffington had been the night before, Gibbon accompanied the quartermaster, Captain Henry W. Foster, as he went to the guardroom to inspect the breakfasts of eight prisoners:

Dickson is tiny, a dwarf of about four feet six, a grotesque figure in a black coat and with curious eyes. McIntyre is of medium height and burly. Leaving the large room we go down a passage to the smaller cell. The keys are fetched and it is opened. It is a tiny cell, Skeffington, with his hands handcuffed behind his back, gets up and bows to us. There is something dignified about the action, though my first impressions are of a slightly ridiculous figure. He is small with a reddish beard and is wearing knickerbockers. These and the Votes for Women badge in his buttonhole suggest the Hyde Park orator … He has a wonderful smile and there is a gentleness about the whole man, in every move, in every word he says.[15]

Colthurst went to the guardroom at 10.20 a.m. and told the duty officer, Second Lieutenant William L. P. Dobbin, who was standing outside, that he was going to take out three prisoners and shoot them as he thought that it was the right thing to do. Dobbin, as duty officer, should never have permitted this, and at the very least should have objected, but he was a young man, eighteen years of age and with no experience, so he deferred to the senior officer, though he noticed that the captain was not his usual self and appeared to be in an excited state. Dobbin called to Second Lieutenant Alexander S. Wilson, 7th Royal Dublin

Fusiliers, a nineteen-year-old, who was standing on duty at the nearby main gate, to cycle the 500 yards to the orderly room and inform the adjutant.

Inside the guardroom Colthurst ordered Sergeant John W. Aldridge of the 10th Royal Dublin Fusiliers to bring Sheehy Skeffington, McIntyre and Dickson out to the enclosed yard at the rear. Aldridge, an Englishman, was an old soldier, fifty years of age, who had re-enlisted for the war. Rifleman Michael Ireland, the key holder, unlocked the door of the detention room and called out Dickson and McIntyre. Dickson quipped ironically, 'I suppose we're going to be shot.' They then collected Sheehy Skeffington from his cell before going out to the yard. The walls were about eleven feet high and the yard itself was roughly 35 by 21 feet. Six armed members of the guard were also brought out and lined up as Colthurst told the prisoners to go to the wall at the far end of the yard. As they turned round he ordered the soldiers to load, present and fire their rifles: the prisoners fell to the ground.[16] Despite a statement to the contrary made by Hanna Sheehy Skeffington, the eyewitness evidence shows that not one word was uttered by the victims after their entry to the yard and that they were shot in the torso, not the head. Hanna claimed of Sheehy Skeffington that 'He refused to be blindfolded and met death with a smile on his lips, saying before he died that the authorities would find out after his death what a mistake they made. He put his hand to his eyes and the bullet passed through his hand to his brain.'[17]

The volley of shots was heard just as Second Lieutenant A. S. Wilson returned from the adjutant, and Dobbin rushed into the yard to see the three bodies covered in blood. He thought he saw a movement in one of Sheehy Skeffington's legs and sent Second Lieutenant Fred S. Tooley, Royal Irish Rifles, for instructions to the orderly room. Tooley returned with orders from Colthurst to shoot again, so Dobbin duly lined up a second firing squad of four men and complied with the order.

Colthurst then went to the adjutant, Lieutenant Morgan, to report the executions, saying that he was afraid that the prisoners might escape or be rescued by the rebels, adding that both he and Morgan had brothers killed in the war and that he himself was as good an Irishman as those he had ordered to be shot. Morgan recalled that, at the time, there was heavy firing going on around the barracks. Lieutenant Morris, who was present, observed that Colthurst 'seemed then rather worse than the night before – he was perfectly stupid ... He was extremely agitated and excited. I do not know Captain Colthurst very well – indeed he did not strike me at the time as a man who should be at any time in command of troops.' Morgan, having visited the guardroom and seen the bodies, made a report to Major Rosborough at about 10.45 a.m., to Major Smith at Irish Command headquarters and to the garrison adjutant, Captain Burton.[18] Sergeant James Geoghegan, Royal Army Medical Corps, then took the bodies to the morgue.

Colthurst's mother justified his actions in the following manner:

He found the explanation of these deeds in the inflammatory speeches and writing which had for some time past come under his notice in his recruiting work and with which the country was flooded. In his heart he believed that the dissemination of such literature had pointed direction and guidance to the spilling of so much blood. He prayed to God for guidance. And in his overwrought state, he forced himself to take the decision which he loathed and hated but which he was convinced was his duty, of condemning to death those whom he held to be, through their writings, in great measure the authors of the revolution and responsible for horrors in the middle of a great war, which the safety of the whole Empire demanded should be won.[19]

Colthurst began to realise that his actions would be condemned and informed Major Rosborough that he had acted on his own responsibility and might possibly hang for it. Rosborough requested a report in writing and ordered him not to leave the barracks, an order that Colthurst chose to ignore. Rosborough did not put any measures in place to ensure that he was obeyed, which, in the circumstances, was a serious error. Soon after this, at about 11 a.m., Colthurst led a group of soldiers to attack rebel outposts located at Andy Byrne's shop and Delahunt's public house, which were located opposite each other at the junction of Lower Camden Street and Grantham Street. Hanna Sheehy Skeffington claimed that other murders were committed that day:

On the same day Captain Colthurst was in charge of troops in Camden Street, when Councillor Richard O'Carroll surrendered (one of the Labour leaders in Dublin City Council). He was marched with his hands over his head to the back yard and Captain Colthurst shot him in the lung. When a soldier pityingly asked was he dead, Captain Colthurst said, 'Never mind, he'll die later'. He had him dragged out into the street and left there to be picked up by a bread van. Ten days later O'Carroll died in great agony. For six days his wife knew nothing of him and when at last she was summoned to Portobello, he could only whisper in her ear his dying statement, which she repeated to me … On the same day Captain Colthurst took a boy, whom he suspected of Sinn Féin knowledge, and asked him to give information. When the boy refused, he got him to kneel in the street, and shot him in the back of the head as he raised his hand to cross himself.[20]

Dick O'Carroll was a quartermaster in the Irish Volunteers and general secretary of the Brick and Stone Layers Trade Union. He was captured at Delahunt's bar, 42 Lower Camden Street, and was shot through the right lung. Hanna's account of the murder of O'Carroll is generally true and was based on statements provided to her by Mrs Annie O'Carroll, Alderman Kelly's sister Mary Bridget Kelly, his shop assistant Michael Brennan, and Mrs Mary Smyth and Bridget O'Connor, both of 38 Lower Camden Street. However, none of them mentioned a boy being shot, although they did describe the shooting of an unarmed Irish Volunteer in uniform just as he was about to bless himself.[21]

Other accounts shed light on the second shooting: 'I then heard that a friend of mine, Patrick Nolan, 2nd Battalion … had been shot by Captain Colthurst. He had been taken by surprise by the military … and was brought down on to the footway and shot out of hand.'[22] Nolan, who survived the shooting, later stated that he was captured at Byrne's shop and was the only person present in the building at the time: 'They just brought me outside the door. The sergeant in charge said I had better say my prayers as he was going to shoot me. He shot me all right [through the chest]'.[23] Nolan and O'Carroll were both members of the Jacob's factory garrison.

A group of Trinity College and Inns of Court Officers' Training Corps men were part of the action at Byrne's and Delahunt's. One of the Trinity College members, Cadet Sergeant Gerald Fitzmaurice Keatinge, wrote to Monk Gibbon many years later:

About six men went as far as Pleasants Street and kept the crowd up there. The Captain then ordered a Second Lieutenant [Leslie Wilson], another Cadet, and myself to search Delahunt's shop, which lies opposite Byrne's … the rebels opened fire on us from across the street. The Captain was undaunted and walked about the street giving his orders as if there was nothing the matter. Finally, he ordered a soldier to run across and break Byrne's window. This was done and a bomb thrown right in. After a few seconds a terrific explosion took place and the inside of the shop was completely wrecked. The Second Lieutenant then called for volunteers to explore Byrne's, so I and one of the Rifles went with him. After searching two rooms we came on one of the Sinn Féiners at a window with his rifle ready. I covered him while the officer disarmed him. The prisoner was brought down and after about three minutes was shot by order of the Captain, but only wounded … A second rebel was found in the shop on the other side of the street and also put on a cart – being wounded – and brought to barracks.

One has to admit that Colthurst seemed quite unafraid and to that not inconsiderable extent in control of himself. When I reported to Colthurst that we had a prisoner and asked what should be done with him, he replied in the most matter of fact way, 'Shoot him. Shoot him'. Whether he saw that I was shaken at this – I was only seventeen years old – I do not know, but at any rate he made the man kneel down to make his peace with God, and then ordered a sergeant to shoot him, which he did at point blank range, but as I have said, did not kill him. All this took place in full view of many people, admittedly a little distance away. Moreover, there was never any question of shooting him out of sight as apparently you were told.[24]

The behaviour and lack of fear that Colthurst displayed at that time may well indicate a death wish on his part. Later that day he allegedly informed Major Rosborough that he had been in communication by telephone with Irish Command headquarters about the murders and was told that everything would be done to help him.[25] He made a statement that evening to justify his actions:

> I have to report for your information that yesterday evening at about 11 p.m., according to your orders, I proceeded with a party of 25 men to 'Kelly's Tobacco Shop' in Harcourt Road. Some shots were fired at us but whether from this shop or not I cannot say. Two men were seen standing in conversation outside the shop who at once bolted inside. An entrance was effected and four men were made prisoners, two of whom were subsequently released, the other two being detained. The two men detained were McIntyre of the *Searchlight* (Editor) and Dickson, Editor of the *Eye Opener*. Sniping was going on and I lodged the two men detained in the Portobello Guard Room … This morning at about 9 a.m. I proceeded to the Guard Room to examine these two men and I sent for them and for a man called Skeffington who was also detained. I had been busy on the previous evening up to about 3 a.m. examining documents found on these three men and I recognised from these documents that the three men were all very dangerous characters. I therefore sent for an armed guard of six men and ordered them to load their rifles and keep their eyes on the prisoners. The Guard Room was full of men and not a suitable place, in my opinion, in which to examine the prisoners. I ordered therefore the three prisoners to go into the small courtyard of the Guard Room. I regret now that I did not have these three men hand cuffed and surrounded as the

yard was a place from which they might have escaped. When I ordered these three men into the yard I did not, however, know this. The Guard was some little distance from the prisoners and as I considered that there was a reasonable chance of the prisoners making their escape and knowing the three prisoners (from the correspondence captured on them the previous evening) to be dangerous characters, I called upon the Guard to fire upon them which they did with effect, the three men being killed ... I have further the honour to report that at 11 a.m. this morning I proceeded with a party of 70 men and examined a house belonging to Mr Byrne, Grocer in Camden Street. A large number (several hundred) of rounds of ammunition were found in this house and Bandoliers, haversacks and 15 rifles of various patterns, were secured in this house and in 42 Camden Street (Delahunt) which is nearly opposite ... One man, name unknown, was found with arms in his hands in Delahunts and was wounded and captured. One other man (name unknown) was captured in Byrne's and as seditious (pro-German) literature was found on him and as he had arms in his possession he was made prisoner and placed in [the] charge of Sergeant Kelly. Later Sergeant Kelly informed me that the man had attempted to escape but was fired upon, wounded and re-captured ... During the whole of the time (about 1½ hours) while these two houses were being searched, my men were being fired upon from Lower Camden Street from some houses which I was unable to locate. The aim was however extremely inaccurate and the shots were spasmodic. The two wounded prisoners together with the arms and ammunition secured were brought back to barracks. I have to bring to your notice the assistance rendered to me on the occasion by CSM Lyle ... No other men were fired upon except the two men referred to.[26]

In considering this statement, it must be emphasised that there was absolutely no possibility of the prisoners escaping from the enclosed yard – they would have had to return through the guardroom, having first gone past the firing party – and the minimal amount of documents found on them would have taken only minutes to read. In addition, Second Lieutenant Gibbon overheard Colthurst encouraging Sergeant Aldridge to say that the prisoners had been trying to escape.[27] It has often been believed that because Colthurst behaved in such a rational and conniving way at times during this period that his mental problems were not genuine. I therefore sought the assistance of Dr Paul Miller, MD, BCh, BAO, DMH, MRCPsych, a consultant psychiatrist, who gave this opinion:

> This pattern of behaviour is consistent with a person who suffers from significant and substantial dissociative symptoms. We can usefully consider our psyche to be made up of a collection of different ego states, rather than just one united self. In other words, the psyche is like a cake shop that sells lots of cakes. These cakes are all recognised by the customers as cakes, but they come in a variety of forms that are suitable for different occasions. They all have slightly different recipes. The wedding cake and the birthday cake are both cakes but will look and taste differently: each one being appropriate for the occasion for which it is intended.
>
> A person may normally move smoothly from one pattern of behaving and thinking to another. The soldier comes home from the war zone and becomes the husband and father; we would hope that he behaves accordingly when home with family. Now in some cases this fails to occur and some individuals with the affective disorder post-traumatic stress disorder (PTSD) have

exactly this dilemma. The person's brain with PTSD tells them that they are still in danger and a door banging in the house can trigger a response more appropriate to an Improvised Explosive Device being detonated nearby.

Now these ego states are normally smoothly transitioning from one to the other, however, in some people the ego states have been generated as a result of trauma and are linked to dysfunctional memories. These dysfunctional ego states can have a pattern of behaviour that is extreme and out of keeping with the person's normal demeanour and behaviour. In the most extreme forms they are operating as separate identities and can be unaware of each other's existence; this most extreme form of dissociation is called Dissociative Identity Disorder. Ego states are triggered by certain environments that cause a switching from one ego state to another, e.g. the door banging loudly causes the person who is in 'husband' ego state to suddenly switch to 'soldier'.

In the case of Bowen-Colthurst the stress of the situation appears to have triggered an ego state switch to a setting that was driven by extreme fear and whose primary aim was the reduction of threat at all costs. Here his mental state could be considered as switching between the 'calm and in control' officer to the 'berserk terrified' officer who had to eliminate the perceived threat at all costs. As far as Bowen-Colthurst was concerned this was a matter of life and death. This is not at all unintelligible and can be understood by considering what is happening in the brain whilst this behaviour is playing out. The perceived intense threat triggers the amygdala, which is the brain's equivalent of the metal detector at the airport. This alarm results in the thalamus, which is acting as the security guard, closing the entrance to the higher brain centres that could bring a more accurate assessment and improved decision-making. At the same time there is a signal sent to the adrenal glands and the body is flooded with adrenalin, which drives the fight–flight–freeze response. All these things mean that the person is now functioning at a more instinctual and less rational level of thinking and deciding. The emotional dissociation means that although the experience is being driven by fear and threat perception the person may be feeling numb. Once the person comes out of this neural setting they may be amnestic for the whole period of the dissociation or they may have fragmentary or full recall: depending on several factors.

If the person is made aware of their actions and if these actions have been at odds with core personality traits then they may insist that they were either 'not there' or state that they acted in a manner other than what they have been accused of doing. At some level the person is convinced that they are being falsely or maliciously accused.[28]

When asked how Colthurst could have had the ability to falsify evidence and yet be insane, it was explained that when Colthurst temporarily regained his composure it could colourfully be called an 'Oh shit!' moment:

Where no amnestic barrier exists, the normal ego state that is usually in control, which is referred to as the Apparently Normal Part (ANP) in the structural dissociation model, may be deeply ashamed or upset and it is conceivable that at such a time the ANP then acts to minimise the impact of the poor choices made by the Emotional Part. The 'Oh shit!' moment would naturally trigger self-preservation drives and in some people lying and the falsification of evidence may be the adaptation that they resort to.[29]

On the afternoon of 26 April Major Vane gave a stern lecture to the assembled officers on the limits of martial law and the exercise of restraint. Colthurst, with his training, would have been well aware of such limits and his failure to comply with them can only be seen as either a deliberate decision or a sign of mental debility.

At about 4.45 p.m. Lieutenant Morris encountered Colthurst in the officers' mess. There were several junior officers present, most of whom were strangers to the barracks. 'Captain Colthurst made a very ridiculous set speech indeed as to Sir Francis Vane doing all sorts of wicked things and being a Sinn Féiner and a pro-Boer. On that occasion he did not seem to be right in the head … He said he should not be allowed in the barracks and that he should be shot.'[30] Morris told the other officers not to pay any attention to what Colthurst had said, and thought the captain was not quite himself at the time. However, Colthurst's opinion about Major Vane was not entirely fanciful, as I shall show later.[31]

Captain Edward A. Gerrard, Royal Field Artillery, a past pupil of Clongowes College and a Gallipoli veteran, had been wounded in an earlier engagement at Mount Street Bridge and taken to the barracks hospital. He observed Colthurst 'raging along the perimeter of the walls. Even then I was told he was quite mad. He was heavily armed. He was shouting and yelling and patrolling the place. That was why the troops were frightened of him. He was the boss of that place and was letting everyone know it.'[32] Yet Monk Gibbon remembered that Colthurst went out of barracks on several other raids and that some of the younger officers liked to accompany him, maintaining that he was the right sort of man to deal with the situation – 'It needed toughness, they said, and he was not afraid to be tough.'[33]

That night, at about 11.15 p.m., the three victims of the earlier execution were buried within the confines of the barracks, under the supervision of Captain Philip E. Kelly, Royal Irish Fusiliers, Second Lieutenant Alfred H. Toppin, 3rd Royal Irish Rifles, and Lieutenant James C. McWalter, MD, Royal Army Medical Corps, who formally identified the bodies. The burial service was conducted by Fr Francis E. O'Loughlin, a local Catholic curate and chaplain at the barracks.

On the afternoon of Thursday 27 April Colthurst and Lieutenant Leslie Wilson were on defence duty in the barracks. Private W. J. Farrell was with them and recalled:

> I was stationed in the far end of the barracks behind the church near that public house on that road that goes up by the canal … We got orders from the Captain to shoot man, woman or child after half-seven that was seen coming toward the barracks from that point. The next morning I went out with a party under Captain Colthurst to Harold's Cross Road to raid Harold's Cross Cottages. On the way we met an old man who stopped to look at us. Captain Colthurst walked up to him and struck him in the head knocking his hat in the road, which he gave a kick and broke.[34]

Meanwhile Hanna Sheehy Skeffington, a daughter of David Sheehy, MP, had been frantically trying to get news of her husband from whom she had not heard since Tuesday evening. Her brother, Eugene Sheehy, a lieutenant in the Royal Dublin Fusiliers, was engaged in the fighting during the week. One of her sisters, Margaret, was the widow of Frank Culhane, a solicitor and former taxing master in the Irish Courts of Justice, and another, Mary, was the wife of the highly regarded Lieutenant Thomas M. Kettle, a barrister, politician, poet and professor of economics, who was on active service in France with 9th Royal Dublin Fusiliers.

By Friday 28 April, after hearing all sorts of rumours about her husband, Hanna asked her two sisters to try to find out what had happened to him. Having failed to get any information at the local police station, they went to Portobello Barracks at one o'clock in the afternoon. Initially they had no difficulty in gaining entrance and began by asking Second Lieutenant Joseph Beatty, 3rd Royal Munster Fusiliers, who treated them well, for news about their brother, Lieutenant Eugene Sheehy. However, when they asked about their brother-in-law Frank, Beatty became flustered and excused himself to go and consult with other officers. On his return he informed them that he regretted he would have to place them under arrest as they were thought to be Sinn Féiners. Despite the sisters protesting the absurdity of this accusation, they were placed under guard and marched across the barrack square to the orderly room, where they remained outside while officers inside discussed the matter. Colthurst then came on the scene and questioned them. When they mentioned Sheehy Skeffington, the captain denied any knowledge of him and ordered them to leave the barracks and not to talk to each other. An embarrassed Beatty escorted them out to Rathmines Road and they then went and told Hanna what had happened.

About four o'clock that afternoon Hanna got word from J. J. Coade's father that when he had seen his son's body in the barracks on Wednesday night it was beside that of her husband. This was confirmed by Father O'Loughlin, who told her he had officiated at Frank's burial. He explained that he had informed Coade's family because the shooting happened on a public street. However, as a military chaplain, he considered he was unable to divulge anything that had happened inside the barracks.[35]

At 7 p.m. that Friday evening, as Hanna was putting her only child, Owen, who was almost seven years old, to bed, a group of soldiers under Colonel Henry T. W. Allatt and Colthurst arrived at her home. According to Hanna, before she could react a volley of bullets was fired through the bay window and the soldiers burst through the front door with bayonets fixed. Colonel Allatt, aged sixty-nine at the time, was a draft-conducting officer and joined the raid on his own initiative.

Hanna's version of bullets being fired into her house was accepted in the later Royal Commission of Inquiry by Sir John Simon after he visited the property.[36] However, Major Gerald H. Pomeroy Colley, a staff officer at Irish Command headquarters, was sent to inspect the house on 17 May. Hanna was absent but he met her sister, Mrs Kettle, and a maid: 'No shots were fired. I searched and could find no traces of bullets anywhere. Door was intact, no signs of forcing it. Troops apparently broke two windows to get in … two cheap locks on cupboards were forced … They will both corroborate the above statements.'[37] Before the war, Colley, a retired major of the 3rd Royal Irish Regiment, was a resident magistrate in County Tipperary.

Sergeant Roger Cooney, a former constable of the RIC who had enlisted in the 3rd Royal Irish Rifles, was posted nearby at the time of the raid. He made a statement on 27 June 1916: 'No shots were fired at or struck Mrs Sheehy Skeffington's house … There was no firing done by the military throughout the day, the rebels were firing continually.'[38] In later years Owen recalled that 'we were having tea in the back room … and we heard what we thought were shots fired into the house. It was in fact a volley in the air because simultaneously then they broke all the ground-floor windows in the front of the house and they poured into the house and the rest of the party went upstairs and ransacked the whole house.'[39]

Along with her maid and her son, a terrified Hanna was held at bayonet point for over two hours while Colthurst searched frantically for incriminating evidence. He took away a huge quantity of papers and books but his search would eventually prove futile. Among the records was a copy of the 'Castle Document', which was not surprising to find in the possession of a journalist, and Colthurst gave it to the adjutant on 4 May, fraudulently certifying that it had been found on Sheehy Skeffington the day he was arrested. The fact that Hanna taught languages and had much German material for educational purposes did not help. Sergeant Maurice Ahern, a detective with the Dublin Metropolitan Police, G Division, examined all the documents seized and 'found nothing useful in them'.[40]

Colonel McCammond returned to Portobello Barracks on 29 April. His wife had informed him of the murders the previous day. By arrangement with McCammond, a number of bricklayers under the supervision of Major Victor E. G. Guinness, Royal Engineers, replaced any bricks in the wall of the yard that had been damaged by bullets. This action is often considered to be proof of a cover-up, but most armies carry out repairs as quickly and efficiently as possible, abhorring untidiness. McCammond later stated that the reason was because other civilian prisoners were being exercised in the yard.[41]

Major Rosborough detailed the events of 30 April, the day the rebellion ended:

Acting on my suggestion and, owing to my anxiety ... lest Captain Colthurst's position had not been clearly understood, my

Commanding Officer accompanied by myself took the full written report of the shooting to Headquarters Dublin Garrison, where my Commanding Officer saw and interviewed the Officer in Command. On making inquiry while returning from this interview, my Commanding Officer told me no further disciplinary action would be taken in respect of Captain Colthurst at the moment.[42]

On Monday 1 May McCammond ordered Major Vane to relinquish command of the barrack defences in favour of Colthurst. This move was intended to keep Colthurst within the confines of the barracks and under observation. Much has been made of this, but the rebellion was over and it was to be expected that the barrack garrison would resume its usual activities. McCammond had not yet realised the true nature of the killings and had probably been advised of Vane's unsatisfactory military record.[43]

Along with many others, Vane had only reported to Portobello at the start of the Rising and would be expected to return to his normal assigned duties. Perturbed at being replaced by Colthurst, he immediately brought the murders to the attention of the higher military authorities in Dublin. However, with some justification from past encounters, Vane was thought by his superiors to be a maverick and so they did not give much credence to his account, Colthurst's family being held in high regard. By a strange quirk, and before the rebellion, Vane had been considered entirely unsuitable as an officer and had been requested on several occasions to resign his commission. He refused, and proceedings had been put in place to have him dismissed instead.[44] Vane made no effort to report the murders until after he was relieved of his duties in the barracks. His motives are questionable and he may have wished to put pressure on the army authorities with whom he was already in conflict. Under these circumstances, and having received Colthurst's as yet undisputed report, it is not altogether surprising that the authorities were dismissive of reports that murders had actually been committed. Nevertheless, given that the Sheehy Skeffingtons had their own military and powerful political connections, it would have been impossible to keep the circumstances of Frank's murder a secret.

Vane went on leave to London on the afternoon of 1 May and reviewed events for Under-Secretary of State for War Harold J. Tennant, who arranged for him to meet Secretary of State for War Lord Kitchener and Sir Maurice Bonham Carter, the prime minister's private secretary, the following day. 'Kitchener was very pleasant, but when he was told the facts, it was clear he could not at first believe them. "Why have I not been informed," he said, "and why is the officer not under arrest?"' According to Vane, Kitchener then directed that a telegram be sent to headquarters in Ireland ordering that Colthurst be placed under arrest pending trial by court martial.[45] The Dublin authorities claimed that no such telegram was received.

In the meantime Colthurst had been detailed by Colonel McCammond to lead an advance party to take over Newry Barracks in County Down. Major General A. E. Sandbach, CB, DSO, commanding the troops in the Dublin area, forwarded Colthurst's report about the killings in the barracks to the Irish Command headquarters on 3 May, adding that Colthurst 'seems to have carried out his duties with discretion'.[46] He had evidently not yet learned of Kitchener's telegram.

The 3rd Royal Irish Rifles then moved to Victoria Barracks, Belfast, and Colthurst was placed under open arrest on 5 May.

A Court of Inquiry was held in these barracks on 10 May, when a new statement written by Colthurst the previous day was submitted:

> A prisoner named Sheehy Skeffington was brought in ... By my order the prisoner was searched, some incriminating documents were found on him and were handed by me to the Adjutant ... I received orders ... to search the premises of Alderman James Kelly. I proceeded to the house with about twenty men and on the way we were fired at. On the premises of Alderman J. Kelly I found two men named McIntyre and Dixon [*sic*]. As they should have been in their homes, and were unable to account for their presence in Kellys [*sic*], I brought them back to Barracks and confined them in the Guard Room. In my opinion the Guard Room in Portobello Barracks was not sufficiently secure for the confinement of these prisoners. It was close to the boundary wall of the Barracks and a rescue from outside would have been very easy. I regarded all three as being desperate men. I got practically no sleep during the night of 25 April. Throughout Tuesday 25th and Wednesday morning 26 April rumours of massacre of police and soldiers from all parts of Dublin were being constantly sent [to] me from different sources; among others a rumour reached me that 600 German prisoners at Oldcastle had been released and armed by the rebels and were marching on Dublin. I also heard that the rebels in the city had opened depots for the supply and issue of arms, and that a large force of rebels intended to attack Portobello Barracks, which was held only by about 150 rifles; the remainder of the occupants of the Barracks were unarmed men including recruits and refugees. There were also numbers of terrified women and children. We had also in the Barracks a considerable number of officers and men who had been wounded by the rebels and whose protection was a

source of great concern to me. I believed that it was known to the rebels that these three men were confined in the Barracks and that probably the proposed attack on the Barracks was with a view to their release.

Rumours of risings all over Ireland and of a large German-American and Irish-American landing in Galway were prevalent; I had no knowledge of any reinforcements arriving from England. I knew of the sedition which had been preached in Ireland for years past, and I was credibly informed that unarmed soldiers had been shot down in the streets by the rebels. On the Wednesday morning all this was in my mind; I was very much exhausted and unstrung after a practically sleepless night; I took the gravest view of the situation and I did not think it possible that troops might arrive from England in time to prevent a general massacre. I was convinced that prompt action was necessary to ensure that these men should not escape, and further spread the disaffection. It was impossible for me to move the prisoners to a more secure place of confinement owing to armed rebels having possession of the streets all round the Barracks. Believing that I had the power under martial law, I felt under the circumstances that it was clearly my duty to order these three men to be shot. Major Leatham, 6th Royal Irish Rifles, who was wounded, had previously informed me that the men McIntyre and Dickson arrested at Kelly's were dangerous characters.[47]

Among other statements taken was that of Rifleman Frederick McGuigan, a member of the firing squad: 'When we had got into the yard, Captain Colthurst said something to the prisoners and … the three prisoners moved over to the wall and turned around facing us … I am perfectly certain that … nothing was said by … the prisoners.' Rifleman Michael Ireland, who had handed over the prisoners and witnessed the executions, corroborated that statement. Bombardier Jack McCaughey, Royal Field Artillery, was in both firing squads: 'When the witness reached the yard he saw the three prisoners standing against the wall. The orders were given by Captain Colthurst: "Load, present, fire" ... the squad fired and the men dropped. Lieutenant Dobbin, when he saw what had happened, put his hand to his eyes and said "Oh, my God".'[48]

Subsequent to this inquiry, with most of the facts having been established, Colthurst was placed under close arrest pending a court martial, but he refused to plead insanity. According to Major Vane:

> It was found out that Colthurst's counsel ... was a barrister called Adams – so I visited him at the Four Courts ... He was told of my interview with Lord Kitchener, and that I had said that Colthurst must be mad, and I asked him to make his plea one of insanity therefore. For if he tried to plead justification I said frankly that I would give evidence against him. Previously a letter had been received from the Hon. Mrs Bowen-Colthurst, the wife, who quite agreed with this procedure.[49]

Vane himself was never called on to testify, most probably because he had not, in fact, been present when the murders took place.

8

CONSEQUENCES

In the meantime, attention was focused on dealing with those who had caused the rebellion. Judge Advocate General Alfred Townsend Bucknill found that the legal powers available were by no means clear-cut. The general officer commanding-in-chief of the forces in Ireland, General Sir John G. Maxwell, KCB, KCMG, CVO, DSO, who arrived in Dublin on Friday 28 April to replace General Friend, wanted to proceed with courts martial and executions under the Defence of the Realm Act, but the act did not provide for a case of armed insurrection, so the rebels were charged with aiding the enemy. When Maxwell was sent to Ireland he was given a free hand to deal with the insurgents but was told by Prime Minister H. H. Asquith that, at all costs, whatever was done would have to be done legally. As soon as the executions began, the prime minister began to feel apprehensive and sent frequent queries as to the basis upon which Maxwell was proceeding.[1]

In the middle of all this, the case of Colthurst began to assume importance, because Sheehy Skeffington had many friends in the Irish Party at Westminster, who were inundating Asquith with questions about the murder. Asquith felt General Maxwell's replies to the questions were unsatisfactory, and under repeated questioning Maxwell admitted that a mistake had been made. 'The reply was a peremptory order from the Prime Minister to General Maxwell that there were to be no more executions pending a personal discussion.'[2] Over the course of ten days up to 12

May, fifteen leading rebels had been tried and executed, with the whole secretive and hasty process polarising and shifting the public perception. On 12 May the prime minister arrived in Ireland for a six-day visit to examine the situation. Maxwell had ignored the telegram from Asquith to halt the executions and needed to be reined in. The speed with which the rebels had been sentenced and shot contrasted sharply with the slow procedure for dealing with the murders of innocent civilians by the British military, of which there were several occurrences. Interestingly, the next rebel listed for execution was Éamon de Valera. It is often thought that he was given a reprieve because of his American citizenship, but Bucknill recollected that this was not the case. In a later interview Bucknill said: 'If any single factor was more responsible than another, it was the murder of Sheehy Skeffington.'[3]

Following his discussions with Asquith, Maxwell wrote to the War Office on 14 May regarding Colthurst:

> This case is arousing considerable parliamentary and public interest, both in this country and in England, and I am most anxious that the trial should not only take place as early as possible, but also that there should be no grounds for any suggestion that political consideration carried any weight either in the framing of the charges or in the selection of the court.
>
> As regards the former, I have therefore transmitted the summary of evidence to the Judge Advocate General requesting him to prepare the charge sheet and also to advise generally in the conduct of the case. As regards the latter, I would most strongly urge that an officer of standing and experience be sent over to act as president. I would suggest Major-General Lord Cheylesmore as the most suitable person, having in view the great experience he has gained in such matters since the commencement of the war.

The question of selecting a prosecutor is one of importance. I am not in favour of making use of civilian counsel, and I would prefer that a specially selected officer, with legal experience, who has had no connection with the recent disturbances in Ireland be detailed ... The Prime Minister attaches great importance to the trial being held in open court.[4]

As the pressure grew, Maxwell asked General Sandbach, who was in command of the troops in the Dublin area, to explain the favourable opinion he had formed regarding Colthurst's actions. Sandbach's reply of 16 May stated: 'I never imagined for one moment that the men could actually have been killed by design. But having since read the evidence ... the act appears to me in quite a different light, and if this letter is true, then the officer in question used no discretion.'[5]

Deputy Judge Advocate Kenneth Marshall advised that the Army Act forbade a trial by court martial if the offence was committed in the United Kingdom, unless martial law was still in force at the time of the court hearing; otherwise a civil court would have jurisdiction. This caused consternation in army and government circles and led to much discussion and correspondence as to how this could be avoided – the reputation of the army had to be upheld at all costs in this time of war. The Irish law officers gave their opinion on 17 May:

In view of public safety and the defence of the realm, and more especially in order to prevent the circulation of reports calculated to spread disaffection and alarm, we are absolutely convinced that it is essential, if possible, that the trial in this particular case should take place before a military tribunal. The delay, excitement and popular agitation which could result from a civil trial of this case in Ireland, where it can only legally be tried, would in our opinion jeopardise the peace of Ireland and possibly lead to turbulence and disorder.[6]

Lord Reading, the lord chief justice of England, convened a meeting in his office the next day. Present were the English Solicitor-General Sir George Cave; the director of public prosecutions; Irish Attorney-General James H. M. Campbell, KC; and Brigadier General J. A. Byrne, deputy inspector-general of the RIC. They agreed that a special Defence of the Realm Act regulation should be drafted to allow civil offences to be tried by court martial.

A further difficulty arose when Timothy M. Healy, KC, MP, indicated that the Army Act did not preclude the possibility of a civil trial after the court martial. The authorities considered this to be totally unacceptable and the new regulation was formulated to exclude such a possibility. The regulation, numbered 58d and inserted on 23 May, read:

Where His Majesty has by Proclamation suspended, either generally or as respects any specified area, the operation of section one of the Defence of the Realm (Amendment) Act, 1915, then any person who is alleged to have committed any offence (whether an offence against these regulations or otherwise) at any place within the United Kingdom or within the specified area, as the case may be, while the Proclamation was in force and while he was subject to military law shall, notwithstanding anything in the Act or law to the contrary, be liable to be tried for the offence by court-martial and not otherwise, and on any such trial the procedure of the court-martial and the punishment to be inflicted in case of conviction shall be as prescribed by the Army Act.[7]

A legal opinion from Sir George Cave and Sir Frederick E. Smith, issued on 6 June, stated:

> It would be impossible to put in clearer terms the justification for the view that the public safety required that the trial should be a military court; and it was upon this view, fortified by the information given to us by the military authorities that, under existing conditions, the trial of soldiers by Irish juries would have a subversive effect upon the discipline of the Army, that we come to the conclusion that the public safety and the defence of the realm required that soldiers should not, so long as the disturbed state of Ireland continues, be tried by Irish juries for certain offences.[8]

Meanwhile, Mrs Anastasia Keating of Inch, Gorey, County Wexford, a sister of Patrick J. McIntyre, had sent a letter on 27 May to Hanna Sheehy Skeffington, stating: 'No inquiry can be of any use except it ends in the death of the man who was the means of these three murders ... I did not imagine that there was [*sic*] such inhuman men at large. I do hope he will be severely dealt with.'[9]

Tim Healy, who was providing Hanna with legal advice, gave his opinion on 29 May:

> It seems to me ... that the officer is certain to be convicted and then there will be little life left in any subsequent investigation, once the guilty man has been condemned. Please think over the case from that point of view, till we meet, as the attention concentrated on it has coerced the Military to show their 'impartiality', and when a man is condemned to death as seems certain here, it will be set-off against every barbarism.[10]

Major Vane gave Hanna a different perspective on 3 June:

> I took rather an active part in making what I believe to be the truth known. Namely that the acts were committed by an officer who was not sane at the time. This is my honest opinion and to that degree I offered to help him to prove it. I am awaiting news in respect to giving evidence. It is most important that I should do so in the interest of Captain Colthurst himself. Of course, if they attempt any justification, I wash my hands of the court martial and will go for the enquiry, which I believe is inevitable. My own opinion as to Colthurst and his employment is not quite yours. I think the authorities knew that in times of excitement he lost all control of his actions and employed him, not anticipating a rebellion, simply to train troops.[11]

Colthurst's mother, Georgina, wrote to her son from 33 Upper Leeson Street, Dublin, on the eve of his trial:

> My dearest Jack. My love to you today, the 5 June, a day of good omen, the anniversary of your release from Pretoria. You had a hard and trying time then, as now, but it was overruled for good then, and I know by God's grace, so will this trial be also. You dear, true soul, you will be given help and strength, and you will know that through the nobility and dignity of your bearing, through your steadiness, and uttermost patience, and gentleness, you will help not only yourself but a great many others. A mother's part is to support her son in every way she can, and if you feel that I can best do this by being absent, you will know that though I am absent by your desire, my thoughts will be with you all the time. I shall pray hard for you. 'In everything, by prayer and supplication, with thanksgiving, let your requests be made known unto God,

and the peace of God which passeth all understanding, shall keep your hearts and minds.' Much love my dear Jack, ever and forever. Your loving and devoted Mother.[12]

The thirteen-member court convened on Tuesday 6 June at Richmond Barracks, Dublin, under the presidency of Major General H. F. Eaton, Lord Cheylesmore, KCVO. The prosecutor was Major Edmund G. Kimber, DSO, 13th London Regiment, and the judge advocate was Kenneth Marshall. Admission to the court was by ticket and about 100 civilians were present, including Sheehy Skeffington's father and widow. Lord Cheylesmore, on opening the proceedings, referred to the loss which the nation had suffered by the death of Lord Kitchener the previous day. Louie Bennett, a friend and colleague of Francis Sheehy Skeffington, observed:

The first General Court Martial held in Ireland in a hundred years … was held in a large, lofty, square hall, bare of all signs of its usual use, the windows high and barred, a large skylight the main source of illumination. The public were allotted deal chairs and forms. The officers and officials composing the Court, sat around a square table, covered in green baize. The space immediately behind three sides of this table was 'reserved for relatives'. The centre of interest was Mrs Skeffington, pale, still, like a stone image of tragedy. She emitted extraordinarily the impression of tense, absorbed interest, every fibre of her being strung to one single point in life. Not even the prisoner – placed as he was in circumstances of tragic interest – could draw interest from her nor arouse the grief and pity which her mute presence stirred … the trial proceeded with the cumulative interest of a carefully framed drama. The nervousness of the witnesses, their reluctantly-given evidence, added to this effect.[13]

The indictment read:

> 1st charge, Section 41 Army Act: Committing a civil offence, that is to say murder, in that he, at Portobello Barracks, Dublin, on 26 April 1916, murdered one F. Sheehy Skeffington.
>
> 2nd charge, Section 41 Army Act (Alternative): Committing a civil offence, that is to say manslaughter, in that he, at Portobello Barracks, Dublin, on 26 April 1916, unlawfully killed one F. Sheehy Skeffington.

Similar charges were made in the cases of Dickson and McIntyre, a plea of not guilty on all counts being entered. The defence team consisted of James Chambers, KC, MP, and Thomas Andrews (instructed by Charles H. Denroche). Major Kimber gave an outline of the prosecution's case before calling Lieutenant Morris, Sergeant Maxwell, Lieutenant Morgan, Second Lieutenant Dobbin, Sergeant Aldridge, Second Lieutenant L. Wilson, Major Rosborough, Father O'Loughlin, Sergeant Geoghegan, and Major Charles A. J. A. Balck (Royal Army Medical Corps) as his witnesses. Their evidence established the facts as already outlined, though only the shootings in the barracks were examined. When details of the first firing squad were outlined, Hanna broke down and Colthurst 'hung his head and turned away'. When Second Lieutenant Dobbin described carrying out the order to shoot again, 'this evidence caused a sensation in court and women shrieked … while the accused hid his face'.[14]

The defence declined to call Colthurst to the stand and proceeded to produce character and medical witnesses instead. Major General Bird, the first to testify, said 'I think that, generally speaking, he was a zealous officer; in a great many ways a good officer. At times he did not seem to be able to concentrate his mind on a subject, and his demeanour was quite eccentric.' In Bird's opinion Colthurst was a man of high character and ideals, an excellent example for everybody, had deep religious convictions and would not be consciously capable of doing anything wrong or dishonourable. Bird then detailed how he had to relieve Colthurst of his command after he broke down during the retreat from Mons. His behaviour at the time convinced Bird that he was quite incapable of taking charge of men:

> Normally he was all right but when he became, as he did on the morning of the Battle of Mons, very excited and fatigued, I don't think he would be responsible for his actions ... I think his mind goes under, and he would not be capable of forming a fair and reasonable judgement ... I know him to be a man of high courage, a fine soldier who would often expose himself unduly to danger. As I said before, in peace time his conduct was an example to his brother officers and, in every moral way, apart from his military duties, his conduct was admirable.[15]

On being cross-examined Bird explained the difficulties of 1914, how he had reported on Colthurst's insubordination and that he was not favourably impressed with certain incidents in his conduct.

Major H. R. Goodman, who had known Colthurst since 1904, stated that he was most kind and always considerate in his dealings with the men and with his brother officers, but had occasionally carried out acts of an eccentric nature. Under questioning, Goodman described the dog-shooting incident in India as an example of Colthurst's eccentricity:

I think all through the retirement from Mons Captain Colthurst was in, as far as I could see, a highly strung, not nervous, but excited tension apparently ... I thought he was inclined to give orders on the spur of the moment ... I believe he would be quite incapable of consciously doing a wrong act ... I have known him to make some very grave errors of judgement as to men's actions, whether they were right or wrong.

Captain Philip E. Kelly, commandant of the School of Instruction at Portobello Barracks, had observed Colthurst at lunch on the day of the executions:

I thought the manner of the man was extremely strange. He was half lying across the table with his head resting on his arm or his hand. He looked about occasionally and stared across the room and then fell forward again with his head on his arm ... I saw Captain McTurk and I said 'For goodness sake ... keep an eye on Captain Colthurst, I think he is off his head'.

Captain James McTurk, Royal Army Medical Corps, found Colthurst very pale and in a highly excited state. He recalled that Colthurst had said, 'It is a terrible thing to have to shoot one's own countrymen.' McTurk felt that Colthurst was not responsible for his actions, was incapable of exercising any sound judgement or of discriminating between right and wrong. 'My opinion was that his condition was due to the belief that he had to shoot them ... I believe he was on the verge of a nervous breakdown ... looking into his eyes you saw that the pupils were dilated.'

McTurk prescribed ten grains of potassium bromide – an ineffective amount – and advised Captain Kelly accordingly.

Unfortunately, McTurk then took no further action and did not report his opinion to a superior officer.

Dr Alfred Parsons had examined the defendant on the previous Friday, 2 June, and found him labouring under considerable excitement and restlessness. The doctor reported that Colthurst was mentally unstable, did not seem to realise his position in regard to the murder charge, and explained the Bible reference that had exercised a very powerful influence on his mind. Parsons said the accused was adamant he had done right in carrying out his duty and that in any other country except Ireland it would be recognised as right to kill rebels. In their discussions, Colthurst said that it was he himself who should have died and not his brother, Robbie (killed in 1915). He could not understand why this had not happened and thought he should have been out at the Front again, for nearly all his brother officers had been shot. He thought General Bird entertained some unkind feelings towards him and that he had gone out to France with a halter around his neck.

Dr Richard R. Leeper, FRCSI, medical superintendent, St Patrick's Hospital, James's Street, Dublin, an expert in mental diseases, had sat in with Parsons during that interview. He reached the following conclusions on Colthurst:

> He seemed to be in a restless, agitated state of mind, pacing up and down the room. He did not appear to be able to control himself, and did not appear, at all, to realise the seriousness of the charge, the nature of the charge against him, or to have the ordinary self-protective feelings of a man having an imminent and serious charge hanging over him ... he seemed depressed and in a restless state; said that his brother had been shot, and why should his brother have been shot if he was still alive himself.

It was a great sorrow to him, he said, that he was alive at all … I came to the conclusion, from the examination I had of him, that he was a man exceedingly nervously shaken; and, if his condition remained as I saw him, he was on the eve of a complete breakdown. He was in a very agitated, restless state … His conversation was quite inconsequent. He kept pacing up and down the room. It was very hard to follow him, even though your whole attention was directed to him. He went from one subject rapidly to another.

Captain R. Wade Thompson, deputy lieutenant for the County of Dublin, stated that Colthurst had been one of his staunchest friends for ten years: 'I considered him a little eccentric in his manner at times, and a little inconsequent in his conversation occasionally. Otherwise he proved himself always a straightforward, kind gentleman in every way, and a man who would be incapable of anything dishonourable under natural circumstances.'

Sir Frederick Shaw claimed that Colthurst was a very fine character and an honourable, straightforward gentleman, but on his return from France 'I should say he was more unbalanced in his mind, more unbalanced than he had been before, as far as I could judge … especially after his brother had died … I considered him a man of very religious ideas. I think that affected his views in an abnormal way.'

Lieutenant Colonel F. J. Hamilton Bell, a former commanding officer, thought Colthurst was a thoroughly honourable, upright, straightforward gentleman, and a very good example to young officers. He was quiet and considerate, took a great interest in his work, and always did his best to carry out instructions. Colonel John S. Brown echoed these sentiments.

Major Arthur V. Weir, who had been with Colthurst as a

prisoner-of-war in Pretoria, considered him eccentric and always wanting in mental balance, someone who would get unduly excited at times, yet also a deeply religious and honourable man.

Major Philip G. W. Eckford thought Colthurst a man of high character, perfectly honourable, quite incapable of meanness yet 'rather gullible in some respects where the men were concerned'.

When one examines the words commonly used by the character witnesses, such as straightforward, honourable and eccentric, it is hard to avoid the conclusion that either they had all been groomed by the defence, or they gave an accurate description of Colthurst's personality.

The court reconvened the next day with Captain George R. Lawless, FRCSI, medical superintendent at Armagh County Lunatic Asylum, giving an opinion of his examination of Colthurst that morning:

> I say he is in a state of mental instability; he is restless and unstrung. His mental weakness has extended over a year. I was at the Medical Board in March 1915 at which Captain Colthurst presented himself … I saw him again last Saturday and was with him for about two hours and had an opportunity of noting his condition … he is at present in a mentally unsound state and is not responsible … I consider it to be coming on for a long time.

Major Francis C. Purser, MD, Royal Army Medical Corps, who was accompanied by Lawless during the examination, was in agreement with his findings.

The judge advocate summed up by saying that, because the defence was not denying that Colthurst had committed the crime, there were only two options available to the court –

guilty of murder or guilty but insane. The accused deliberately took the lives of the three men and there was nothing in the evidence to reduce the crime to manslaughter:

> The one question is, whether at the time he ordered these men to be shot, he was capable of knowing not merely the difference between right and wrong in the abstract, but of knowing that it was wrong for him to have these men shot. Now with regard to the question of insanity you have had various doctors called before you, two of whom, at least, were experts ... you may not go entirely on their opinion. You must take into account the conduct of the accused.

Colthurst was found guilty of murder but that he was insane at the time of the commission of the offences. The finding was confirmed by General Maxwell, following which 'the King was pleased to direct under Section 130 of the Army Act that the accused be removed to a Criminal Lunatic Asylum for safe custody during His Majesty's Pleasure', i.e. until it was officially decided that it was safe to release him.[16]

Dr Sheehy Skeffington told me he considered that Colthurst was not mad in the sense of being a raving lunatic:

> It seems to me that to express an understanding of Bowen-Colthurst's actions, one is not compelled to prove that, through madness, he had no culpable responsibility for them. The question, in my opinion, is not a simple dichotomy, mad or not-mad. That would imply that if mad, he was not culpable, and if not mad, he was fully culpable. The guilty-but-insane verdict would seem to imply a clear-cut absence of culpability at the time. I think the truth is more complex than that ... The passage quoted from

Luke 19:27 could even be taken to mean that he thought that all those who favoured Irish freedom should be taken out and shot. That rage seems to me to be the main explanation for his actions that morning. But the evidence shows that he immediately had some sense that he had done wrong. He told his commanding officer that he thought he might hang for it. He framed his reports, verbal and written, padded with lies, in such a way as to cover up his guilt and make it appear that he had done the right thing. Such rational behaviour has been quoted as reason to put him in the 'not mad' category. I do not think it does, but I do think it shows a degree of culpability that makes it inappropriate to put him simply in the 'mad' category and leave it at that. I would moderate my view of his degree of culpability if he had shown any sign of remorse afterwards ... war makes monsters of ordinary people, and violence begets violence. In that sense, Jack Bowen-Colthurst was a victim of war as well as a perpetrator of it. How ironic that he murdered a man, one of whose life's principles was the pursuit of that very idea.[17]

Louie Bennett, who also thought that Colthurst was himself a victim of militarism, commented:

A strange incident occurred. In the midst of the evidence about the 'hostage' episode, a terrific hail shower came on ... It battered upon the roof and the large skylight with such force that every other sound was inaudible. For some minutes the trial was suspended and all sat in tense stillness ... After that it was difficult to listen to prisoner's Counsel labouring to build up his theory of insanity. No doubt of the prisoner's guilt could be maintained. And I, for one, needed no further proof of his mental deficiency than the fact that he could sit and listen to the evidence without standing up to acknowledge his guilt and his regret, if he felt any, or his faith in the rightness of his deed. An element of greatness made Sheehy Skeffington's final experience tolerable to the imagination – but to see a man placed as Bowen-Colthurst was placed, was an ugly pain, a pain to be hidden away, forgotten … I went out into the great bleak barrack's space, stupidly wondering if I was in the real world.[18]

Tim Healy, who later became the first governor-general of the Irish Free State, wrote to his brother Maurice:

As regards the defence of insanity raised on behalf of the prisoner two things impressed me; First: that Colthurst was proved to have become a 'Bible convert' in India after a wild life. Second: that in 1914, in the retreat from Mons, he refused to go back, and led his men towards the Germans. He sat throughout the trial with clouded brow, gazing downwards. I do not think he was shamming madness, although I at first suspected it … Everyone is satisfied that we have done better than we had a right to expect.[19]

Not everyone was convinced that the correct outcome had been achieved. Public opinion, which had initially opposed the rebellion, was now shifting after the execution of the leaders. The failure to execute Colthurst, who was portrayed by parts of the media as evil rather than mad, helped in no small way to entrench anti-British feeling. Joseph McIntyre, brother of Patrick who was shot alongside Sheehy Skeffington, sent a letter to Hanna on 8 June:

I never expected what the result of the court martial would be and I, for one, am not satisfied with its result. My sister Mrs

Keating wished that the extreme sentence could be carried out with this so-called man Colthurst. But when I looked at the face of my murdered brother, when I raised him from Portobello Barracks, I could not wish otherwise than the fate he meted out to these poor men that he murdered should be meted out to him.[20]

Major A. V. Weir, who had appeared for the defence, wrote to Colthurst on 9 June:

I find it is very difficult to write what I feel. I know you will bear yourself manfully in the trials to come as you have in the past. You know you have the sympathy of all your brother officers, this may not be such a consolation to you as it would be to one less strong. It is very hard to say that all is God's will but I always feel this. All will come right soon. These dark days will pass, bright days will come and endure. I wish I could impart some of my phlegmatic temperament to you in exchange for some of your noble nature.[21]

Colthurst's military service was terminated on 10 June, and he was admitted to King George V Hospital, Dublin. On 19 June General Maxwell contacted the War Office: 'I am of the opinion that in the present state of feeling in Ireland the transfer of this officer to England would be advantageous.'[22] On 5 July Colthurst started his journey to the high-security Broadmoor Asylum for the Criminally Insane at Crowthorne in Berkshire. Wade Thompson had sent him a message on 2 July:

We know that God is with you in this hour of trial ... Our loving Father has His own way of teaching us all that He would have us know of His mind and will. It's hard to understand all His ways at times, but He asks us to trust Him in the darkest hour and to know that there are no circumstances in which we may be placed where He cannot make the light to shine and give His perfect peace … I trust that these few lines of sympathy and love may reach you.[23]

The committal sheet, completed by Major William R. Dawson, FRCP, Royal Army Medical Corps, inspector of lunatic asylums, then serving as mental specialist to the forces in Ireland, gave the supposed cause of Colthurst's problem as 'Hardship during retreat from Mons; later grief for a brother who was killed, and chagrin at being passed over for promotion; lastly excitement and anxiety during the Sinn Féin rising. There is some heredity, a cousin having been insane.' Other comments included:

> Does not seem to appreciate the seriousness of his act, nor to feel the nature of his position. Is inclined to be restless, and in talking jumps about from one subject to another, and is illogical in his ideas. Said that he felt no remorse or contrition for shooting the three prisoners, but also gave an instance of his humanity to show that shooting prisoners was not the sort of thing he would have done if sane. Seemed unable to form a just judgement where his emotions were engaged.[24]

Photographs of Colthurst taken on his admission to Broadmoor show the face of a shattered man, with bags under his eyes and aged beyond his years. His mother petitioned King George V unsuccessfully to have her son transferred to a hospital for shell-shocked officers in England.

Intense pressure fell on Major Rosborough for his apparent failure to control events properly at the barracks. On 2 July

General Maxwell reported to a War Office inquiry that was being held as to the responsibility of Rosborough during the rebellion. It was considered that Rosborough did not exercise his command effectively during this period. Even allowing for the natural excitement generated by the rebellion, the constant, anxiety-generating work, and a want of rest, there was an utter absence of control, so much so that it was possible for armed parties to leave the barracks on missions without the knowledge of the commanding officer. Colthurst had left the barracks, taking Sheehy Skeffington with him, and Adjutant Morgan had reported this immediately to Rosborough, who did nothing and stated that he could not recall this report. Maxwell's report noted:

> Major Rosborough is apparently rather deaf, and his comman-
> ding officer states that he is slow to appreciate events and take ac-
> tion, though in other respects he is a good officer. I consider that
> events show that Major Rosborough is inert, wanting in quick
> and sound judgement, and unfitted to command troops.

Maxwell recommended that Rosborough be placed immediately on the Retired List, while the War Office demanded that he resign his commission. In Rosborough's defence, Colonel Henry V. Cowan, CB, CVO, assistant adjutant-general (AAG) Irish Command, stated that the 3rd Royal Irish Rifles was one of the best two, if not *the* best, of the twenty-eight draft-finding battalions in Ireland recruiting and training soldiers for the war. Colonel McCammond was given credit for this and he stated that he was assisted by Rosborough. Cowan supported Rosborough, claiming he should be retained and that confidential reports on him were satisfactory. Following

127

representations it was proposed that no action be taken until the impending Commission of Inquiry had reported. That inquiry completely cleared Rosborough of responsibility in the affair and the order to resign was cancelled.[25]

Unfortunately, this was a most unsatisfactory outcome from the point of view of public perception and led to a large body of opinion claiming that justice had not been done and that Colthurst was found to be insane by arrangement. The British authorities avoided responsibility and blame attached to no one but Colthurst, who was deemed to be insane. Major Rosborough had failed in his duty as commanding officer to exercise proper control. He was told, on the night it happened, that Colthurst had taken Sheehy Skeffington out as a hostage, yet took no action of any kind. Lieutenant Dobbin, as duty officer, was responsible for the safety of the prisoners in his care, but rather than keeping them safe, he in fact participated in their deaths. If Rosborough had made it clear the night before that no prisoners were to be taken from the guardroom without proper authorisation, then the murders might have been avoided. Rosborough also failed to ensure that Colthurst remained in the barracks as subsequently ordered. Despite the public's reaction, no one else faced any charges for the deaths caused by Colthurst, and Rosborough and Dobbin both remained in the army – Rosborough was discharged in 1921 and Dobbin was killed in action in 1918.

Georgina de Bellasis
Bowen-Colthurst.
(*Courtesy of G. Sutherlin*)

Robert Bowen-Colthurst in the
uniform of vice-chamberlain to the
lord lieutenant of Ireland.
(*Courtesy of G. Sutherlin*)

The family home at Oakgrove, Coolalta, Killinardrish, County Cork. The
picture is thought to show John with his father. (*Courtesy of G. Sutherlin*)

Second Lieutenant J. C. Bowen-Colthurst, having been commissioned into the Royal Irish Rifles, 1899. (*Author's collection*)

The British transport lines and camp at Gyantse, Tibet, 1904. The fort in the background had just been captured. (*Author's collection*)

Colthurst (*centre*) leading a Bible-study group at Miss Sandes Soldiers' Home, Chakrata, India, 1907. (*Author's collection*)

Officers of the 1st Royal Irish Rifles at Meerut, India, 1907. Colthurst is standing in the centre of the back row. (*Author's collection*)

Colthurst with Lieutenant A. E. Peebles and NCOs of C Company at Tidworth, 1914. (*Author's collection*)

John's children in 1915: Robert St John, Theobald and Dorinda. (*Courtesy of G. Sutherlin*)

Colonel W. D. Bird.
(*Courtesy of the Royal Ulster Rifles Museum*)

Colthurst dressed as he probably would have appeared in 1916.
(*Author's collection*)

Alderman J. J. Kelly's shop just after the Rising. The damage to the premises on the right has been boarded up. (*Courtesy of B. Rainey*)

Above: Francis and Hanna Sheehy Skeffington.
(*Courtesy of F. Sheehy Skeffington*)

Left: Lieutenant M. C. Morris, who arrested Sheehy Skeffington.
(*Courtesy of M. Morris*)

James Joseph Coade (*right*). (*Courtesy of Kilmainham Gaol Archives, KMGLM 2015.0703*)

Thomas Dickson. (*Courtesy of Kilmainham Gaol Archives, KMGLM 2015.0704*)

Major F. F. Vane. (*Courtesy of the Irish Labour History Society*)

Photographs taken on admission to Broadmoor show Colthurst appearing much older than his nearly thirty-six years.
(*Courtesy of the National Archives, Kew*)

Colthurst in 1940, aged sixty. He is wearing his Silver War Badge. (*Author's collection*)

Rosalinda Bowen-Colthurst outside the family log cabin at Terrace, British Columbia, 1928. (*Courtesy of Lord Dunboyne*)

Colthurst with his second wife, Priscilla, at Penticton in 1959. (*Author's collection*)

9

BROADMOOR

The superintendent at Broadmoor, Dr John Baker, sent a memo to the Home Office on 23 June:

> If this officer is to have exceptional privileges would it not be preferable to send him to a private institution such as Virginia Water, where he could be ensured of privacy and a certain degree of liberty that could not be given him at Broadmoor. I think this is a reasonable view more especially owing to the fact that he is now apparently sane and not likely to be dangerous. If removed to Broadmoor we can give him a single room and he can have his own belongings in it, within reason. He could also have a patient as servant. He would be located in one of the blocks, and necessarily must come in contact with the other patients more especially at exercise in the airing court. I do not see how this can be avoided … Should it be decided to transfer Captain Colthurst to Broadmoor I trust that no strict stipulations will be insisted on as regards exceptional privileges, etc., because it may be found difficult to carry them out. I hope that he will go to a private institution as exceptionally privileged patients are viewed here with jealousy by other inmates.

The phrase used above that 'he is now apparently sane', so soon after the Rising, does not imply that Colthurst was never insane: the stress of being in a conflict situation had abated and he was in a quieter and calmer environment. Harry Butler

Simpson, CB, assistant private secretary to the home secretary, replied the next day:

> He is a Criminal Lunatic and instructions have been given for his detention in an asylum ... General Byrne, who had to deal with the case, spoke to me about it. The case is a sad one: Colthurst's mental equilibrium broke down at the front and he was sent home to Dublin where, presumably, it was thought he would not be exposed to any great mental strain and then came the Irish rising putting on him as severe a strain as well could be. There is no question of him being given preferential treatment at Broadmoor, but I told General Byrne that he will be treated there as a patient, not as a criminal, and that inmates of Broadmoor who have an income of their own are allowed to spend some of it on special comforts. There was no suggestion of any stipulation as to how he should be treated.

Dr Baker, in responding, explained that he was under the mistaken belief that Colthurst's committal was due to political expediency and that he did not actually need treatment:

> I had conceived the idea that he would be regarded as a political prisoner for whom special arrangements would be required. Should he come here I shall endeavour to make him as comfortable as circumstances will permit. It will depend on his mental condition. If he is amenable and quiet it will be possible to locate him in Block 2 where there is a good library, a billiards room, and an excellent airing court.[1]

Colthurst's friends rallied around him after his trial, and the following letter, from the Reverend J. Stuart Holden, is typical of the support he received:

I need not tell you how much you have been in our thoughts and prayers during this sad time of trial, and I want you to know how entirely my belief in you, and affection for you, are unaltered by all that has happened. Personally I can have no thought of blaming you in anything you did, and I am very sure that The Lord who knoweth our frame, and remembereth that we are but dust, takes every circumstance into account in judging our actions. I know how overstrained you have been ever since getting back from the Front, and how distressed in mind over your brother's death and your own regimental difficulties, that if I with my limited knowledge can make allowances, how much more can He with His perfect understanding of us ... Life is not yet over for you, nor are its possibilities exhausted. Someday the light will break.[2]

As a form of occupational therapy, Colthurst painted water-colours of flowers, and on the advice of his friends maintained a schedule of religious studies. He wrote down this prayer on 6 August:

For my past confidence in self and pride I ask forgiveness Lord!
For my proud ways I now before thee kneel.
Pardon my pride, my fall.
Here I ask pardon, and in thy riven side find love, thy word.
Lord I am nothing and thou art come to heal, to be my all in all.
Thy blood-bought child I stoop, just at thy feet, in all humility.
Henceforth not I but thou until we meet.
My life, thy charity.[3]

A Royal Commission of Inquiry into the murders was held at the Four Courts in Dublin from 23 to 31 August 1916, under the chairmanship of Sir John A. Simon, KCVO, KC, MP, a former attorney-general and home secretary under Asquith. Hanna Sheehy Skeffington was a major instigator of the inquiry, having refused the offer of a large monetary compensation from Asquith. During the inquiry Tim Healy, acting on behalf of the Skeffington and Dickson families, emphasised that the affair was an Irish matter, stating that 'in a time of war like the present, we should eliminate all topics of racial prejudice by making it clear that we are here concerned with an Irish regiment and Irish officers and the discredit which must indelibly remain on them would be a discredit to my own country [Ireland], and therefore not appertaining to Great Britain'.[4]

Nothing particularly new came from the inquiry apart from a more detailed account of events and an examination into the shooting of Coade. Regarding Coade's case, Lieutenant Leslie Wilson claimed that Colthurst 'meant to shoot the boy in the legs, but the shot lodged in his abdomen'.[5] No other killings came within the scope of the inquiry, but the commission did conclude that there may have been one more murder (on the way to Alderman Kelly's shop), that Colthurst planted evidence and that his statements were full of lies. Tim Healy complained that not all the officers concerned were compelled to attend: 'the officers of the guard were more guilty than Colthurst, who was a lunatic'.[6] However, he later added, 'I think it right to say that, as some doubt prevails in the public mind, I am satisfied also that the military have discharged their duty frankly and fairly'.[7] The commission concluded that 'apart from the defence of insanity, there can be no excuse or palliation for his conduct from first to last, a state of things which was frankly recognised by those who appeared before us on behalf of the military authorities'.[8]

Opinions were polarised, with Colthurst's attackers demonising him and his supporters being blind to the evidence, especially that the victims whose deaths had been investigated were not rebels but entirely innocent and blameless. No consideration seems to have been given to the feelings or plight of their next of kin. Elsie Mahaffy, daughter of the provost of Trinity College, Dublin, thought Colthurst was 'one of the best young men I have ever met', while Sheehy Skeffington was 'a man whose life and principles were vicious' and the other two were 'ruffians, editors of seditious and indecent papers'.[9]

Almost immediately a campaign for Colthurst's release was instituted. British newspapers regularly carried stories, comments and pleas on his behalf, particularly the conservative *Morning Post*. A letter to the editor by S. Bartholomew (perhaps his brother Robbie's widow) in September stated:

> It is the authors of the Rebellion who must be considered primarily the cause of the death of Mr Sheehy Skeffington and of all the other tragedies connected with that terrible week. It was small wonder that the horror of Irishmen, bribed by German money murdering Irish soldiers of the Empire, was sufficient to unhinge the brain of a man, admittedly rendered liable to such collapse under sudden strain by earlier sufferings in the war.[10]

Despite all the evidence against him, there were many who chose to see Colthurst in a heroic light. Miss H. Evelyn Hunt, of Oaklands Red Cross Hospital, Cranleigh, Surrey, wrote to him on 15 October:

> I am a complete stranger to you... a mutual friend thought that it might cheer you in your unutterably sad surroundings to hear something of what your world is thinking – those, that is, who

know the truth of what happened. May I say that I often think of you, and though I have never seen you, what you have done brings a lump in my throat when I think of it – the greatest instance of pluck and self-sacrifice in this war, where both have been conspicuous. The deliberate sacrifice of a career, with his life in his hand, in order to save the country – that surely is the great love on which the immortal blessing was pronounced ... I can only think that your friends must have given their evidence to save the death penalty, because they felt they could not let you go ... You saved our country by your action, knocking the bottom out of the rebellion.[11]

A letter from William Henning Corker, a solicitor for the Colthurst family, appeared in the *Cork Constitution* on 20 October:

Your issue of yesterday contains a report of Mr T. P. O'Connor's speech in the House of Commons in which he charged Captain Bowen-Colthurst with making false entries to shield himself, and affected to ridicule the finding of the court-martial that he was insane at the time. The many friends of Captain Bowen-Colthurst, including myself, who have known him all his life, are satisfied that he was absolutely incapable of any dishonourable act, and the evidence ... given at the court-martial is convincing that he was completely off his head during the rebellion just as he had previously been after the battle of Mons. Under these circumstances it is not logical to hold him accountable for what he said or wrote.

On 5 November Dr Baker informed the Home Office that he had been served with a writ the previous day as the person in charge of Colthurst. Alderman Kelly was claiming damages, including costs, for trespass and damage to his premises during the Rising. This caused considerable anxiety to Colthurst, because he had not been briefed as to what was happening, even though his wife, Linda, was named as his guardian and representative. The claim was eventually settled by the British government by way of £3,250 paid as an 'act of grace', with both parties paying their own expenses, Kelly already having received £1,400 compensation for damages.[12]

Linda petitioned the Home Office on 22 December for her husband's release. She promised to keep him under supervision and to report immediately any relapse should this occur: 'My husband is suffering a fate worse than death and bearing it grandly. I believe we have your sympathy – will you give us your help?'[13] Colthurst himself argued vainly with the Home Office that he should have been indemnified from any charges under the *Manual of Military Law*: 'Any soldier who takes … such measures as he honestly thinks to be necessary for carrying to a successful issue the operation of restoring peace and preserving authority, may rely on any question as to the legality of his conduct being subsequently met by an Act of Indemnity.'[14]

In the meantime, Hanna Sheehy Skeffington increased the pressure on the British authorities and went incognito to the United States to deliver her lecture 'British Militarism as I Have Known It' and to raise sympathy and funds for Sinn Féin. Over a period of six months from December 1916 she spoke at more than 250 venues, opposing the war and British rule in Ireland, and laying particular emphasis on the murder of her husband and how the matter had been handled.

On 27 February 1917 the War Office asked the Treasury for permission to divert Colthurst's pension to his wife, who was at that time living at Newnham Lodge, Wokingham, Berkshire. Up to this point his pension was being used to pay for his maintenance at Broadmoor. A letter to the Ministry of Pensions sought a pension grant of seven shillings per day to Linda, who was 'in urgent need of funds', less £1 per week deduction for the cost to the public of maintaining Colthurst in Broadmoor. The problem was that this could only be done by the Army Council if Colthurst was mentally incapable of managing his affairs, but the superintendent at Broadmoor would not certify him as being so incapable. The Treasury devised a solution, inserting a new paragraph into Article 517 of the Pay Warrant that reduced the amount of the pension available for the maintenance costs and allowed the balance to be given to Linda.[15] The governor of Broadmoor was told of the situation and replied, 'It would probably be inadvisable that the officer should be advised of this decision.'[16]

Following the government's decision to release the interned rebels, a campaign began to have Colthurst treated similarly, with many representations being made to the Home Office. A letter to the editor of the *Morning Post* from 'A Loyal Irishwoman' (probably Colthurst's mother, Georgina) appeared on 25 June:

> Captain Bowen-Colthurst ... suffered, as many another brave soldier has done, from severe shell-shock, and while in this state tried to shoot some of the prisoners in France. He had to be sent back to England, but instead of being granted sick leave or being sent to a sanatorium to recover, he was immediately appointed to what was called 'quiet home duty' in Dublin, at the time that a rebellion was daily expected ... He was tried and sentenced before his brain had had time to recover, and is now doomed to

a living death, the result of fighting for England ... It seems as if England will pardon anything in Irishmen except loyalty.

The following day, Athelstan Riley, a prominent Anglican hymn writer and translator, added that 'the Government has to consider votes, and there are at this moment more votes behind the Sinn Féiners than behind Captain Bowen-Colthurst'.[17]

Internal Home Office memos discussed what should be done:

28 June 1917: It is unlikely that this patient will be taken back into the Army from which he has been discharged and equally unlikely that he will again be subjected to such circumstances as those in which he lost his mental equilibrium in April 1916 – at a time when he had not fully recovered from shell shock. He has now recovered his mental balance and ... there seems no *medical* reason for his continued detention ... Captain Colthurst has not been convicted; Irish convicts have recently been released and it is more than likely that an agitation for Colthurst's discharge will arise. Further, it would no doubt help to soothe the Ulster party in the proposed Convention, if this man was also discharged; and it would be better to do so not as a result of agitation. The case is an exceptional one and could not be regarded as a precedent. Signed L.S.B.

Sir Edward Troup, KCB, permanent under-secretary in the Home Office, responded on 3 July:

If this had been an ordinary murder, there could have been no serious question of releasing him now. I think that after six or eight years would be the earliest date for release in such a case

– probably the time could be longer. The question is whether there are political reasons for releasing earlier – even at the risk of relapse into a condition in which a similar murder might be committed.

(1) I do not think the case is parallel to that of the Irish rebels just released. They were all men captured in open rebellion. Mr Duke was satisfied that none of them could be proved guilty of an individual murder. Captain Bowen-Colthurst caused an unarmed and untried man to be shot in cold blood.

(2) There is no reason to think his release would 'soothe Ulster' – he is a Cork man – and I understand Ulster takes no great interest in him.

(3) I think the effect of release in the USA could be bad. The answer to Mrs Sheehy Skeffington's propaganda is that, if her husband was murdered, the British Government at least did its best to punish the murderer; but it would be vain to say that, if, after a verdict of murder committed while of unsound mind, the murderer merely spent a year in comparatively comfortable conditions in Broadmoor and was then set free.

I am sorry for Captain Bowen-Colthurst who, apart from outbursts of excitement which completely upset his sound judgement, was a good soldier, but it seems to me that to discharge him now out of the ordinary course would not be in the public interest.[18]

Dr Baker made his annual report from Broadmoor under the Criminal Lunacy Act 1884:

On admission he may have been said to be suffering from melancholia. He was unsettled and very apprehensive. He appears to have felt very much the shooting down of the recruits he had trained. Under the even regime of Asylum life he became resigned and tranquil. Then ensued a short period of morbid religious questioning, this phase passed away and for the past six months he has been rational and tranquil, occupying his time with gardening and games. Latterly he has been employed in the carpenter's shop ... He cannot be certified insane at present.[19]

Chief Secretary for Ireland Henry Edward Duke, KC, MP, raised the matter with the home secretary on 11 July:

These communications, like many others which I have received, appear to compound two classes of cases, namely, the class in which the punishment of a criminal offence is remitted; and the class in which an insane person who has committed a homicidal act while insane is kept in custody for reasons of common safety. You will, I think, agree with me that the reasons of policy and even of administration of the criminal law, which had weight in the case of the prisoners of the Rebellion lately released have no application in the case of the unfortunate gentleman who is found to have committed an act of homicide while insane.

It appears to me ... that it is not unlikely he might at an early date be given either qualified or absolute freedom without any danger of an attack by him upon any other person. In replying to the various communications I have received upon this subject I have not in any way suggested what your decision as to the case may be. I should be glad, however, if you are able to see your way to direct an examination of Captain Bowen-Colthurst by experts well qualified to pronounce a decision as to the present state of his mind and nervous system, and if the result is of the favourable kind, I hope it may be found possible either to discharge Captain Bowen-Colthurst to a sanatorium or to set him at liberty, either conditionally or absolutely.[20]

Colthurst wrote a large number of letters to Conservative members of parliament and anyone else of influence who could help him. By the autumn of 1917 many representations were being made for his early release, including those by Anglican Archbishop of Armagh John Crozier, Sir Frederick Milner, Lord Henry Cavendish-Bentinck, Lieutenant Colonel Leslie Orme Wilson, CMG, DSO, MP, and Charles Bathurst, MP.

Dr Baker reported to Sir Edward Troup on 19 September:

The following extracts written by Captain Bowen-Colthurst in a letter to his wife of yesterday's date may be of interest as serving to show his views on the events in which he was concerned in the Dublin Rebellion, and also his grounds for believing he ought to be released.

(1) 'I am perfectly well again, physically and mentally.'

(2) 'Any nervous breakdown I sustained was due to severe wounds incurred in the course of active service for the country.'

(3) 'Anything I did was done openly and with the best intentions. I have an absolutely perfectly clear conscience about it all, but of course I am not an informer, and I cannot go and say that I consulted others, as they would only be made scapegoats too. Where I was wrong, as I see quite plainly now, was having the men shot in barracks instead of in the street.'

(4) 'The men who butchered my boys, and the Notts and Derby boys, are all free again.'

(5) 'I'm an Irishman, and it is not fair to compensate and reward those who have been over-rebellious while making things as black as possible for one who has been over-loyal.'

(6) 'There was a rebellion in progress so it was not exactly the King's Peace. I wasn't represented at Sir J. Simon's inquiry, while what inquiry has there been into the shooting of any of the soldiers and police? At Castle Bellingham the rebels put Dunville and some police who were quite unarmed and had taken no part in the fighting up against the wall and shot them. Dunville, however, had not been killed, but has since, I think, been killed in France. The police were killed. There has been no inquiry into the shooting of any of our soldiers who were home on leave, and were shot practically before their wife's eyes.'

(7) 'While possibly a few of the extreme Nationalist Members of Parliament may object to my being released, still I think that most of them will be glad to let bygones be bygones for the good of Ireland.'

I think paragraph (3) is important.[21]

It is apparent that this was not a normal letter to Linda, but a case being put forward for dissemination to those who were fighting his cause, and he would have been well aware that his letters were being read by Dr Baker. There is no evidence that he consulted anyone before the murders, and the third paragraph demonstrates a cunning side to his nature in trying to establish that he acted heroically and sacrificed himself to save others.

The Duke of Bedford, military aide-de-camp to King George V, advised Linda on 1 October that 'the only course open to you is, I think, to petition HM The King for your husband's release through the Home Office'.[22] The Reverend J. Riversdale Colthurst, of Cowper Road, Dublin, petitioned the home secretary on behalf of his cousin on 12 October 1917:

> I am supported in this appeal to you by a very large body of opinion, not only in Ireland, but also in England, as shown by numerous letters in the *Morning Post*, *Spectator*, *Times*, etc., of which I enclose a specimen. We appeal to you for justice to be done to my cousin, not only on the merits of the case, but also on account of the 'amnesty' which this summer released numerous prisoners who had been sentenced to death for murder and other crimes.

> Our appeal, then, is based on the following grounds:

> (i) At Easter 1916 Captain Bowen-Colthurst was suffering from the direct effects of the hardships he had undergone in the service of his country …

> (ii) The responsibility for the shooting of Sheehy Skeffington, etc., should in strict equity be placed on the shoulders of those who placed Captain Bowen-Colthurst in a responsible position, knowing that he had not quite recovered. Though most anxious to get back to his own regiment in France, he was not allowed to do so.

> (iii) Assuming the very worst that his enemies urge against

him – assume that he *was* responsible for his actions at the time, and that the deed *was* murder; it was surely a strange kind of justice that keeps him in durance and unconditionally releases Edward de Valera, the Countess Markievicz, the late Thomas Ashe, and others who had been sentenced to death.

Such a one-sided amnesty, that acts only in favour of rebels, traitors to their country, and avowed friends of Germany, and ignores a man, who for many years had faithfully served his King and country, is a spectacle new to British history. The feeling is growing in both Ireland and England that, in the case of my cousin, justice is being subordinated to political expediency, and that clemency is shown to every crime in Ireland except that of loyalty to the Crown.[23]

The Home Office, in response, pointed out that Colthurst was not in prison or undergoing punishment, that an amnesty would not be applicable in his case as he was detained in consequence of the verdict of insanity and that the suggestion of political expediency was wholly without justification.

An article in *The Spectator*, 13 October 1917, pleaded for his release:

Captain Colthurst's act can be excused and forgiven on only one ground – the unbalanced state of mind in which he has since been proved to have been at the time. On this ground, and on this ground alone, we make our appeal. Most of those leaders in the rebellion who were convicted on the clearest evidence not only of treason but of being accomplices in murder were released last Christmas ... They were in full possession of their reason. He admittedly was not ... If, therefore, Captain Colthurst has recovered from the unhappy condition of mind which accounted for his deeds during the rebellion, he is surely not fit for further detention amid the deplorable surroundings of Broadmoor Asylum. It may be said that there is no precedent for releasing a person from Broadmoor after such a comparatively short term of confinement. In answer to that we would say that there is no precedent for the confinement at Broadmoor of a person who was suffering from shell-shock at the time he committed his offence. We might also answer that there is no precedent for the release of men convicted of treason against the State and of open crime in the streets. We appeal not only for clemency but to a sense of fairness and justice ... We think that now or then he ought to receive a 'free pardon'.

A summary of Captain Colthurst's military record will show how strong a claim he has on the magnanimous consideration of the Government and the whole nation. He is a member of a very well-known family of soldiers in Ireland who have fought for Britain for generations. The names of the family appear in the battles of the Peninsular War, at Waterloo, in the Indian Mutiny, and in almost every campaign since then ... Not many soldiers have a cleaner record of hard professional work and conscientious devotion to duty.

It will be obvious to everyone that an officer who was not allowed to return to the front owing to his nervous condition was not the man to take control with the wisdom and judgement required at any one of the extraordinary situations which developed here, there, and everywhere in Dublin during the rebellion.

Dr Joseph Bartholomew Skeffington, MA, LL.D., JP, of Belfast, former senior inspector, National Education Board, and father of the unfortunate Francis, issued a printed circular that was much closer to the truth and in direct opposition to this article:

> The *Spectator* ... makes an appeal for the release of Bowen-Colthurst (backed by anonymous letters), founded on plausible but deceptive arguments, which may mislead the public, which he thinks perturbed in his favour: evidently overlooking Ireland, where the insanity theory found little credence, and where many public bodies have been calling on the Government to have Colthurst tried for the killing of Coade, and other crimes not put before the Court Martial.
>
> The first argument is, that Colthurst was in a terribly trying position, (1) in Command of the troops, (2) responsible for their safety, (3) in a position of extreme personal responsibility, his commanding officer being in hospital, (4) he was not the man to take control of the extraordinary situation, (5) cut off from all communication, (6) on duty without sleep for two days and nights. Will it be believed that these *bare facts* as they are called, are chiefly fancies and mostly false. For he was *never* in Command, nor in control of, nor responsible for the Troops, the Commander being Colonel M'Cammond, and when he went to Hospital *not* Captain Colthurst but Major Rosborough was in command, and was responsible during the Colonel's absence. Surely the *Spectator* should be better informed, the Court Martial evidence and the Commission Report are open to all. Again, he was not cut off from Communication, being in touch by telephone with Headquarters and Dublin Castle all through. Nor was he two days and nights on duty without sleep; he was like another liable to be called on; he stated himself he was up till 3 a.m. on Tuesday night reading dangerous papers found on these prisoners, but Sir J. Simon's Commission found that

these papers were quite harmless, and could be read in a *few minutes*. The only charge Colthurst had was a troop of forty men to raid Kelly's shop on Tuesday night. So the whole argument is baseless, and instead of *having responsibility*, he sought, and took control of the Guard, etc., quite unauthorised, as he made the raid on Skeffington's house unauthorised. 'There was no charge against Sheehy Skeffington,' said the Adjutant; 'there was no case against him,' said Mr Asquith. 'Sheehy Skeffington had no connection with the Rebellion,' says Sir J. Simon; 'there were no incriminatory papers.' But the *Spectator* omits such *trifles* as the murder (an illegal act the *Spectator* calls what was declared Murder by the Court-martial), of two other innocent Editors, McIntyre and Dickson: the brutal slaughter of Coade going home from his Devotions, and others suspected by the Commission; while Sir F. Vane asserts that two others were similarly slain on Wednesday afternoon. There is no mention of the *unauthorised* cruel torture of Sheehy Skeffington, his hands tied behind his back, in the centre of forty soldiers with rifles and bayonets, kept on the Bridge for an hour at midnight as a Hostage, threatened with instant death to protect Colthurst from Snipers. There is no word of the *unauthorised* raid on Skeffington's house by his murderer days after, blowing in the windows, terrorising widow and orphan [*sic*], ransacking and robbing invaluable documents, papers, and manuscripts, a life's labour destroyed; no feeling for the widow of his victim, no pity for the orphan he had made fatherless. What a subject for pity is this heartless murderer! Further, there is no word of those cunningly-devised lying Reports to excuse his crimes, the false endorsement on a document to incriminate his victim, which made Ireland sceptical of his insanity. Instead of consulting his Commander *before* the murder, he merely told him of it

146

after, saying he 'might hang for it': the fact seems to be he was afraid the Commander (Rosborough) would prevent him from murdering Sheehy Skeffington, which he had aimed at in taking him without authority as a hostage the night before.

The other principal argument is that Colthurst is now sane, but surely he was thought equally sane then by his superiors and fellow-officers, including medical men – until many days after the murders: may not his present apparent sanity be equally deceptive? Can anyone guarantee a homicidal maniac against future criminality? Have not the public a right to protection against such a criminal Lunatic? Look at his history told by his friends at the Court-Martial: General Bird had to suspend him for dangerous conduct in the field after Mons, a fortnight *before* he was wounded: 'at times,' says the General, 'he did not seem able to concentrate his mind on a subject, and his demeanour was quite eccentric, when unusually fatigued or excited he is not quite responsible for his actions.' Major Goodman, who had known him for twelve years, says 'I have known him to do some very eccentric things': the only instance he gives occurred years ago in India, namely, his shooting of a dog, and leaving him to die howling in torture, just as he left Coade weltering in his gore on the street in Dublin; thus cruelty is his eccentricity, the extent of which in Dublin has not yet been measured; for he claimed the right to do as he liked under Martial Law, and to kill those he *called* rebels. Dr Parsons says, 'excitement, fatigue, any strain would cause his mind to go completely off its balance.' Dr Leeper, 'it is perfectly evident that he has been for some years a man of a very weak nervous system, who held his sanity by a very uncertain tenure.' Major Weir, who knew him for sixteen years, considered his character very eccentric and wanting in mental balance.

Shall innocent victims be again exposed to his savage rage, to be again palliated by a plea of insanity!

The last argument is that accomplices in Murder were liberated after rebellion, nameless correspondents called them Murderous Sinn Féiners. This is also a false plea, as all these men were stated officially to be free from personal criminality or moral turpitude.[24]

Despite this, more support for Colthurst came from an editorial in *The Daily Graphic* of 17 October:

To keep him in confinement as a concession to Sinn Féin clamour for vengeance upon their fellow-Irishman would be an atrocious act in any case, but specially atrocious in view of the way in which the Sinn Féin criminals have themselves been treated. Numbers of them who were guilty of capital offences were sentenced instead to terms of imprisonment; all of them have now been released. It would be monstrous if, while this wholesale clemency is extended to enemies of the Empire, who at once set to work to organise fresh plots, clemency should be refused to a distinguished soldier who had risked his life in helping to suppress the rebellion, and who only sinned by a momentary act of madness under the greatest provocation.

John B. Atkins, assistant editor of *The Spectator*, wrote to Colthurst's wife, Linda, on 18 October:

I am delighted to hear that you were pleased with the article. Whenever I have written anything on the subject I have felt rather apologetic towards you because I cannot help feeling how terribly cold-blooded these judicial articles must seem to you in your time of sorrow and anxiety. I can only repeat that I am quite certain that the method I have adopted is the right one. If we provoked and let loose political passions and the fury of wild partisans, we should lose our cause.[25]

A report in the *Weekly Freeman* on 27 October, stated that Matthew Keating, MP, Kilkenny South, had asked the chief secretary, Mr Duke, if it was the intention of the government to have Colthurst tried for the murder of Coade and other crimes and was told that 'It is not intended to take any further proceedings.'

The initiative for *The Spectator* article is explained by a letter from Reverend J. S. Holden, Colthurst's friend, to Linda on 1 November:

> I feel sure that God is going to bring him out, and am greatly interested in the efforts which my friend, Mr Strachey, is making in the *Spectator* to this end. I do feel that we need to continue in prayer that God's will may be done, and that the Authorities may not be terrorised into letting things remain where they are.

Giles Lytton Strachey, a famous writer and conscientious objector, had been an associate of Robbie Bowen-Colthurst at Cambridge.

It was about this time that Colthurst wrote 'Faith':

> Fret not poor soul whate'er befall thee
> Through all thy sorrow Jesus is at thy side.
> Have faith in Jesus, it is His love that calls thee,
> So trust with patience thine Almighty Guide.
> Thou art His, and He is thine!

Art thou fretting o'er a loved one's loss,

Has promotion passed thee by,

Hast thou other worry, other cross?

Have faith in Jesus.

Thou art His, and He is thine!

Knowest thou not that He is now in power?

And coming soon, for thee and His own bride?

Thy light affliction lasteth but an hour,

So live by faith in Jesus glorified.

For thou art His, and He is thine![26]

Ronald J. McNeill, MP, advised Solicitor-General Sir George Cave on 9 November:

[Sir Edward] Carson has received a very strong protest from Sir Frederick Milner against the continued detention of Colthurst as a criminal lunatic, and has enclosed for Carson to see a letter from Colthurst to Lady Dunboyne, which is a clear, closely reasoned, and temperate letter, which nobody would believe to be the work of a lunatic. There is a growing feeling among Colthurst's friends that he is detained for purely political reasons ... Sir F. Milner suggests that, if Bowen-Colthurst cannot be at once released, he should be moved into some hostel or private establishment, where he could receive special treatment, instead of keeping him in a criminal lunatic asylum where the associations and treatment will probably end by driving him *really* mad ... Though this letter is not written for Carson, it is written after consultation with him and his approval.[27]

An offer had been made to accommodate Colthurst in Sir James Craig's private hospital at Craigavon, County Down. Sir

Frederick Milner, a former member of parliament and strong advocate on behalf of ex-servicemen, in responding to further representations made by Linda, promised to do everything in his power to help, but added that 'It is all this rotten fear of the Irish that causes the difficulty.'[28]

Also on 9 November Linda received advice from the Reverend Colthurst:

> If, by the end of the year, our efforts are still unsuccessful, I should advise that a full statement be drawn up, printed, and sent to every decent member of Parliament and newspaper, and anywhere else that might occur to us ... It seems quite clear to me now that it's no good appealing to any sense of justice in the Government, for they have none![29]

In the meantime, Ralph D. Blumenfeld, editor of the *Daily Express*, took up the case, informing Linda on 7 November: 'I am greatly interested in the case of your husband, and if I can be of any service towards effecting his release I shall be delighted to do so. Kindly let me know how I can help with further publicity.'[30] An article appeared in that newspaper on 14 November:

> If it was right to release the Sinn Féin murderers, it must also be right to release Captain Bowen-Colthurst, whose offence was due to a temporary derangement of his reason. We cannot believe, as has been suggested, that political considerations are involved in the continued detention of this man. If there be any truth in the suggestion, then British justice is being dragged in the mud. The matter is one in which the Home Secretary should act without further delay. The amnesty is in operation. Sinn

Féiners are parading the streets of Ireland's towns and villages in triumph. Let it no longer be true that the only victim of the rebellion remaining under punishment is a British soldier.

In the same issue, a Mrs Margaret Bedford, of St Andrew's Rectory, Holborn, had her letter published:

I do not know the man or anyone belonging to him, but … I feel how cruelly and unjustly he has been treated. A brilliant, brave, courageous soldier, he suffered for England. Nerve-shaken and unstrung, he was sent to Ireland, the authorities, no doubt, thinking that anywhere in our Dominions a brave man could enjoy rest from strife. But, alas! he found treachery, and, striving to cope with it, he did a foolish thing; but in time of war treachery has to be dealt with quickly … What are our sons to think of England's justice? Are women expected to bear sons to be treated thus? If Captain Bowen-Colthurst has a mother living, what can she think of the justice of England which treats the son she has willingly given to serve his country with such gross injustice?

John B. Atkins wrote to Linda again on 22 November: 'It may interest you to know that I was talking to Arnold Bennett, the novelist, last week, and I asked him to say something about Captain Colthurst. It would be useful if he would for he writes for a Home Rule paper, the *New Statesman*.'[31] Bennett's article appeared on 24 November:

I am glad to see that the agitation for the release of Captain Bowen-Colthurst is still active … He had Mr Sheehy Skeffington killed, and naturally became thereby an object of the contumely of two continents. He was adjudged, no doubt rightly, to be of unsound mind. It is certain that he was then still suffering from shell-shock intensified by his later experiences in France. But it is equally certain, unless all unbiased accounts are quite valueless, that at the present moment he is of sound mind. Yet he is still imprisoned in Broadmoor. Broadmoor is an asylum for criminal lunatics. Anybody who has ever seen even a decent lunatic asylum can imagine what the Broadmoor scene is. Why is Captain Bowen-Colthurst imprisoned in Broadmoor? Is he a criminal? A nerve-shattered victim of the war, worn out by forty-eight hours continuous, maddening duty, his mind unhinged, he undoubtedly made a grave error of judgement; but in no reasonable sense of the word can he be called a criminal. All his career speaks in his favour. He is imprisoned because of the political bother aroused by the very lamentable death of Mr Sheehy Skeffington. He is imprisoned because the authorities cannot, or will not, think clearly. His tremendous misfortune is due to the fact that he insisted on serving his country. Even if he is not absolutely recovered from his shell-shock, Broadmoor is the very last place in the world where he ought to be, and that he should remain there is a monstrous shame. The people who ought to be in Broadmoor are those who allowed Captain Bowen-Colthurst, with his notorious medical history and mental trouble, to hold any responsible military position at all in the Dublin operations.

The final sentence above is disingenuous in that Colthurst did not hold a particularly responsible position within the barracks and took upon himself duties that had not been delegated to him or authorised by his commanding officer.

Major Martin Archer-Shee, DSO, MP, Gloucestershire Regiment, who had recently returned from France, took up the matter with the home secretary on 6 December:

Personally, I believe that Bowen-Colthurst is neither a criminal nor a lunatic … He himself informed me the other day that he would far rather have been shot than sent to his present place … If I am alive after this war, I shall personally leave no stone unturned to arouse public opinion to have this man reinstated in the Army, and an Act of Indemnity passed for what happened during the rebellion. The Royal Commission on the subject, a political move if ever there was one, was an entirely ex-parte enquiry, on which the prisoner was not represented in any way, and it is my opinion, which is only a personal one at present, that it was an absolute outrage that this man should have been treated in the way he was treated … I had half an hour's interview with him the other day and, although I am not a doctor, I cannot believe that he is any less sane than the majority of the members of the House of Commons.[32]

Arnold White, a right-wing prolific author of social commentaries, had argued the case in *The Referee* on 14 October, using the pseudonym Vanoc, in a rambling article entitled 'Unscrambling Scrambled Eggs: de Valera and Bowen-Colthurst'. He was then approached by Linda to make further efforts on her husband's behalf. Having been refused a visit to Broadmoor, unless he kept it private, White had this diatribe published in *The Referee* on 11 December:

Bowen-Colthurst was sentenced to torture that recalls the worst deeds of Torquemada. Wholly sane, if not wholly cured of the after-effects of shell shock, the result of heroic efforts during the retreat from Mons, Bowen-Colthurst has won the Mons Star. Will it be given to him, to his wife, or will it be withheld because Sinn Féin resents justice to the King's friends … Bowen-

Colthurst lives in a block of Broadmoor Criminal Asylum. He is herded with seventy criminal lunatics in that block. His companions at meals are three criminal lunatics seven days a week. Such treatment, if he is sane, is un-English and inhuman. His sanity ought not to rest on official certificates because his enemies and ours have eighty votes at their disposal. If the Government is wise it will liberate Bowen-Colthurst. He does not hunger-strike nor complain. But he is distressingly ill, caged and insulted by politicians every hour of the twenty-four.

The article fails to mention that the Mons Star was given to all members of the original British Expeditionary Force and was not an indication of bravery.

Dr Baker reported to the Home Office in December 1917:

Since my last report nothing has occurred in the condition of Captain Bowen-Colthurst to call for special comment. He has shown a certain amount of impatience at his continued detention, comparing his lot with the Sinn Féin prisoners who were released.

With regard to his bodily health, he has lost a certain amount of weight, but otherwise he is in good condition. Touching his mental state, nothing has been observed in the nature of delusive conceptions. He is in possession of his reasoning faculties and can transact ordinary business; his letters are lucid and frequently expressed with a certain amount of literary ability; his talk is rational, but at times he seems unable to maintain a sustained or prolonged conversation, due probably to an exhaustion of psychic energy dependent on enfeebled nerve tone.

No exception can be taken to his conduct whilst in the Asylum; if he has felt any repugnance to his fellow patients he has concealed it, and has taken his part in the social life of the place. He has his meals and exercise in common with the other inmates of the block in which he resides. He is employed with a few other patients in the carpenter's shop; he shares in their amusements, he has played cricket with them, he is now engaged in a billiards tournament which he originated for his ward, and he is to take the chair at the Christmas Concert for the whole of the inmates of the Block. It will thus be seen that his time is not altogether passed in morbid introspection and cavilling at his surroundings.

In further estimating the complement of his mental endowment, and in probing deeper, one cannot fail to observe certain defects or deficiencies which betray themselves from time to time; they include a want of judgement and a lack of willpower combined with some degree of emotional sensibility; hence he is easily swayed by the opinions of others, appears irresolute, and occasionally displays alternations of apathy and activity. All this does not connote insanity, but rather a mental disharmony, a lack of mental poise, and a predominance of spontaneity over reflection and volition. It is not to be implied that these conditions, now considerably mitigated, are ordinarily in evidence, but they are apt to appear under stress or worry, and were no doubt largely responsible for the events in which he was concerned during the Dublin Rebellion, when he was placed in circumstances with which he was, both temperamentally and constitutionally, totally unable to cope, and which in all probability will never recur.

These conditions may be regarded as partly inherent, and as partly acquired by reason of exposure to stress, to sorrow and to shock producing nerve exhaustion. Should his removal from the Asylum be contemplated, the suggestion to transfer him to a convalescent home or hospital for nerve shock cases is deserving of consideration. It would serve as a transition period from Asylum to ordinary life, and the modern therapeutic equipment of these hospitals might be advantageously employed in supplementing and possibly completing the rehabilitation of the patient's nervous tone.[33]

Following this report, the Home Office deliberated on the matter. It was considered unprecedented that a man charged with murder should be released so soon, but the circumstances of the case were exceptional and, in view of Baker's report, it was decided to place Colthurst on conditional release. It can therefore be seen that his release was not the result of the British government being soft on the issue, but based on advice given by his doctor.

Sir James Craig, MP, sent a letter to Linda on 28 December: 'I find your most welcome letter awaiting my return to Town and write at once to say with what genuine pleasure I learn the joyful news.'[34]

Colthurst was finally released from Broadmoor on 26 January 1918. J. B. Atkins sent a note to him on 7 February:

> I cannot tell you how pleased I was to hear that the Home Office had allowed you to go to a private Home, as they ought to have done long ago. What you say about loyalty to your friends is very generous and you may be assured that I for one have complete confidence in your words.[35]

Reverend Holden also joined in:

> It is indeed a great and gracious answer to prayer, and I do trust that the next step of His Will may unfold with much clearness,

so that you shall have no doubt whatsoever as to what He wants you to do ... I am just home from a visit to the centres of the Soldiers' Christian Association at the camps in France, and could not help thinking while there what a splendid sphere one of those huts would make for you and your wife, if you were only free to go. There is constant soul-winning work going on in every one of them, and the opportunities are perfectly boundless.[36]

Also on 7 February, the Right Honourable William Drennan Andrews of Dublin, a retired High Court judge and member of the Privy Council of Ireland, contacted Linda: 'There are no two opinions here amongst all people whose opinion one cares for as to the wisdom and propriety of the government's action. All seem to think that the only mistake is that it has been so long delayed.'[37]

A bombastic Arnold White wrote to Colthurst on 8 February:

Your enemies are German swine, Irish renegades and their German paymasters and the foul clot of contemptibles known as politicians. If you had shot 3,000 instead of 3 too many, you would have been a national hero, for there would have been no Irish question. Some of your social enemies have crabbed you, probably because you 'wiped their eye' out shooting or some such cause. Your wife has been magnificent and stands as a model for all time as to the best way of extricating a husband from a d—d tight place.[38]

Reverend Colthurst communicated with Linda on 9 February:

I think all decent Nationalists will be glad he is out – the thing was so patently and monstrously unfair ... The leading Dublin papers reproduced the bare announcement without any comment at all – except that the *Independent* published a photo of Jack! I wonder where they got it!

He enclosed a letter for Colthurst, which read:

> Everybody over here is expressing the greatest pleasure at your release. Of course I don't know about the Sinn Féiners, as I don't number many of them among my acquaintances! Still I fancy that most of them even will not grudge you your freedom, as I think they must realise that you have suffered enough. Things are still bad enough over here. Scarcely a paper but contains news of raids for arms by Sinn Féiners through the country, and yesterday they seem actually to have held up the Post Office at Banteer. It reads more like Oregon or Nebraska than Ireland![39]

Perhaps surprisingly, in general terms the reaction in Ireland to Colthurst's release appears to have been muted.

10

TOWARDS FREEDOM

Following his release from Broadmoor, Colthurst became a patient in a private asylum at Grantbourne, Chobham, Surrey, being placed there involuntarily as a condition of his release. He was under the care of Dr Herbert C. Crouch, MRCS, LRCP, of St Michael's, Ascot, Berkshire, who specialised in nerve cases. In a letter dated 21 February 1918 to Fred Crawford advising of his new address, Colthurst noted:

> Everything comes right in time. Some day, before too long, I hope we'll meet again, and I'll be able to tell you more. My wife and her babies are with her mother at Ascot, six miles away. I've been to see her once since being here. They are all very fit I am glad to say.[1]

Dr John Charlton Briscoe examined Colthurst on 19 March 1918, the interview lasting an hour and a half, and reported that he was not suffering from any demonstrable form of neurasthenia, that he exhibited no signs of mental abnormality and was physically sound in every way:

> From information supplied I gathered that he had written one or two letters which were not tactful and rather tended to bring him before the public. These letters and his general attitude indicated that he is a man of faulty judgement ... I understand from Dr Crouch that his physical condition at the commencement of his

residence with Dr Crouch was rather low and that he has made very considerable improvement in the last two months.[2]

An internal Home Office memo on 15 April considered the matter:

> It seems to me too soon to allow of his release. He is a person of unbalanced mind who is liable to become altogether insane at a time of excitement, and though he may be perfectly tranquil and reasonable now, we can have no assurance that under the influence of strain and excitement he might have a dangerous relapse. The present time, when Ireland is in a state of ferment and another rebellion is possible, would be very unfavourable for discharging him from medical control and still worse for allowing his return to Ireland.[3]

Having had him under constant observation for three months, Dr Crouch gave his judgement of Colthurst to Sir Edward Troup, the under-secretary of state, at the Home Office on 1 May:

> In my opinion he is absolutely sane, but of a highly nervous and erratic disposition, a man of impulse, who is always liable to commit actions without considering their results, easily influenced, and where the influence is good, capable of extremely good work.
>
> His work, unless supervised, will be of a spasmodic character, before one job is finished he is inclined to think he would like to start another, but will return to the old work at once on friendly pressure. He was put by me on parole, and has behaved in the most honourable way the whole time, never breaking my instructions

either by spirit or letter. He himself is very anxious to engage in some national work, and I am sure if this were permitted, and it were made plain to him that he must take no part in public affairs, his word could be relied upon.[4]

It was believed by Colthurst's supporters that he had practically recovered and was to be released in the near future. They planned to place him into an officers' shell-shock home or a convalescent home. His pension continued to be paid to Linda on the understanding that she became responsible for settling his expenses. Sir George Cave, who by this time was home secretary, and Troup had a meeting with Crouch on 14 May. Troup recorded:

> He [Crouch] says the chief difficulty with regard to the patient comes from his wife – he is perfectly reasonable and quiet except when he is excited by her. Bowen-Colthurst is in ordinary circumstances quite normal, but he is liable to outbursts of excitement when he 'sees red'. It would be most dangerous, for instance, to let him go to Ireland at a time when there is risk of Sinn Féin disturbances. He is strictly honourable and always observes his parole.
>
> He brought a letter from Mrs Bowen-Colthurst in which she asked him to tell the Home Office that if her husband was not at once released she would open a press attack on the Government. Dr Crouch was doubtful about keeping Bowen-Colthurst longer as he was costing him a good deal.
>
> The Secretary of State arranged that Dr Crouch should keep him till the end of the six months. In the meantime try to find outside work to which he could go daily on parole. No promise to be given as to what could be done at the end of that time.

The reply to Mrs Bowen-Colthurst was to be that the Home Secretary paid no attention to such threats as that in her letter.[5]

The next day Crouch brought Linda up to date on developments:

I imagine that your threat, which you asked me to give to the Home Secretary, is now seen by you and your husband to be a very wrong and unreasonable one, and of course you will understand that the moment any such step is taken by you or your husband or by others acting for you I shall be unable to continue to be your surety, and the whole matter will have to be reconsidered de novo. I strongly advise both of you to accept the Home Secretary's offer, which you must clearly understand binds the latter to nothing in the future ... although I am satisfied, after the most courteous interview he gave me, that he is acting entirely in the best interests of everybody concerned.

Finally I strongly urge you to exercise a more moderating influence over your husband in future than you have done in the past. You must remember that he is a man of impulsive temperament, and that he has gone through considerable nervous strain for an extended period, and that in consequence his judgement is not as sound as it might be. And it is for you to bear this constantly in mind, and to use your undoubted influence with him to persuade him to remain where he is, and where after all he is perfectly comfortable, and to dismiss all future movements from his mind, and to be content to leave the management of his affairs in the hands of the Home Office who are actuated by nothing but the best intentions towards him.[6]

Colthurst set about deciding what to do with the rest of his life, and wrote to a cousin, MacGregor Greer, of County Antrim, who had been a prominent recruiter for the 36th (Ulster) Division, about the possibility of renting land from him. Greer responded on 23 June:

> Now remember this, the door of this house is always open to you and yours and all you have to do is to walk in at whatever time is convenient, so just come along as soon as you can and we'll be most delighted to see you. As far as I can see I think you would be wise in carrying out your idea about your Estate in the South. As to Tullylagan, I am just now negotiating for letting it, but if it falls through I shall have very great pleasure in going into the matter with you, and I need hardly say how very delighted we would be to have you there.[7]

Colthurst complained to the Ministry of Pensions on 4 July that his pension had been reduced and he could not support his family and pay the private asylum fees. He requested the reinstatement of increased payments, especially as he was being kept in the asylum 'under the instructions of the Home Secretary'. He added that he had been certified perfectly well and trusted that his detention would not be continued for too long:

> Dr Crouch's charge for professional attendance is at the rate of four guineas per week; I have the honour therefore to request that my former pension of £280 per annum granted to my wife under your letter dated 10 September 1917, may be continued to me until such time as I am fully released and permitted to return to my family, for the following reasons:
>
> 1   I am compulsorily detained here under the order of the Home Secretary, for treatment under Dr Crouch's direction.

2 I did not ask to be sent here … and the fee of 4 guineas per week was arranged with Dr Crouch, at a time when my pension was £280 per annum.

3 It was believed that my pension would cover the cost of my detention, and it was not understood that my pension was going to be reduced from £280 to £180 per annum while my expense for professional attendance remained the same, and could naturally not be reduced.

4 Dr Crouch has, I understand, only charged me for his professional attendance at an exceptionally low rate. I explained my dilemma to him and have told him that my combined income and pension do not amount to his fees at present. He has charitably offered to reduce his fees still further, but I do not consider it fair to him to accept his offer until I hear quite definitely from the Ministry of Pensions, after bringing my case before them.

5 When your medical adviser surveyed my case on 19 March 1918, it was then understood that under your letter to Dr Crouch dated 23 February 1918 I would shortly be removed from Dr Crouch's charge and come under Dr Lumsden's scheme, which would of course be considerably cheaper to me.[8] I would beg therefore to point out, that in granting me temporary retired pay at the rate of £180 per annum, after the medical survey of 19 March 1918, the fact that I would still continue to be under Dr Crouch's care was not taken into account.

In further proof of this I would beg to point out that I received a letter … asking me if I desired to come under Dr Lumsden's scheme, to which I replied in the affirmative on 5 April 1918.

I have the honour, therefore, to point out that in attending Dr Lumsden's scheme, under which it was understood I was to come shortly, when my pension was being fixed at the rate of £180 per annum, and in continuing my treatment under Dr Crouch, it is only fair to Dr Crouch and to myself to also continue my pension at the former rate, viz. £280 per annum.

6 My private income, apart from my pension, is very small indeed. My income from investments (before deduction of income tax) only amounts to £20/5/4 per annum. Particulars of my income have been sent to the Paymaster General. I am separated from my wife by the order of the Home Secretary. Her private income ... amounted last year to under £300, before deduction of income tax, and out of this she has to support herself and 3 children. I may add that in addition to my current expenses I have to meet two insurance premiums shortly, amounting to £42/5/3. It is not I think fair on my wife to ask her to assist towards meeting my expenses here.

7 My property in County Cork is at present, owing to political agitation, quite valueless. I am not permitted to reside there by the Home Secretary's orders. In fact, by today's post, I have received a letter from my solicitor asking if I want to sell my land there.

8 I would again beg to point out that my ill health has been entirely due to wounds and losses sustained in the service of the country ...

9 I have been asked not to rake up any incidents of 1916, so do not desire to refer to them: if requested to do so my solicitors can supply particulars.

10 In conclusion I would like to point out that the Home Secre-

tary has promised to reconsider the question of my complete release on or about 26 July 1918. If, therefore, my release is granted on 26 July 1918 the amount additional to my pension of £180 to bring it up to £280 for … April, May, June, July, would only be about £30.

This may not seem a large sum, but it is a sum which will make all the difference to me, and as to whether I can meet Dr Crouch's fees and my insurance premiums, and be overdrawn at the bank or otherwise.

11 I do not, of course, ask for a continuance of the pension of £280 for a day beyond my present detention under Dr Crouch's charge, and if released and permitted to earn my living. But I would beg to point out that while I am continued under Dr Crouch's charge I am on 100% disability.[9]

His appeal appears to have been successful.

Crouch wrote to Troup on 18 July, requesting a meeting to discuss Colthurst's case:

He has carried out your instructions, and for the last two months has worked at a controlled establishment at Sunningdale. That, of necessity, has to come to an end because the Carpenter's and Joiner's Union [*sic*] have ordered him out, or they will call all the men out. He has been allowed a week's grace, which expires on Saturday. He has loyally carried out all my instructions in the meantime.[10]

Colthurst had been cycling to the factory each day.

Troup met with Crouch on 23 July and reported back to the home secretary on his meeting:

He tells me that he has now ceased to work at Norris's Factory for munitions boxes, Sunningdale. The Carpenter's and Joiner's Union [*sic*] objected to the employment in the factory of national service workers, and they were all (43 of them) dismissed, including Bowen-Colthurst. He worked well in the factory, making 10 boxes to 7 made by union workmen, and this was the reason for his being turned out.

The six months which Dr Crouch undertook to keep him have now expired, and he cannot retain him any longer as he is losing heavily by taking him instead of a good paying patient. Bowen-Colthurst must either be discharged from supervision or go back to Broadmoor. Dr Crouch says that Bowen-Colthurst is not now insane. Moreover he is an honourable man who keeps his word and would carry out any undertaking he might give. He is an Irishman with wild ideas, who spreads out his tail for anyone to tread on, and he suffers a good deal from ill-advised friends who will not leave him alone.

His wife is always apt to disturb his equilibrium, but his mother and sister are sensible and have a good influence. Dr Crouch's view is that he might now safely be relieved from supervision by a further conditional discharge: he thinks he should still remain liable to recall to Broadmoor in the event of a relapse and that he should certainly be precluded from going to Ireland or from taking any part in politics. He says Bowen-Colthurst himself quite understands this and would be willing to give an undertaking and would abide by it. It is necessary to come to a decision soon, as Dr Crouch says he has now kept him for the full time which he undertook and cannot afford to do so longer, though he regards him as an excellent patient, always amenable to rules and instructions and thoroughly to be trusted.[11]

Troup advised Linda, by then living at Ringstead House, Bridport, Dorset, that the home secretary would allow her husband to be released from strict supervision and would agree to his living in a quiet place in England, preferably in a doctor's house, if close medical supervision was provided.

Meanwhile, the political situation in Ireland continued to deteriorate, especially in the Cork area, as Colthurst's mother explained on 13 August:

At least I must send you a few words of most loving greeting by Pixie, as I cannot go with her as I had hoped to do. Meanwhile I shall hope to be able to come over later on. Pixie will tell you about the post, how diffident one is forced to be about entrusting anything to it of a confidential nature. That is the reason I have not been able to write so many things to you that I wanted you to know … The country is in an appallingly unsettled state. Pixie will tell you. The Dripsey Police Sergeant has just come back from Waterford looking very much the worse for wear; one of the men with him was badly injured – the Sergeant escaped injury but looked worn out from strain and stress. Near Macroom last week Sergeant Butler and a constable were attacked and seriously hurt. A company of soldiers is stationed at Macroom now and one never knows what is going to happen next. Do not think of coming over, nor must you on the other hand be uneasy about me – no one would harm me personally, being old and a widow. To harm me would bring so much discredit it would not pay to do it, but it is impossible for anyone to live here now without feeling the continual strain and a certain amount of nerve tension, nor do I think it will be otherwise for many, many years to come. I will do all I can to get strong enough to come over. I am longing for a sight of you and a real talk. My dear, dear Jack, Pixie will do

Queen's messenger for me and tell you at least some of the things I want you to know.[12]

Crouch updated Troup that same day:

I have written fully to Dr Oliphant of Bridport about the supervision of Captain Colthurst, and the former has acknowledged my letter and said he is quite willing to undertake the job. I made it abundantly clear that I was not writing as an official representative of the Home Office. At the prospect of being able to join his family Captain Colthurst's spirits are absolutely different, and he is only looking forward to doing so. He has no intention whatever of taking part in politics at all of any kind.[13]

He added on 21 August: 'I am quite sure Captain Colthurst will give no anxiety of any kind to the Home Office as he is a scrupulously honourable man.'

Although Dr Oliphant had undertaken to see Colthurst at least once a week and to advise the Home Office immediately of any symptoms of mental disorder, this arrangement was not acceptable. The Home Office did agree to Dr Crouch's later proposal that Colthurst would remain under his supervision, while being employed on the land of a Mr Minchin, a substantial Ascot farmer, and that Linda could live with him provided she moved to that area. In the meantime Colthurst applied, and was approved, for the Silver War Badge issued to those who had to leave the Army as a result of war service.

Following representations made to him, Sir James Craig, MP, had been advising Colthurst's family as to how they should proceed in securing his release, but then found himself at odds with how things were progressing. Minutes of a meeting held at the Home Office on 13 September state:

> Sir James Craig MP called today. He said he understood Bowen-Colthurst's family were about to make another strenuous attempt to secure his complete freedom. He (Sir J. Craig) advised Secretary of State, and still advised him, to keep Bowen-Colthurst under restrictions for a further period; and he was at the same time advising the family, and Bowen-Colthurst himself, to acquiesce in this. In view of the advice he was giving the family, Sir James Craig hoped that the Secretary of State would not at any time decide to release Bowen-Colthurst without giving him (Sir J.C.) some warning: otherwise he (Sir J.C.) would be made to look rather foolish. He said that the Ministry of Pensions had recently sent down a Medical Board to examine B.C., and they had passed him as in thoroughly sound physical and mental health. The family would probably make great play with this certificate, especially as the Ministry had reduced his pension by £100 per annum in consequence of it.[14]

On 16 August, in a letter to Minister of Pensions John Hodge, MP, Colthurst had sought assistance from the King's Fund for the Disabled, advising that 'My property in Ireland has been temporarily ruined owing to my loyalty.'[15] An internal note to the parliamentary secretary from Mr C. M. Wynne, dated 18 October, reported:

> This is a very difficult case, and we know it well. To begin with, we are not concerned with the article in *The Referee* or the contention that Bowen-Colthurst was in his right mind and was justified in his action. I would only observe that, had his sanity been

accepted, he might have fared worse. The court-martial found him insane at the time, and he was retired for medical unfitness and placed in Broadmoor, a confinement which secured his own safety as much as that of others. The disability was considered to have been aggravated by service in France.[16]

On 18 October Colthurst arrived at Ascot Heath Lodge, where his family joined him, but the campaign for his full release continued. Those who responded positively to his representations included the Earl of Mayo; Brigadier General Thomas E. Hickman, CB, CMG, DSO, MP; Brigadier General Herbert C. Surtees, DSO, MP; Lord Henry Cavendish-Bentinck, MP; Commander Sir Edward Nicholl, MP; Major John R. Pretyman Newman, MP, DL, JP; and Admiral Lord Charles Beresford.[17] Brigadier General Edmund J. Phipps Hornby, VC, CB, CMG, responded on 3 December: 'Personally I shall be very glad to see you exonerated as I feel certain that in the same circumstances, nine men out of ten would have acted as you did.'[18] Here again we see that no consideration was given to the absolute innocence of the victims.

Colthurst complained once more to the Ministry of Pensions on 18 December, this time about the fact that he was forced by the home secretary to live at Ascot and that he could not leave England or return to Ireland. The cost of living at Ascot was too high for his income, he was not allowed to take up paid employment and his property in Ireland was not let: 'I am still a prisoner of the State.' Linda had advised him that their weekly expenditure was the minimum on which she could manage and did not include any sundries. His pension of £280 had been reduced to £180 and he wanted it reinstated 'until such time as I am released'.[19] The War Office advised that his retired pay was set at the level of his disability and could not be increased.

On 6 January 1919 Crouch reported to the home secretary:

When he first arrived from Broadmoor his nervous condition was unstable, he got unduly excited over trifles, to a certain degree had lost his sense of proportion, and was not sleeping well. His weight was also lower than it should be. He stayed with me at my nursing home at Chobham until 18 October 1918, and during that period he steadily improved. For the first part of his stay he had a great deal of rest, then he was put to work in the garden gradually increasing in extent, and during the final period of his stay at my Home he was working at Messrs Norris's builders at Sunningdale, on war work.

By 18 October 1918, he had regained completely his normal health, and, with your consent, he joined his wife at Ascot in a house adjoining mine, so that he could remain under my supervision. I have seen him frequently under all conditions, and his mental and physical condition have remained normal in every respect, and there is no reason whatever to suppose that he has not completely recovered from the state of psychasthenia in which he was at one time. I have never at any time seen any trace of insanity, though he has of course the Celtic temperament. He is a man of a very sweet nature, unselfish, absolutely honest and always extremely courteous especially to his social inferiors. All those brought into contact with him, either his nurses, the servants, his fellow patients, or, at Ascot, ordinary acquaintances have conceived a very real affection for him.

From time to time he has received extremely foolish advice, both in letters and verbally, from people who thought they were in a position to assist him, and it has only been on these occasions that he has ever given me any anxiety at all. His sense of injury has been deliberately worked upon by these people, and that at times he did succumb and write foolish letters was, I think, only to be expected. But he himself was afterwards the first to realise that he was not assisting his own cause in so doing.[20]

A letter from Edward Shortt, KC, MP, the new home secretary, dated 10 January 1919, advised Colthurst that he 'felt justified in allowing you to leave Ascot if you wish and to reside elsewhere in England'.

Despite this, on 13 January, Colthurst wrote to the Home Office complaining that he had not been allowed to make a submission to the Royal Commission of Inquiry: 'I have not hitherto taken any steps to publicly refute the allegations made at that time by hostile and partisan counsel.' The reply advised that the inquiry was closed and could not be reopened, and that the decision not to give him permission to reside in Ireland stood.[21] Then, on 4 March, Colthurst requested an appointment to appear before a medical board as his intention was to move to Canada at the earliest possible date. His address at that time was given as Crugmeer, Stanpit, Christchurch, Hampshire.

A cousin, Admiral Sir Robert Swinburne Lowry, KCB, of Wickham Lodge, Wickham, Hampshire, whose wife, Helen MacGregor Greer, was also a cousin of Colthurst's, wrote on 16 April:

We hear that you are soon leaving England for British Columbia to look for a ranch … I think you are very wise to go now, and that doing so offers the best prospect of happiness for you all … May you find her and the children able to go out too before long. The work of providing a home for them will give you many

strenuous days, and I hope prove such a keen interest that many
sad memories will weigh less on your mind.[22]

Clearly, although he went to Grantbourne asylum involuntarily,
Colthurst had developed a real friendship with Dr Crouch and
appreciated all he had done for him. This is evident from the
following letter, which Crouch sent him on 30 April:

> I have not written to you before because I wanted to see the
> mirror first, so that my gratitude for your kindness would be in
> strict proportion to the value of the gift! That you should give me
> anything at all was extremely kind, but you have, with the genius
> which all Irishmen show, given me something that is exactly what
> I wanted, though I did not realise it before it came. My wife and
> I quarrelled as to where it should be put, and I ended the victor
> and for once in my life I was allowed to have my own way, and it
> is now in my bathroom, and I shaved with it for the first time this
> morning … If you come back later to fetch your wife and child, I
> hope you will give us the opportunity of renewing what has been
> to my wife and to me a very valuable friendship.[23]

True to his intention, Colthurst soon left for British Columbia,
Canada, to check out the situation, leaving his pregnant wife
behind. He arrived at Vancouver Island in May 1919. By this
time the War of Independence in Ireland was intensifying.
Since the 1916 rebellion, a boycott had been put in place
against the Colthurst family by those with a nationalist outlook
and, in Cork, the focus fell on Dripsey. An anonymous note was
circulated, which highlighted the wisdom of the Home Office's
decision not to let Colthurst himself return to Ireland:

For Those Who Forget. There are some things which Irishmen and women must never forget as long as life lasts and the spark of patriotism burns. One of them is the massacre at Portobello Barracks in Dublin in 1916. The guilty murderer of the innocent men and boys, convicted by British laws but saved from the hangman by British strategy, was Captain Bowen-Colthurst. Nothing in the faked records of Turkish or Bolshevik atrocities exceeded the brutality of that crime and for it the House of Colthurst will ever bear the stigma.

Who fraternises with them insults the memory of the dead. Beware then. No intercourse with the House of Colthurst. Remember that John Kelleher of Myshall threshed for Mrs Colthurst last season and she has glorified in the bloody deed of her ghoulish offspring. John Kelleher has outraged national feeling by his conduct and therefore no Irishman must hire his engine for threshing, crushing, or in any way avail of his equipment without incurring the same risk. This decision has been come to after grave consideration and the public are warned to observe it faithfully. Lest We Forget.[24]

The Irish Times reported on 18 September 1919:

At a Crimes Court, held at Douglas, Cork, yesterday, three young men named James O'Leary, Denis J. Murphy, and Jeremiah Hinchion were charged … with unlawful assembly on the 24th August at Aghabullogue, in that they, with others to the number of about forty, assembled with intent to intimidate one John Kelleher, who owns a threshing machine, from threshing for Mrs Bowen-Colthurst, Dripsey Castle.

The accused were not personally represented. Sergeant Culhane stated that on the date in question he was at Aghabullogue and saw a notice on the notice board of the chapel wall. Witness gave particulars of the notice, which spoke in strong terms of a family in the district, and condemned John Kelleher for having threshed for Mrs Colthurst last season. Witness pulled down the notice and subsequently one of the accused, O'Leary, held up a paper against the board and witness searched him. O'Leary refused to give his name, and witness placed him under arrest. When he tried to take away his prisoner the crowd obstructed him. The other two defendants were in the crowd. Father Shinnick, Catholic Curate, then came on the scene and asked what was up. Witness told him. Father Shinnick, addressing the crowd, asked 'Did you hear my sermon?' and Hinchion replied 'I did. You take the sergeant's part; you recruited for the Army in Coachford, but I will recruit for an Irish Republic, and train up our sons to fight for it'. Witness was obliged to let the accused go. … The witness, replying to Mr Carroll, Crown Solicitor, said that within the last few months there were about thirteen outrages in his sub-district, consisting of the breaking of milk cans belonging to persons supplying milk to Mrs Bowen-Colthurst's creamery, smashing of windows in the suppliers' houses, destruction of harness, carts, and so on. Five or six men supplying milk to the creamery had been tied and gagged on the road … O'Leary and Hinchion stated that they refused to recognise the court. O'Leary and Hinchion were convicted, and the former was sentenced to three months' imprisonment, and the latter to one month's imprisonment with hard labour. The case against Murphy was dismissed.

Michael O'Sullivan, an engineering officer with the IRA, told how this story concluded:

There was a project to take Inchigeela Barracks by a ruse in June 1920. The owner of a threshing set, a wild irresponsible type, had been boycotted for threshing for Bowen-Colthurst and to try and have the ban removed came to us and offered to bring in a bottle of poteen to the Barracks if we would put a drug in it. We thought it a dirty kind of trick but at length consented and a doctor friend of ours and a Volunteer put morphia in it, just enough to send the police – there were fourteen of them there now – asleep and enable us to get in and capture everything when the poteen maker would emerge. We assembled about the Barracks at the time appointed and in due course he came out letting on to be drunk and when we got him away some distance, by cross-examination, he admitted there were seven police unaffected by the poteen so we decided not to proceed with the venture, as it seemed as if their would-be betrayer might in reality be walking us into a trap. We brought him away from the scene and gave him the benefit of the doubt, partly as a nephew of his, a good young lad, was in the Battalion.[25]

On 31 October 1919 Linda delivered Colthurst's third son, David Lesley. As he was then without a stabilising mentor to guide him, Colthurst wrote to King George V on 8 November from the Red Triangle Club (YMCA), Vancouver, complaining about the Royal Commission of Inquiry ruling that he had lied about a document found on Sheehy Skeffington:

Material evidence has been withheld. With regard to the statement in Paragraph 52, that I afterwards added a specific document. This would have been impossible for me to do, as all papers found on the men subsequently executed, were handed over by me to the Adjutant, and were held by him until produced before

Sir John Simon. Such action would have been unnecessary, as two motorcar loads of documents, many of them seditious and incriminatory, in connection with the men executed, were forwarded to Dublin Castle.[26]

This was forwarded to the Home Office and one of their internal comments read: 'This does not give a very favourable impression of the writer's present mental condition!'[27] It may well be that his memory of events during the Rising was sketchy, but it is also obvious that he had not faced up to the facts of the murders.

On 22 March 1920 Colthurst returned to Britain. He had sailed from St John, New Brunswick, arriving in Liverpool, and rejoined his family at Carnarvon House, Swanage, Dorset. A confidential letter sent from Assistant Commissioner Basil Home Thompson, Director of Intelligence, Metropolitan Police, to Edward Troup on 22 May 1920, stated:

> I had a long talk with Bowen-Colthurst yesterday and found him quite reasonable. His reason for wishing to go to Ireland is to see his property. He has a house and 120 acres of land, but he seems inclined now to sell them, and when I told him that it would be an embarrassment if he went to Ireland he promised not to go. He will probably buy a farm in Devonshire and settle down there. He does not seem to be mentally disordered, though he is undoubtedly excitable when you get him on to the subject of the Irish Rebellion, and from what he said I should judge that under the same circumstances he would act exactly in the same way.[28]

Meanwhile Hanna Sheehy Skeffington continued to turn the screw and claimed that Colthurst was employed in an important position by the government. This raised questions in parliament on 16 December 1920, where the home secretary denied the rumour. Kathleen E. Royds, secretary of the Women's International League for Peace and Freedom, wrote to Hanna on 18 January 1921 regarding the matter, because she had learned from a few reliable sources that the allegation was untrue: 'Would you very kindly contact us with the details on which you base your statement, as it is of course a difficult position for us not to be able to support statements made by our speakers which are criticised in this way.'[29]

Peggy Scott, daughter of Colthurst's late brother, Robbie, described the atmosphere during the War of Independence and the difficulties for Colthurst's family back in Ireland:

The troubles in Ireland were building up. Stories of the terrible happenings never reached the nursery, but it must have been a tremendous strain on my mother having to take momentous decisions on her own. We had police protection at one time, and I can remember milking my beloved Dexter cow in the upper yard with an RIC man standing beside me ... The Black and Tans, reckless, recently demobilised young soldiers, tore round the roads trigger-happy. I remember one lot tossing out sweets as they passed us on the road, and our nursemaid snatching them from us, saying that they were probably poisoned ... My mother must have had some definite warning that the house was to be attacked, as we all moved suddenly up to Dublin in 1919 ... Oakgrove was burnt to the ground shortly afterwards. This was not done by local people, but by agitators who came down from Dublin stirring up trouble all round the country. The same agitators let it be known that they would blow up the fountain which my mother was planning to erect in Carrigadrohid in my father's memory. There was no tap in the village, only a well from which buckets had to be carried, and a running water system would have been a godsend to the cottagers. My grandmother lived on at Dripsey Castle on her own, experiencing several raids by masked men. She would interview them in the drawing room, and often recognised the local boys, and shamed them by addressing them by name. In 1921 she was told that if she sold the house to Mr O'Shaughnessy, the owner of the Dripsey Woollen Mills, it would not be burnt. There was really no alternative, and she moved over to London, where she only survived for a few months. Her body was taken back to Aghinagh to be buried. It was a brave decision by her family, as the Civil War was raging in County Cork by then, bridges were down, and ambushes were a constant hazard. But, like all funerals in Ireland, it was followed by hundreds of neighbours, and politics were forgotten for the day.[30]

Oakgrove was actually burned on 4 July 1920 by local members of the Macroom IRA commanded by Captain Ned Neville: 'I was in charge of about fifty men from Rusheen Company when we burned down Oakgrove House, as it was feared that it would be occupied by British forces. We cleared out the caretaker and cattle from a farm belonging to the Bowen-Colthurst family who owned this house, as they were being boycotted at the time.'[31] Despite Neville's explanation that the house was burned to stop it being used as a barracks, Lieutenant Jeremiah Murphy stated that he organised its destruction as a reprisal for the murder of Francis Sheehy Skeffington: 'It was a big house and we drenched the vital places, such as the hot press, with petrol and then set fire to it. Some of the furniture was taken out first by the Volunteers. I actually put the match to the house to start the fire. Only half a mile away at Carrigadrohid there were R.I.C. and Tans but they came along too late.'[32]

In the autumn of 1920 the London branch of the IRA made an attempt to kidnap Colthurst. Five armed men travelled to Three Fields Farm, Colchester, Essex, where they wrongly thought he was living and, in the darkness, surrounded the house. The alarm was raised by a dog barking and a woman came to the window. The effort was then abandoned.[33]

On 19 April 1921 the War Office granted Colthurst permission to travel to British Columbia again, provided he went as a civilian and kept them informed of any change of address. He had been granted passage by the Canadian Government Overseas Settlement Board with a view to settling permanently in British Columbia as a 'Soldier Settler'. As his home had been destroyed, and in view of the current state of affairs in County Cork, he no longer wanted to go back there even if he had been allowed. His address in Canada would be Toronto General Trust Corporation or c/o Canadian Bank of Commerce, both in Vancouver. However, contrary to many accounts of that time, he did not have a career in banking.[34] Colthurst sailed from Southampton aboard the SS *Scandinavian* on 26 April 1921, the fifth anniversary of the murders. Linda telegrammed: 'Our love and best wishes for new home goes with you.'[35]

Back in Ireland, Michael Mullane, an officer of the IRA in Cork, recalled that 'the majority of the members of the company took part in the burning of two houses at Dripsey to prevent their occupation by enemy forces. The houses were the property of Miss Bowen-Colthurst. The operation was carried out under Tim Twomey and myself.'[36] According to *The Irish Times* of 5 November 1921:

> Mrs Georgina Bowen-Colthurst, of Dripsey House, whose son, Captain Bowen-Colthurst, had such a tragic connection with

the rebellion of 1916, and her daughter, Miss Peggy Bowen-Colthurst, of Dromgowna House, Dripsey, each lost their dwellings by fire and were left practically homeless. The latter conducted a successful dairy industry for a time in a most hostile atmosphere, until the dairy buildings finally shared the same fate as the mansions.

According to the UK Probate and Cork death registration index, Georgina died at Victoria Hospital, Cork, on 21 November 1921 and her funeral took place three days later:

> The first part of the Service, at which the Bishop of Cork officiated, was held at St John's Church, Cork, and the funeral procession had then a long 22-mile drive to the ruined Church of Aghinagh, where Mrs Bowen-Colthurst had expressed a wish to be buried near her husband. The route had to be a circuitous one, through fields and rivers, as the main roads had been rendered impassable earlier in the year, but in spite of the difficulties, many old friends of all classes joined the procession as it neared Aghinagh. The hymns sung at the graveside included one written by Mrs Bowen-Colthurst, and many wreaths were laid on the grave.[37]

In December 1921 a meeting was held in London between members of the IRA. One of those in attendance, Seán McGrath, later claimed that it was agreed to carry out the execution of three people: Sir Henry Wilson, John Bowen-Colthurst and a woman who had betrayed people in Cork. His version of events was, however, denied by others who were present.[38]

In May 1922 Linda made a visit to Canada to see the home Colthurst had prepared for the family. She returned to England in March 1923 and was soon ready to emigrate with her children. She wrote from St Andrews, Brockenhurst, Hampshire, on 25 May:

> Darling one, it is quite a long time since I've heard from you. How are you? And how goes the farm? And how are the animals? Has Betsy-Ann calved yet? Well did I tell you in my last letter that the *Ansonia* (the ship in which I've booked our passages) has postponed her passage to Montreal from August 3rd to August 10th? Not a very serious difference! How lovely that we'll be together again so soon! Are you glad, darling one?
>
> I'm hoping to stay with Peg for a few days, next month. At present she's in Denmark, attending some farming conference. Heaps of love darling one and God bless you. Be a nice, gentle husband to me always, darling one, and I'll try to be a good, helpful wife to you always. Heigh ho! Good night, Jonathan Jones, from Rosalinda.[39]

11

CANADA

By 1924 the Bowen-Colthurst family was living at Kitsum-kalum, immediately west of Terrace, in the remote Skeena River Valley of northern British Columbia. They kept a summer cabin at Waterlily Bay on nearby Lakelse Lake, where Linda Bowen-Colthurst had purchased sixty acres. For a time she was also part-owner of the local Hot Springs resort. She 'found life in the wilds not a little foreboding, but with fortitude, she managed to survive with the help of the family retainer – a Miss Holtham – and learned to milk cows, tend chickens and bring up her family'.[1]

Andy Kelleher emigrated to Canada that year and encountered Colthurst. Andy was the nephew of John Kelleher, who used to thresh the corn at Dripsey Castle until the IRA boycott. Colthurst is reported to have told Andy about Lieu-tenant Colonel McCammond's action at the start of the Easter Rising. 'The OC ... went over the head of my superior officer, Major Rosborough, in sending me a private message from his home to stamp out rebellion in our district in his absence.'[2] There is no evidence to support this statement, but it does seem to clarify his implausible earlier statements, which implied that he took full responsibility for his actions in order not to implicate others.

In the summer of 1925 Robbie's widow arrived on a visit with her daughter Peggy, who remembered:

Before going out to join Uncle Jack in Canada Linda had lived a very easy cosseted life, with a maid to do everything for her, even to brushing her hair. Here, in Canada, with a selfish husband who went off for days on end, fishing and hunting and shooting, leaving her with three schoolchildren and a new baby David, she was worn out and very conscious of her lost looks … A Chinaman came once a week, to help her with the washing, otherwise she did everything on her own in the most primitive of conditions – no hot water and cooking on wood fires. Uncle Jack had built one timber house and was still working on a second. Slippery duck-board paths over very muddy ground, which must have been desperate in the snow in winter. She was intensely religious and had hymn singing on Sunday evenings. An itinerant preacher came round the scattered farms occasionally but she was completely cut off from civilised company or conversation. As a fifteen year old I found Uncle Jack marvellous company. We camped in the woods beside hot springs. We shot and fished together.[3]

Possibly Linda was a little less precious than Peggy would lead us to believe. Her father worked for a living – he was a lawyer leading a fairly middle-class existence at Old Windsor in England. When he inherited Knappogue Castle on the death of his brother in 1899, he had to continue working in London until he retired, using much of his income to maintain the castle and estate. Linda's siblings – four brothers and three sisters – were far from being a weak bunch, and all her brothers served in the Great War. Robert, who had given her the land at Vancouver Island as a wedding present, had built and lived in a log cabin there from 1910 to 1914. He earned the Distinguished Service Order (DSO) and the Military Cross as a sapper and was one of the first-ever tank engineers. Leslie commanded the 2nd Irish Guards as one of the founding officers of the regiment, was awarded the DSO and made a Companion of the Order of St Michael and St George, being mentioned in dispatches six times. Theobald 'Toby' served in the Royal Artillery and was also awarded the DSO. The eldest brother, Fitzwalter 'Fitz', was a captain in the Royal Navy and had taken part in the punitive expedition against the Sultan of Witu in East Africa in 1890.[4]

Patrick Hegarty, a former IRA officer who had emigrated to Canada in 1925, recalled an incident when he was at Anyox, British Columbia:

Archie Moore, a mechanic by trade, of Scottish ancestry, had a homestead ranch reclaimed by himself along the Frayer [*sic*] river. His wife lived on the ranch and Archie came to Anyox to work every winter. In the Spring of 1927, he went home on a visit and learned from his wife that a gentleman by the name of Captain Colthurst had purchased a ranch or was given one by the Government close to his own ranch, and that his wife (Colthurst's wife or the woman living with him) told her that he had grown a beard as he wanted to appear old and was afraid to go anywhere. He was in Victoria before going there and was well known as a remittance man and was mixed up in some affair in Dublin City, Ireland.

The Captain had borrowed some farm machinery from Mrs. Moore and, knowing nothing about farming, broke the machines lent to him. The cost of repairs, Archie informed me, was about 200 dollars, a big sum of money in 1927. Mrs. Moore had asked the Captain to make good the damage and he bluntly refused to pay for or repair the machines. The wife wrote to Archie and asked him to come home and straighten out the matter. Archie went home and called on the Captain. An argument arose and Moore hit him and said: 'I'm coming back in a short time with some Sinn Feiners who are in the camp'...

Moore looked me up when he got back and I was only too delighted to have an opportunity to accompany him on his mission and meeting [*sic*] Captain Bowen-Colthurst face to face. He wrote his wife to say the day we would arrive and, by return, he had a letter from her to say that Colthurst was gone for an unknown destination, leaving a message for Mrs. Moore and 100 dollars in currency with another homesteader requesting that she would not tell those Sinn Feiners in Anyox anything about him.[5]

In 1930 the Colthurst family moved to Milne's Landing, near Sooke, a small town on the south-western tip of Vancouver Island, but they continued to spend summers at their lake cabin near Terrace. The property at Milne's Landing was named Coolalta after the family's old home in Ireland, and was built on the land they had been given as a wedding present. Being a devout Anglican, Linda was active in the Women's Auxiliary at Holy Trinity Church, Sooke, in support of the Missionary Society of the Church of England in Canada.

Despite the beneficial changes in Colthurst's home life, the episode on the Aisne continued to prey on his mind. He sent a long, rambling letter to General Bird on 15 June 1930:

I believe I know your honourable character well enough, to declare my belief, that unless you sincerely believed that I had attacked without orders, and had valid reason for so believing, you would not have sent in the exceedingly bitter report referred to. The words 'exceedingly bitter' were used in my presence by the C. in C. in Ireland, 1915, General Friend, reading your report.

On the advice of General Friend I secured the sworn statements of six Warrant and Non-Commissioned Officers ... who had heard Major Spedding personally order the attack nine months previously. Incidentally I took no affidavits from any rank under Sergeant. Again on the advice of General Friend, I asked for a personal interview with the then Military Secretary, and was granted such an interview. I showed the Military Secretary your report and told him that your report was mistaken in its statement that I had attacked without orders. I informed the Military Secretary that my whole company was present when Major Spedding, who was actually commanding the Battalion on the morning in question, personally gave me orders to attack

... The reply of the Military Secretary may be of interest to you, and was as follows: 'It is evident from this very bitter report that Colonel Bird is bitter against you for some reason. It is either Colonel Bird or you; one of you is finished. It is the policy of the War Office to support the CO. If, however, it can be shown that Colonel Bird's report on you, that you attacked without orders, is contrary to the facts, then Colonel Bird is finished.'

Under such circumstances what would you have done? What I did, however, may possibly be of interest to you. You may not recollect, or you may not have known, that the morning of August 1914, when the Royal Irish Rifles marched out of Bhurtpore Barracks ... when at the head of my Company, I passed Mrs Bird, who had come out to see the Regiment off, and whose natural and commendable emotion was such that when I passed she was weeping. I called out to Mrs Bird these exact words 'Cheer up Mrs Bird! We'll bring your husband back a General!' possibly Mrs Bird does not recollect these careless words; possibly she never heard them. That does not alter the fact that I said them.

My lightest word has however always been my bond, and nearly a year afterwards, in the office of the Military Secretary at the War Office, London, England, I had to make an instant decision, if it was to be you or me. I do not claim to know if my decision was right or otherwise, but I decided to do nothing to prevent my pledge to your wife from being fulfilled. I knew in any case that to you, honours, title, rank, decorations, promotion, rewards, counted for much, to me as a Christian and an Irishman, the objects of life are found more in duty and in sacrifice.

Would any Englishman ever say like Daniel before the King 'Let they gifts be to thyself, and give thy rewards to another'? Would any Englishman ever have turned down decorations, rewards, rank, like Lawrence of Arabia?

On 11 April 1914 I was rude to you. It was the day before Easter Sunday. I was wrong. From your point of view as an Englishman apparently unpardonably wrong. You could have ordered my instant arrest and trial by Court Martial; that would have been an open and straight-forward course. However, you did not do so, and I apologised to you. Outwardly you accepted my apology. It would have, of course, been better if I had resigned my commission immediately, or asked for a transfer. Unfortunately I did not do so. And next day, Easter Sunday, 12 April 1914, you knelt beside me at the Sacrament of our Risen Lord and Saviour, in the communion of fellowship as Christians. Apparently, however, you never forgot or forgave my rudeness, it still rankled. Even the Declaration of War, and a common enemy, could not obliterate my rudeness.

My rudeness to you was, apparently, at the back of your mind in your 'very bitter' report. It was again on your mind and specifically referred to at my court martial ... 'A root of bitterness springing up, troubling you, whereby many were defiled' (Hebrews 12.15). You certainly smashed my career, probably more completely than any Officer's career in the whole history of the British Army had ever been smashed. It may be of interest to you to know that, at my court martial in Dublin in 1916, I could have taken up an entirely different line of defence; however, my career was ended not by sentence of court martial ... but by the 'root of bitterness' due to my rudeness on 11 April 1914. Please correct me if I am in any way wrong, but I would like to know your motives.

As my Colonel (Lt.-Col. McCammond, a militia-man) said in Dublin in 1916: 'Thank God that I am not in a career that may be ended at any moment by a bitter and untrue report sent in nine months afterwards.'

I have three sons and they are growing up into stalwart Canadians. I have many friends, and I shall probably leave a few notes on various incidents in my life. I believe in the honourable character of Englishmen as a whole, and I certainly believe that you would not have sent in the report you did against me unless you had believed it true. If, therefore, you will favour me with a letter or memorandum, explaining your motives for acting as you did, I shall be glad to get it. On the other hand, of course, you need not reply to this letter, if you do not so desire. Should you still feel in any way bitter against me, I beg of you in Christian charity to forget it. We have both, I believe, the highest ideals of what a soldier stands for. Possibly the mistake lay with the War Office in sending you, an Englishman, to take charge of Irishmen.

All mistakes are, however, over-ruled for eventual good by Almighty God, and so everything works out right in the end. Your report helped to bring about self-government for Ireland. After all, no portion of the world desires to be governed by Englishmen and we in Canada would certainly not permit it for a moment. 'I am content with Canada, and ask no better life than has been given me. No greater joy, no more inspiring task than to up-build and share her destiny.' Of course I send my sincere personal regards to yourself and Lady Bird. You can tell the world that it is due to your wife that you stayed and I went out.[6]

Bird took up the matter with the Secretary of State for Home Affairs on 2 July: 'it is not necessary for me to make any comment on what is said in his letter'. Not waiting to see if he would get a reply, Colthurst lost the run of himself again on 15 July:

> I … am pleased to see that you are still accumulating decorations and rewards, and that you have just been made Colonel of the Queen's Royal West Surrey Regiment. It was a great pity that you ever left The Queen's even for a short period. Your appoint-

ment as CO of an Irish Regiment was just about as suitable as appointing a Brahmin to command a regiment of Pathans. We never understood you, you never understood us.[7]

Bird forwarded this to the Home Office on 1 August: 'I enclose a copy of a not un-amusing letter from Captain Colthurst, which reached me today. But I hope that he is not going to make a hobby of writing insults to me.' Another followed on 16 April 1931, with Bird noting 'I attach another letter ... I propose not to answer it':

> RMS *Oroya*, Callac, Peru. 14 March 1931. I wrote to you last year to ask if it would be possible for you to tell me how it came about that you believed that I attacked without orders ... but in case you do not care to write have you any objection to my bringing the whole matter to the notice of the Army Council and asking them to apply to you for the required information? I believe that you once publicly expressed your contempt for 'Colonials' so that as I am now a Canadian, you may consider replying to a letter from me beneath your notice. There may of course be some other reason.[8]

That year Colthurst had embarked on a four-month trip to South America, taking in a British Trade Exhibition at Buenos Aires, and returned home in June. On his many travels he would regularly contact members of the local Freemason Lodge and be well looked after. For him, the attraction was the camaraderie with a group of men he could trust.[9]

More letters to Bird followed: '27 July 1931. As you have not replied ... I am forced to the conclusion that you have no reason to give, and that the report originated in the bitterness

of your own nature.'[10] Bird complained to the Home Office on
11 August:

> I wish now definitely to protest against the continuance of these
> insults. My reports on Captain Colthurst's behaviour in France in
> 1914 were instrumental – as you can see from the minutes of his
> trial – in saving his life in 1916. It seems to me, therefore, to be
> intolerable that I should be subjected to these wild accusations.
> Captain Colthurst's action on 15 September 1914, about which
> his letters are concerned, was not that of a sane leader … With
> one company, then, Captain Colthurst began to attack a trench
> held by at least two battalions, who were supported by artillery,
> which we were not.[11]

He continued on 21 August:

> I suppose that, to be worried by a man whose mind was certainly at
> times unhinged, is the penalty that one pays for having discharged
> an invidious duty. I was, I may say, similarly pressed in 1915 by
> Captain Colthurst's powerful relatives. But in 1916 they turned
> round and begged me, as a favour, to give evidence as to his lack of
> mental balance.[12]

Bird's comments seem to confirm that there was no co-ordinated
attempt to pervert the course of justice in 1916. The Home
Office advised Bird that 'you are right in thinking it proper
to communicate … anything which throws light on Captain
Bowen-Colthurst's present state of mind'.

Another bee in Colthurst's bonnet was the Provincial Game
Laws. He wrote scathing letters to *The Daily Colonist* throughout
1933:

The Game Department has just appointed a game warden whose principal qualification was that he once mistook a farmer's black pig for a bear and shot it ... The woods of Vancouver Island are full of vermin which have destroyed the grouse and pheasants. The North Country is overrun by wolves, those especial pets of the Game Department, which has cancelled the farmer bounties on these animals.[13]

In March 1934 he addressed the Overseas League about 'The British Empire, Past, Present, and Future', arguing that 'the two glories of the British Empire are Bibles and newspapers' and that 'Canada holds the key position to establishing the friendship of the British Commonwealth of Nations and the United States of America, which friendship is the best hope for the peace of the world'.[14]

Despite these distractions, more letters to Bird were to follow:

Terrace, 29 May 1934.

When I survey the wondrous cross / On which the Prince of Glory died
My richest gain I count but loss / And pour contempt on all my pride.

My dear Bird ... I would value a reply, but if not answered, I have neither self-pity nor resentment. I have been much helped by the Oxford Group Movement. Will you accept its challenge? I would be glad to hear.[15]

The Oxford Group Movement aimed for absolute standards

of love, purity, honesty and unselfishness. Above all, this evangelical group was a Christian fellowship, which held regular meetings and carried their message aggressively to others. Part of Colthurst's activities involved travelling around British Columbia in a caravan distributing Bibles. Unfortunately, these high ideals did not extend to those against whom he harboured a grudge, while his regrets over the murders in Dublin seemed only to arise in the context of their consequences to himself, rather than to the acts themselves.

During this time he fell under the influence of, and befriended, William 'Bible Bill' Aberhart, who had been broadcasting popular fundamentalist religious programmes on the radio for many years. In September 1935 Aberhart became the premier of Alberta as leader of the Social Credit Party. Colthurst was an enthusiastic founder member of the party in British Columbia. In a speech to the movement's supporters at the Union Building, Victoria, on 1 December 1934, he stated that 'the grim choice businessmen have to face today is either enormously increased taxation or a complete change in the social order'. The party was concerned at the discrepancy between the costs of production and the purchasing power of individuals, believing that the remedy was to supplement individuals' purchasing power through direct grants.[16]

On 2 May 1935 he wrote again to Bird: 'Dear Bird, as I am leaving Canada today for the Orient to study the economic situation in Japan and the military situation in Manchu Kuo, I am writing once again to ask you to let me know why you wrote that … I had attacked at the Aisne without orders. I am entitled to an answer.'[17] Linda accompanied him on his journey around the Orient and they arrived back in Vancouver on 12 August.

An anxious Bird made these observations to the Home Office on 14 June 1935:

> I hope that you will recognise that my position on this matter is one of considerable difficulty, because I conclude that it is my duty to take into consideration the interests of my wife and family ... For 14 years after his trial Captain Bowen-Colthurst kept silent. I only heard of him twice: in the winter of 1917–1918 when his wife came to lunch with us, and, in 1921, when he visited the battalion of the Royal Ulster Rifles that was then in camp in Hyde Park. Since 1930, however, he has written to me a series of letters that progressively become more menacing and insulting. Knowing him as I do, I think that it is now not impossible that he may decide to cease writing and resort to direct action, and, if so, there will be no letters to forward to you.[18]

Here again, Bird demonstrates that he had no doubt as to Colthurst's mental instability. The pinnacle of Colthurst's series of letters was this extraordinary outburst of 15 June 1936:

> The English do only what's done – by the English
> And so may be censored by none – but the English
> Though frigid they are suave and polite – to the English
> In everything flawlessly right – being English
> They eat in the moderate way – of the English
> Subsisting on five meals a day – like the English
> How stylish when in Vanderhoof – are the English
> From the natives they keep well aloof – for that's English
> It's correct if you learn only English

And proper to spurn all not English

Because as admitted so long – by the English

You cannot be in any way wrong – when you're English

Dear Bird, May I have your permission to dedicate the fore-going Tribute to the English to you. I want to congratulate you on going back to the Queen's Regiment but a Prussian Regiment is the right place for you. God never meant you to go to an Irish Regiment. This was just an intrusion on the part of the devil to upset the purposes of the Almighty for the welfare of humanity. The malice of Satan is however over-ruled for good. I have one fixed rule in life Bird: I TAKE NO ORDERS FROM AN ENGLISHMAN.

I have met many a poor Englishman out here, and invariably seek to recompense your malice by the only way a Christian can act – and that is by kindness. Sometime and somewhere – you will be called to account to answer the question I have asked – 'Why did you send in that report to the War Office of my having attacked without orders?'

A Contrast between English and Irish Soldiers and Sailors:

Englishmen: Bligh of the 'Bounty' and Bird of the Queen's Regiment – The disciplinarians, cause of mutiny and murder.

Irishmen: John Nicholson, General Dyer, the only two Britishers ever made Sikhs – Beloved by their men.

Englishmen: Townsend the Englishman surrenders Kut and 10,000 men – the biggest surrender in British history. Buller the Englishman advises White the Irishman to surrender Lady-smith. White's motto 'No surrender'. Maude the Irishman has to recapture Kut surrendered by the Englishman Townsend.

Englishmen: Sir Arthur Paget (Pomponius) by his pompous manner causes Bulgaria to declare war against Britain. Braddock's incompetence causes destruction of a British Army in North America. Whitelock's incompetence at Buenos Aires.

Irishmen: Kitchener, Roberts, Sir William Butler, Sir Henry Wilson, Wolseley, French, the Goughs, Admiral Sir Edward Beatty, Lord Charles Beresford, Admiral Lowry commanding Rosyth during war. All splendid and beloved officers.

Would any Englishman ever have behaved like Lawrence of Arabia and refused honours and decorations, and thought only of his men? You have made getting decorations the main object of your existence, as was shown by your ordering me to march on Belfast in 1914. Now Bird, if you've got any ideas on this subject you might pass them along.[19]

It is very revealing that Colthurst considered General Reginald Dyer to be one of his heroes: Dyer is notorious for the Amritsar Massacre of 1919 when, in putting down civil disobedience, he ordered his troops to fire on unarmed civilians – over 400 Indians were killed and over 1,000 wounded.

Colthurst outlined his case to the military secretary on the same day:

> I … received an order from an Englishman who had just been appointed to command the Battalion … to get mobilised for active service in Ulster. I was commanding C Company and was rude to the Colonel. The CO could have had me tried by court-martial, no doubt for insubordination, disobedience of orders, or any other charge he cared to have drawn up, for saying that I belonged to a Belfast regiment and was not going to order my men to fire on their brothers and sisters and fathers and mothers to please Messrs Asquith, Lloyd George, Sir John Simon, Winston Churchill, or other politicians.

I was an Irishman first, last, and all the time and told Lieutenant-Colonel Bird that he did not understand the Irish and never would. Whoever appointed Bird to command an Irish Battalion was capable of appointing a Brahmin to command a regiment of Pathans. Bird never forgot this.

In April 1915, Colonel Bird sent in an entirely false report to the Military Secretary that I had attacked without orders on the Aisne. I saw General Friend (Commanding, Ireland) and he read Bird's report, and he said 'this is a particularly vicious and bitter report, better see the Military Secretary personally'. I crossed from Dublin to London, and sent in six affidavits to the Military Secretary to the effect that I had received definite orders from Major Spedding to attack. From that day to this I have never heard a word and would like to make a report on the subject to HM The King.[20]

Bird commented on 3 July: 'You will no doubt observe that I am now coupled with Bligh of the *Bounty* as cause of mutiny and murder. You will also observe that "sometime and somewhere" I am called to account to answer a question.'[21]

In June 1937 Colthurst stood in the provincial election as the Prince Rupert candidate for the Social Credit League of British Columbia. Hanna Sheehy Skeffington, in the intervening years, had joined Sinn Féin and been elected to the executive of the party. She had been appraised of the situation in Canada by Robert Boyd Matier of Victoria on 28 April:

He is running against the Premier of the Province and has not a chance, but I want to spoil any small chance he may have … He is an Oxford Grouper and is in my opinion cracked, no matter what he might have done in 1916 … He writes letters to the papers but no one takes him on.[22]

A handbill for a political rally at Moose Hall, Prince Rupert, on 20 May outlined Colthurst's political views:

> Come and hear about the political situation in the Province of British Columbia, and the truth about Social Credit. Social Credit demands in this Machine-Age that Money should Equate Production. Social Credit holds that no Individual, Province or Nation can borrow their way to prosperity. A vote for **Bowen-Colthurst** is a vote for **B.C.**[23]

A republican contact in London, who had just heard of Colthurst's selection, wrote to Hanna Sheehy Skeffington on 30 May:

> The London Irish Republican Unity Committee is in touch with various sections of the electorate in Canada that this monstrous outrage must be exposed … It will come perhaps as some surprise to the devotees of Social Credit in Dublin to hear of this nomination. But to us who have always pointed out the fallacy of this economic Reformation among the bankrupt middle classes it comes as no surprise that a decadent like Colthurst espouses their cause and aspires to leadership in the Party ranks.[24]

It could be argued that their campaign was partially the reason that Colthurst received just 14 out of the 2,918 local votes cast. A letter from Matier, dated 4 June, advised Hanna of the result and added: 'I know him to see, but have never spoken to him, nor do I desire to. He is often at one of the chain store counter restaurants talking to all who will listen.'[25]

At one stage Colthurst, still not facing up to the truth, considered taking legal action for libel against Hanna for some article she had written, but was advised to ignore her by his lawyer, J. Stuart Yates of Victoria, on 5 February 1938:

> Mr Skeffington seems to have been in open rebellion against the constituted authorities, while on the other hand you were acting under the said constituted authorities in putting that rebellion down. The only mistake you possibly made was in shooting Skeffington against the wall instead of shooting him on sight. Had you taken the latter course nothing could have been said, but because you gave the rebels a wall to lean against you were decried. This paragraph is just a squawk from a 'lady' who still seems to glory in rebellion.[26]

It is obvious that Colthurst had given Yates a warped version of the facts.

In 1938 Mrs Anna Helene Askanasy arrived with her children at Sooke, having fled Nazi persecution in Austria. She was a Viennese Jew and niece of the composer Gustav Mahler. An acquaintance of Hanna, Mrs Katherine Gillett-Gatty, a left-wing political activist and freelance journalist, was touring Canada in the spring of 1939 and visited Askanasy. In examining the situation of refugees on Vancouver Island, Gillett-Gatty learned that Colthurst was living nearby and determined to find him. Her purpose was to check if he was 'mad' and whether he was running in the next election. While on a bus from Victoria to Sooke she asked the driver if he knew the captain. He didn't, but a youth who overheard said he knew him well and that they called him 'The Crazy Colonel':

> Someone else on the bus began to laugh about him and say 'He's nuts, nuts alright ... and gets up to antics' said the first. 'Yes, that's

him, big tall chap. Awfully conceited … His wife goes along and tries to keep him in order when he gets going on crazy.'[27]

Having received directions, Gillett-Gatty drove to Colthurst's home accompanied by two male refugees and Askanasy:

We got to his place, most beautifully situated in the virgin forest, where some clearing had been done. There were two small white wooden houses. I got out of the car and went and tried to get in at the farthest house. He came out of the other. He had on a frightfully shabby old khaki uniform minus all its buttons. He is a big, bony, tall fellow with a red face, a dolichocephalic skull [much longer than it was broad], hair the colour of damp hay, an unclipped, straight, damp hay-coloured thin moustache, small ratty eyes, at once very shrewd and very stupid in expression. He was full of suspicion and twisting with curiosity about us.[28]

Gillett-Gatty introduced herself as a freelance journalist and told Colthurst she wished to interview him about his intentions of standing again in the next general election. She declined his invitation to meet Linda, have dinner and stay the night:

'I'll drive you back to Victoria tomorrow – I drive most frightfully badly' (with a loud laugh and all very genially) … 'No, I'm not standing.' (He laughed a great deal at this, I saw no other sign of want of balance). 'Oh! Dear me no.' (More laughter). 'Fact is I'm moving soon to New Zealand. Going away from Canada. Are you interested in Social Credit?' (More prolonged laughter).[29]

Gillett-Gatty explained that she wanted his opinion about Social Credit and he laughed: 'My opinion: I haven't got an opinion.' Gillett-Gatty then made her excuses to leave as there were people waiting for her in the car. Colthurst then ran ahead of her and asked all the passengers to come in for dinner. He recognised Askanasy as a new neighbour and asked her to stay, laughingly saying, 'I drive shockingly badly, you know.' As they drove off Gillett-Gatty detected that Colthurst appeared worried about her visit. When asked by her companions if she thought he was mad, she said that she couldn't detect anything except that he didn't laugh normally, or at normal things – he seemed stupid, but had a clever way of not answering questions and of asking them. She then went to Askanasy's house for lunch.

> We just got the lunch cleared ... when a car came along and, to prove how badly he did drive, it bumped into our gate post and in stalked Captain Colthurst, all dressed up for a call.[30]

Gillett-Gatty went upstairs and made herself unavailable, asking Askanasy to tell Colthurst that she was too busy writing some letters. He repeated a request to speak to her, but without success:

> At last he left, long after our dinner hour. At dinner she told us (her daughters and I) that he had behaved most strangely. He told her that he hated editors ... that he was a murderer (but he didn't mention Ireland), that in the Boer War, when he was in Africa, he had murdered dozens and dozens of Kaffirs. But it was all right. He had to. It was his Father's business. He had to do his Father's bidding. God Almighty, his Father, told him to.[31]

Askanasy began to laugh at him for this and told him that her

Father didn't talk as he was an ape! So they had drifted into an argument about fundamentalism and he was horrified to find that she didn't believe in God:

> Then he began on Fascism, in which, of course, he believes, but not for long, as Mrs Askanasy said she never discusses politics and doesn't want to talk about European affairs ... Then he began to talk of the Jews and that they are all immensely fond of money and all immensely rich. So she told him of her family ... I don't suppose he listened. She said he kept reverting to his dislike of editors and wanting to know my name ... I don't know when, or how, but Mrs Askanasy told us he stood up and took down one of the two swords placed as ornaments over the fireplace ... and began to brandish it over his head. 'Remember this! You are among friends. If anyone comes here to annoy you, you just tell me and I'll kill him. I'll run him through the body like this.' Fortunately she saw it wasn't unsheathed, but it was horribly unpleasant.[32]

As he took his leave, Askanasy told him that he could hardly expect her to shake his hand since he said that he was a murderer and she was a pacifist. Her elder daughter later said that she had seen him standing on the counter of the shop at the village behaving in a most absurd way – 'quite, quite mad'.

The next day Gillett-Gatty had lunch with Dr Baillie, president of the Democratic Book Club. Though Baillie had no knowledge of the murders in 1916, he did have definite opinions about Colthurst:

> 'That great blond brute,' he said, 'Oh! Indeed I know him – a most wicked fellow. A fully-fledged fascist who belonged to the

Oxford Group. Is now mixed up with the British Israelites. A very dangerous fellow. Got a wretch of a poor down-trodden wife.[33]

Gillett-Gatty relayed her experience to Hanna Sheehy Skeffington, adding, 'it will help you, perhaps, to know that he is mad. What I can't understand is his being allowed about, for he is, quite obviously, unsafe.'[34]

On 14 November 1939 Linda had an operation on a tumour in her neck, which was diagnosed as malignant, and the strain told on her husband, as can be judged by his next series of letters. He took up his cause with the military secretary again on 31 January 1940, despite the fact that Britain was once more at war and had more serious things to consider:

> There is an old saying that 'in order to have a happy regiment it is necessary to have a happy Colonel' – this is absolutely correct, but it is essential to choose a Colonel capable of understanding the men whom he is to command … Bird had been for ten years at the War Office … He had little understanding of men and absolutely none of Irishmen. He was pitch-forked into the command of my Regiment, with a view to giving him accelerated promotion … As a Colonel of an Irish Regiment Lieutenant-Colonel Bird proved himself by a thousand different follies an impossible individual and in April 1914 his crowning folly was volunteering the Royal Irish Rifles he commanded for active service in Belfast and Ulster. Entirely also on his own responsibility he ordered me and the other Company Commanders to prepare our Companies immediately to fight in Belfast.
>
> As far as I was concerned this was the final breach. I immediately informed Lieutenant-Colonel Bird that his order was

an impossibility, that the Regimental Depot was at Belfast, and that I as an Irishman declined to give my men orders to fire on the peaceful citizens of Belfast … It is only necessary to add that during the retreat from Mons that [*sic*] Bird was on many occasions a gibbering, incoherent maniac, his highly strung nervous system gave way completely under the strain. After Mons he broke down and wailed 'I've got no orders, I don't know where to go, I'm going to take refuge in Maubeuge'; the intention was fortunately prevented … Due allowance should have been made for Bird's temperament and his allegations checked.[35]

These latter accusations against Bird are absolutely scurrilous and more closely describe Colthurst's own state of mind at Mons than anyone else's. The War Office replied that the matter had been carefully considered in 1915 and that, in consequence, the matter was closed. Apparently Colthurst had forgotten that he had been told in writing at the time that his plea had been rejected.

In March 1940, on another trip to the Far East, Colthurst met Priscilla Marie Bekman, a missionary teacher at Ferris Girls School, Yokohama, Japan. She was born in 1906 at Orange City, Iowa, the daughter of Dutch immigrants. Her father was a tailor and she had been in Japan since 1935. She remembered: 'One Sunday, when I attended Japanese church in Yokohama, I met a retired British Army officer who was on a Japanese steamer in the harbour. He sat through the Japanese church service, not understanding a word. I invited him to our house for dinner. He was on his way to China. In a month he returned, giving us the news of China.'[36]

He was in Tokyo on 10 April 1940, when he sent a petition to King George VI seeking redress, but this got nowhere.

He pestered Bird, constantly trying to get an answer about the allegations of 1915. On board *Hie Maru*, 22 April, he wrote: 'As you are aware in your case the report … was a pure tissue of lies, and was sent in by you, solely as the outcome of personal bitterness. You had left the Regiment already almost nine months, and were reporting on a situation at which you were not present.'[37] Bird informed the Home Office: 'The statement regarding the delay of nine months is nonsense. I was dangerously wounded at the battle of the Aisne and I made the report as soon as I had recovered sufficiently to do so.'[38] On his return to Canada, Colthurst found the War Office letter stating that the matter was closed and sent a scathing reply on 27 May:

> To say that I was astonished at its contents is to state matters very mildly … if the Army Council of 1915 reached a decision, why was I not informed? Am I to assume that the Army Council of 1915 supported the then Military Secretary in his decision that a lie told by a Lieutenant-Colonel who is a War Office pet, outweighs the truth told by a Regimental Captain and six Regimental Non-Commissioned Officers? You are in error in assuming that the matter is closed.[39]

He also wrote to Bird: 'I am now taking this case up with the Military Secretary … It is a pity that you are so ego-centric, but it is an Englishman's failing, you were unsuited to command an Irish Regiment, or in fact any Regiment.'[40] Bird submitted that 'it was my evidence in regard to his conduct in the field in 1914 that was material in saving his life, that is in showing his lack of balance and responsibility in times of crisis'.[41] More letters from Colthurst followed, the first to the military secretary, dated 1 June 1940:

You incompetents at the War Office seem to think that it does not matter what happens to the fighting man so long as War Office pets and Staff College favourites get plenty of honours, decorations, rewards, and pay. I am charging that bastard military adventurer Wilkinson Dent Bird with malicious lies. I have proved Bird to be a malignant liar ... In upholding a lie (even if told by a War Office pimp) you are pandering to treason. 'Be not deceived, God is not mocked, for whatsoever a man soweth, that shall he also reap.'[42]

He sent a particularly nasty letter to Bird on 7 June, which questions the level of his mental stability around that time:

To Sir Wilkinson Dent Bird OA, BJI. Sir, OA stands for Order of Ananias, BJI stands for Brotherhood of Judas Iscariot. Here is an Irishman's hand across your lying mouth and the toe of an Irishman's boot to your dirty back. You contemptible War Office Pimp and lick-spittle. Without any regard for your men you collected so-called honours. You are a disgrace to yourself – the name of an Englishman. There are of course many honourable Englishmen. You are a dishonourable liar. Go and read my report on you to the Military Secretary, you filthy bastard imitation of a soldier. And don't forget some day you will have to answer for your mendacious lies before God Almighty ... What a Judas you are![43]

Ananias, a member of the first Christian community, lied to St Peter about the amount he had received from the sale of a piece of land and dropped dead on hearing Peter's rebuke. Not surprisingly, Bird protested to the Home Office:

I am sorry, in this crisis, again to trouble you, but consider that it is my duty to enclose a copy of another letter that I received today from that lunatic Bowen-Colthurst ... I wish that your department, or the War Office, would institute the enquiry that Captain Bowen-Colthurst professes to desire, and so put a definite end to his pestering. Captain Bowen-Colthurst's family were, as he is now, prodigal enough in accusations against me until, in 1916, he committed murder, but, after that, they turned round and, as you are aware, did not scruple to beg for my assistance to give evidence on his behalf when he was tried in Dublin.

After several more complaints, the Home Office told Bird that there was nothing they could do and that there was no point in forwarding any more letters 'unless it appears that he intends to return to England'.[44]

Colthurst sent another curious letter to the military secretary on 18 June, which must have caused some bewilderment to the mandarins in the Home Office:

Let me point out to you that if you Staff-barnacles and brass-hat-limpets in the War Office uphold Bird's malicious lies you pander to a traitor. I use the word traitor advisedly. A traitor is a person who betrays the King ... for the sake of personal gain or personal revenge or malice ... You are only fooling yourself in imagining that anything closes with a lie ...

CLOSED

Help for the Army Council, their spotless spirits hurt,
Help for the English War Office sore trampled in the dirt.
From Pall Mall to Piccadilly, O listen to my song,

The honourable gentlemen have suffered grievous wrong.

Their noble names were mentioned, O burning, black disgrace,

By a loyal Irishman in an English Colonel's case,

They sat upon it full score years, then steeled their hearts to brave it,

And 'The matter's closed', the Military Secretary gave it.

Bear witness, Heaven, of the word told by a lying Colonel

Straight from the pit of Tophet to his devil's work infernal.

Bear witness of that canting pimp kneeling by altar rail,

Bear witness of that Judas friend, bear witness to his tale.

'Closed' in the face of all mankind, in spite of honest word,

Hiding in Hyde Park (and what hid there) they leave the Truth unheard.

Go, shout it to the Seven Seas, give word to England now:

Her War Office gentlemen are 'Closed' and this is how.

They only pay a canting pimp his parasitic price,

They only help a Judas with the Council's best advice.

Their brass-hat tuft-hunters in obsequiousness kneel down,

Their battening smell-feast stooges fawn on snobs in London town.

Sir Pertinax MacSycophant toadys to lick-spittles,

Sir Ananias Judas Bird a ghoulish jackal hunting victuals.

As all their Yes-men flunkeys, a snivelling, grovelling bunch,

Are prostrate on their marrow-bones, toad-eaters wanting lunch.

'Closed', honourable gentlemen? Be thankful it's no more.

A soldier's curse is on your house, the dead are at your door.

On you the shame of open shame, on you from North to South

The hand of every honest man flat-heeled across your mouth.

'Closed', you that guard your honour, go guard your honour still,

Go help to make the Army's laws that break God's laws at will,

One hand stuck out behind your back to signal 'OK, boss',

The other on your medal to show your double-cross.
If black is black, or white is white, in black and white it's down
You're only traitors to the King and rebels to the Crown.
If print is print, or words are words, the Army Council tends
To love an Ananias and act like Judas to its friends.[45]

This letter was ignored.

By July 1940 Linda's health was declining rapidly and she was admitted to the Royal Jubilee Hospital in Victoria. Nevertheless, Colthurst continued his correspondence campaign by contacting Secretary of State for War Anthony Eden on 11 July, still complaining about not being given the chance to refute Bird's allegations:

> I charge Major-General Sir Wilkinson Dent Bird with being a War Office favourite and with making use of the last war and of his high rank by sending a bitter and mendacious report, solely out of personal malice ... I now charge the Military Secretary ... with action contrary to the principles of honour, honesty, and truth in endeavouring to maintain that a lie told by a senior officer outweighs truth told by a junior officer.[46]

It is difficult to see how he thought that these outbursts could have possibly been considered to aid his cause, or even if it was clear to the recipients what exactly was the nature of his complaint.

12

FINAL YEARS

Rosalinda Bowen-Colthurst died on 1 August 1940, having been in hospital for just three weeks. Within days, Colthurst wrote with a proposal of marriage to Priscilla Bekman, who had just returned to the United States from Japan. They were married on 15 January 1941 at Christ Church Cathedral, Vancouver. Priscilla recalled:

> I went to visit a girlfriend in California where I received letters from this gentleman, telling us of his wife's passing. On my birthday, 17 August, I received a proposal of marriage. Twenty-six years difference of age seemed a bit much at first. I did not give my answer until I had gone east on a speaking church tour and family visits. In January we were married in Vancouver and went to live in a village called Sooke, twenty-six miles west of Victoria, on Vancouver Island. We shocked the church people by getting married so soon after his wife had passed away, but I had no job and my husband needed someone to look after him. He built a new house, but the damp climate gave him bronchitis.[1]

Colthurst was still anxious about his reputation, and a hurtful attack came from an unexpected source when a cousin, Elizabeth Bowen, published *Bowen's Court* in 1942:

> Hard upon this return to Dublin came the affair of our cousin, Captain Bowen-Colthurst, whose distracted mother, Cousin

Georgina, forthwith arrived at my father's flat. Henry, being a lawyer, was taken by his family to know all – but his specialisation in Land Purchase hardly qualified him to deal with this fevered and ghastly breach of the rules of war. He did what he could to calm Cousin Georgina, in a position he thoroughly deprecated, and assisted her to find other advice.[2]

When General Bird died in January 1943, Elizabeth became the focus of Colthurst's attention and he wrote to her on 19 June that year:

My fair, unfair and learned cousin. It is with great interest that I have been reading what the *New York Times* calls your 'revealing study of three centuries of life in Ireland' – *Bowen's Court*. In your passing reference to me on page 438, you assume knowledge of the 'rules of war'. I have had much experience of wars, but have not been able to discover the rules. I agree with Sherman, who said 'War is Hell'. If, as you say, I committed a 'fevered and ghastly breach of the rules of war', I did so unwittingly. As the daughter of a distinguished lawyer, you should recognise that there are two sides to every story, even mine … Could you please send me a copy of the 'rules of war' and send them also to Hitler, Mussolini and Tojo.[3]

Not unexpectedly, no reply was received.

In the meantime, as Colthurst spoke ten languages and Priscilla spoke six, during the Second World War they were both engaged as translators of documents from the camps where Japanese-Canadian civilians were interned for the duration of the war.[4] The couple also had two children: Georgiana (Gee) was born on 12 April 1942 and Alfred Greer on 22 January 1946.

At home, among his friends, Colthurst was a raconteur, with a wonderful sense of humour. He had many visitors to his house, where he entertained his guests with jokes and stories, regularly promising to write his life story with the title *The Wrong Side*.

Ever the man to mull over a grievance, Colthurst wrote to Elizabeth Bowen again on 22 February 1946:

> My dear Bitha, If I may call you by the name I knew you by many years ago, and still call you … On the same page where you condemn me you sneer at your own father for not 'knowing which was his right hand and which his left'. You disparage my mother as distracted – your own mother was 'not a capable soul'. Your grandmother, Mrs Colley, was 'hard'. You have not a kind word to say of anyone. You seem to have forgotten or never learnt the first rule of speech and writing. To ask yourself three questions: Is it kind? Is it necessary? Is it true? With the exception of the family tree at the end of the book where Mary Gwynn is shown as your father's second wife, you omit all reference to your step-mother. I have always understood that it was entirely due to your step-mother's brother, Stephen Gwynn, that Bowen's Court was not burnt. In writing a book about Bowen's Court why do you not give your step-mother credit that there is a Bowen's Court to write about? I could not say anything worse about you than you say about yourself. Would it be possible to get you to believe that in spite of your condemnations, sneers, disparaging dislikes, vituperations and invectives, your family is not as bad as you make out.[5]

On his file copy of this letter, he crossed out 'Bitha' and entered 'Bitch'.

Not one to keep a low profile, Colthurst regularly attended Boer War veteran gatherings, and in 1946 attended an official dinner given in honour of His Excellency Viscount Alexander, Governor-General of Canada, by the United Services Association of Victoria. It was in this same year that Hanna Sheehy Skeffington died.

By 1949 Colthurst was experiencing increasing problems with bronchitis and, on medical advice, moved to the much drier climate of Penticton, British Columbia. The family bought a house with one acre of land at 1507 Naramata Road, on the corner of Three Mile Road. Priscilla recorded:

> We missed the salmon, which my husband used to catch, and other things. However, we did not miss the twenty-six miles of difficult road to and from Victoria. ... We planted fruit trees and the garden was very good. I had my first greenhouse, and it was a joy to behold. The view of the lake and the hills was interesting ... This was an ideal place for the children, especially Greer. He enjoyed going down to the lake or going up into the hills.[6]

That year, Colthurst's sister, Pixie, then Mrs Mary Cottingham, came for a three-month visit.

In 1950 Colthurst entered the following on the end pages of his copy of *Bowen's Court*:

> Extract from *One War is Enough* by Edgar L. Jones of the *Atlantic*, February 1946:

> 'We Americans have the dangerous tendency in our international thinking to take a holier than thou attitude toward other nations. We consider ourselves to be more noble and decent than other peoples, and consequently in a better position to decide what is right and wrong in the world. What kind of war do civilians

suppose we fought anyway? We shot prisoners in cold blood, wiped out hospitals, strafed lifeboats, killed or mistreated enemy civilians, finished off the enemy wounded, tossed the dying into a hole with the dead, and in the Pacific boiled the flesh off enemy skulls to make table ornaments for sweethearts, or carved their bones into letter openers. We topped off our saturation bombing and burning of civilians by dropping atomic bombs on two nearly defenceless cities, thereby setting an all-time record for instantaneous mass slaughter', etc., etc., etc., to 'the blackest depths of bestiality'.

Jungle Law is tooth and claw / With ambush, rob and kill.
The Laws of War quite similar are / With bullet, bomb and steel.
Battles prove not who is right / But only who is left to fight.

Dedicated to Elizabeth Bowen who has not yet replied to my letter asking her 'What are the Laws of War'.[7]

The family had a small fruit farm beside their house, which Colthurst ran as a hobby and he was also fond of playing bridge with his friends. He was by then in receipt of both a military and an old age pension, in addition to investment income derived from the sale of his lands in Ireland. Around this time he turned against organised religion, feeling that some of his problems stemmed from his religious beliefs. Occasional approaches were made to him by members of the Orange Order, but he declined to join or have anything to do with that institution.[8] His daughter Gee told me:

We never had any extras when we were growing up ... My Dad talked about all of his adventures and wars. I was more like a granddaughter than a daughter. I would sit on his knee and he would talk for hours … Dad had really got upset with the British Army and government. He said he was on the wrong side of every war. He thought that he would live to see a united Ireland. He also thought of himself as Irish, not British, and had many Irish friends. My father was influenced by a philosophy or belief called British-Israel, weird stuff … I never could figure out why my father had to be so visible in public. The only thing is that Canadians like their eccentric people. People used to come and listen to my Dad's stories for hours. Our house was always full of people from different countries speaking many languages. You can imagine how interesting or exciting my childhood was. When I was growing up in Canada all our neighbours' parents were hiding from somebody. One of my neighbour's father (German) was head of a concentration camp during World War 2 … My Mom was religious and dragged us to church – Dad didn't go very often. I am a 'fox hole' Christian so I don't go near a church much. Because my mother was so bossy and a troublemaker we had to change church every five years.[9]

In 1955 a plot was hatched to kill Colthurst, and the police, acting on a tip-off, put the family into protective custody for four days until the assassin was apprehended. The information had been provided by a priest, who was a family friend and felt that Ireland's problems should remain there. This episode was to have a long-lasting effect on Gee, leaving her anxious that she could be a target. I have not discovered the identity of the intended assassin, or the organisation they belonged to.

An interview published by the *Penticton Herald* in 1959 gives an interesting insight into how Colthurst looked back on the events of his life:

If he had never laid eyes on an Irishman named Francis Sheehy Skeffington, his life would have followed a different course. Not that the tall, 79-year-old ex-British army officer ever frets about it. 'Nothing happens by chance' he is fond of reminding a listener as he mulls over the ups and downs of a vigorous, drama-studded life ... His comfortable home on Naramata Road is jammed with mementoes of his doings on almost every continent in the world ... the first dollar – and last, he claims – he ever earned in Canada, buckskin rifle scabbards picked up on a hunting trip in B.C.'s north, jade from China and books, books, books ... A shoulder injury suffered in a fall this year has slowed the Captain down somewhat ... His father, Robert Bowen, had proved his mettle as a lad of 13 when he went to Australia in 1853. Knocking about there and in New Zealand, he came home with a modest fortune and settled down to the life of a gentleman farmer on the 3,000-acre estate ... he was a second lieutenant in the Royal Irish Rifles fighting the wily Boers in South Africa. 'Good people, the Boers, good people,' muses Captain Bowen-Colthurst. 'Taught us how to shoot' ... Garrison life was dull mostly, but it had its moments. Captain Bowen-Colthurst still chuckles at the memory of the soldier who stood up in the open-air mess to complain about his meat. Before he had a chance to open his mouth a scavenging kite swooped, clutched, and left an empty plate behind. No complaint ... Then came the climactic moment of his life. Angered by postponement of long-awaited Home Rule, Southern Ireland's Sinn Féin movement struck on Easter Monday, 1916 – the Easter Rising.

That morning there were seven of Captain Bowen-Colthurst's men lying dead in the streets, and many more wounded. A prominent Irish newspaper editor and writer named Francis Sheehy Skeffington was among the first picked up. When incriminating documents were found in his possession, Captain Bowen-Colthurst had him shot. He still says he had verbal orders to do so, and he has no regrets over what he still considers his duty. But a conciliatory British government court-martialled him and sent the young captain to prison. It was nineteen months before a friend pulled the right strings that freed him and brought him to Canada.

Perhaps it was just as well he did come to Canada. The Sinn Féin had him marked for death after his release, and failing several attempts, made up for it in part by burning ancestral Oakgrove in 1920 ... Soon he will resign as head of the local Social Credit organization, severing ties which began in the 1930s when as a friend of the late William Aberhart he helped organise the party in B.C. He's enjoyed it all, says the grey-haired captain, and regrets nothing. 'The triumph of right' is his motto, and he sticks by it. [10]

That interview clearly shows that Colthurst did not face up to or admit exactly what had happened as regards the murders and, on the contrary, sought to present himself in the most heroic manner possible. The fantasy of influential friends arranging his release and emigration would have added fuel to the theory that a cover-up had been perpetrated.

Tragedy struck the family when Colthurst's son, Greer, drowned in a boating accident on Okanagan Lake on 15 May 1960. Priscilla recorded, 'But when he was fourteen years of age he was taken from us. We were devastated at the time, but later on we began to realise that God makes no mistakes. As his father said, "We will see him again".'[11]

In 1962 Gee, while at Whitworth College in Spokane, Washington, was courted by Douglas Sutherlin, who remembered:

I had given Gee a number of rather epic poems I had written about her, and also some rather 'high wit' political/social satire (which is one of my interests), and Gee shared these with her father. John thought I was quite the witty fellow, and long before he met me, he advised Gee to marry me. Gee had taken several young men home to meet the folks, from the U.S. back to Canada, and her father had not approved any of them. So I was and am grateful to John for approving me. I did not know the family dynamics then, but her mother did not want Gee to marry. She wanted her to return to Canada from the U.S. and be her lady's companion. She said we were too young, though we were in our early twenties. The old lady did not approve of anyone or anything, but in spite of her, we got married ... John Bowen-Colthurst was the most brilliant person I have ever met. He was fascinating to talk with.

John and I had some long conversations. He was in his eighties then, mind clear as a bell, brilliant and articulate ... Another reason I loved him and still do, was he was very generous with Gee and I. He and his wife had rather separate financial accounts, and he gave us some money, not a great deal, when we were first married, which was a great help.[12]

This one I can attest to personally: when I met John in 1963, he had come to believe in something rather crackpot, cybernetics. He had purchased a number of hardbound books entitled *Cybernetics, Canadians it's time you knew!!!* Cybernetics theory was that soon machines would produce incredible wealth, cars, houses, whatever, and a means of redistribution must be found to spread this stuff around. It seemed rather crackpot to me, and still does, but I went along with it. John and I would attend hockey games in Penticton with a supply of these hardcover books, and attempt to give them away for free to folks, most of whom did not want them. John had boxes of these books, which he had purchased with his own funds. One of John's main themes to me, when I was in my twenties, he would say to me 'don't worship money. I have known some of the wealthiest people in the world, aristocrats, they were the unhappiest people in the world'. He insisted that the last part of his life, when the castles were gone and he lived very modestly, were the happiest years of his life ... On the subject of women, I have no *proof* but I definitely think that John Bowen-Colthurst was a womaniser and probably never turned down an opportunity, of which Georgiana is well aware and not in the least embarrassed.[13]

President John F. Kennedy paid a visit to Ireland in the spring of 1963 and officiated at a ceremony at the grave of the executed leaders of the 1916 Rising at Arbour Hill, Dublin. Colthurst, a great admirer of the president, was very upset over this as he thought the grave contained the bodies of the civilians he had executed.[14]

He sent a final letter to Elizabeth Bowen on 3 August 1963:

You can relax! I was court-martialled not by the War Office but by the personal order of Mr Asquith. My crime in the eyes of the politicians ... was far worse than any breach of the rules of war. It was a breach of their rules of politics. The Right Hon. Sir James O'Connor, in his *History of Ireland 1798–1924* writes as follows: 'The history of every country, England included, has its dark and shameful chapters, but I doubt that any civilised community in modern times can show anything which for cowardice, wickedness, stupidity and meanness can equal the handling by the British Government of the situation created for them by a couple of thousand Irish peasants and shop-boys.'[15]

Doug Sutherlin observed:

There is no doubt whatever that John Bowen-Colthurst was unstable and flighty and had some crackpot ideas. Into old, old age I witnessed that myself. One of his favourites in later life, he had a dispute with the Provincial Assessor, so he would write letters to the assessor and print in huge letters on a big envelope Provincial Ass, rather like the eccentric letters he wrote to Elizabeth Bowen and military figures with whom he disagreed. Perhaps he was lacking in the insight that most people have, if we can truly say that most people have insight. I think the more insight people have, the more they can weigh their actions beforehand and not blunder forward. I had not thought of this before, but a lot of his problems could have been lack of insight. He certainly seemed convinced, most of the time, that he was right, and he did not seem to see the other side. I think it is best to have as much insight as possible into our own behaviour, and to try to ponder why other people are acting as they are. I think that makes for a more sane and reasonable approach. Insisting on the absolute truth of the born again dogma, railing against his perceived enemies, taking up some rather crackpot theories. Perhaps all of this was part of the lack of insight.

It is true he dressed for dinner each evening, under very modest circumstances, I might add. I was not used to this. The dinner plates were at his place at table, and he doled out the meat, etc. Things did not always go well. He and my mother-in-law had a huge garden, and one evening the vegetables were not prepared properly, and there in the veggies were a very large number of well-cooked fuzzy caterpillar creatures. Things like that.

I did find John to have a rather dazzling intellect, but I have to admit that most people I have known with a dazzling intellect can tend to be eccentric, and not always in the best sense of the word. Perhaps unstable, overly volatile, too. Fortunately, he liked me and was very good to me, so that coloured my opinion of him. Also, Gee adored him.[16]

In 1964 Gee and Doug married and Colthurst walked her down the aisle. All the sons from the first marriage attended, together with some of their children. Doug recalled:

In old age, he sometimes fell, but he had learned to roll rather than come down kerplunk, in the military, and he never broke a hip or any other bones. In his last years, he was rather bent and moved slowly. He always had a walking stick with a silver top, made out of a gnarled branch, somewhat like a shillelagh. In the reception line at our wedding, many of my relatives came from the U.S. to Canada, and John had the stick and kept pounding it up and down as he met people, and he got many of the women on the foot, and they talked about it for years later.

He had a huge garden, where he puttered a great deal, a hen house, raised a lot of vegetables, and had fruit trees. He was very social and had a lot of friends in the masons, etc. He was definitely a ladies' man and very courtly, right up to the end. He wore rather rough woollen clothing and a lot of it, in the winter. In his younger years he was not used to central heating. The house, a few miles outside Penticton, was a large, old rambling add-on place, one storey, with a basement. It sat high on a magnificent hill overlooking Lake Okanagan, a very large lake in the interior (south) of British Columbia, a truly glorious setting. In those days, water was short and came from a well. John would buy scrap wood during the summer and throw it down into the basement; wood with bark left on it, left over from logging, etc. The wood was piled all over, he bought a little coal, the old furnace did not have an automatic stoker, but was fed entirely by hand. While very generous in most areas, John was close with the fuel. The fire would go out completely at night, in the cold winter, and the house was freezing in the morning, before a new fire was started. If Gee or I or Priscilla would sneak down into the basement before bed, and throw a lump of the precious coal on, to keep the fire going, he would know it next morning, as the house would be five degrees warmer than otherwise.

To sum things up. I thought that John was absolutely brilliant and charming and what a privilege for me, starting in my early twenties, to meet someone right out of 1880 and part of European history, World War One, South Africa, Tibet, India, so generous. Of course, the fact that he liked me, and told Gee to marry me, was definitely a plus. If I had a very few words to describe my impression of John, and I knew him in his last years, old age: a man of dazzling intellect.[17]

John Bowen-Colthurst died of a coronary thrombosis on Saturday 11 December 1965, at Penticton General Hospital. He was eighty-five years old. Priscilla observed: 'He was ready and willing to go and meet his Lord and his family who had gone on before.'[18] The following January she sent a memorial letter to their friends and relations:

Little did I know when I sent my Christmas letter that John would be spending Christmas with Greer in the Homeland.

After a happy week of meeting friends in various ways, he had a sudden heart attack on 11 December at 4 a.m. I finally got him to the hospital at 8. He was in his usual good humour, joking with everyone, in spite of severe pain and difficult breathing. He talked with me until noon, telling me who I was to notify, etc., and to tell the pastor to preach a gospel sermon because 'a life without Christ is nothing'. He named his loved ones and friends he was looking forward to seeing on the other side. The doctor did not seem to think the end was near because of a strong heart beat and good blood pressure. I left so he could rest and planned to return later. At three o'clock after another hypo, he said he was going to sleep and breathed his last.[19]

The *Penticton Herald* of 14 December reported the loss of the city's last Boer War veteran and described him as a 'colourful figure'. The funeral service was conducted at Our Redeemer Lutheran Church, Penticton, on 15 December, with the small church being filled to capacity. Priscilla detailed a portion of the sermon:

At the turn of the century, a young officer asked his God one simple question: 'What must I do to be saved?' That was the same question asked by another soldier centuries ago. That ancient soldier directed his question to the Apostle Paul. The modern soldier got the same direct answer – Believe in the Lord Jesus Christ and you shall be saved, and your house.

We do not know the further history of the ancient soldier. But the other soldier holds a special place in our thoughts today. Blessed with the curious Irish sense of destiny, John Bowen-Colthurst left no doubts about the kind of message he wished for this day. His Saviour meant more to him than anything else in life. Whatever honours were his, he took it to be of more value that he was counted as a Christian. It was also his concern for others in this regard that will be remembered by many of us. If it wasn't his first question to any conversant, it was not far behind. He witnessed abundantly to his Saviour. It was this phase of his varied life that he would want us to remember ... In his life he walked through the pleasant pastures, and also knew the shadowed valley. He was touched by deepest tragedy, by moments of terrible injustice. But he knew that his anchor would hold, for his trust was in Jesus Christ. His wish for you today would be that you share his faith with him, that Jesus be more in your life, that you would find the joy in serving in the Lord's Army that he found, and that you receive the Crown of Life that is now his.[20]

Members of the Orion Masonic Lodge acted as pallbearers, and the Royal Canadian Legion, of which he was an honorary life member, conducted the Last Post at Lakeview Cemetery. He was buried in the veterans' Field of Honour, wearing his Master Mason's apron. Each of Linda's children inherited around £20,000, but Priscilla was refused a widow's military pension as the marriage took place after he had retired from the Army.[21]

As regards his sisters, Pixie married Major Edward Roden Cottingham, mvo, Royal Marine Artillery, in 1909 and died on 28 February 1967. When Peggy, who married William Greer in 1939 and lived at Brick Wall Farm, Layer de la Haye, near Colchester in Essex, died on 11 May 1970, the *Essex County Standard* of 15 May described her as 'A pioneer of organic farming and a colourful figure known to many local people as the woman who drove a tractor because she couldn't drive a car ... Mrs Greer moved to Essex during the First World War when the county agricultural committee wanted her to train land girls at Layer.' Layer was where Robbie's widow originated and it was to here that Pixie had also moved.

Colthurst's second wife, Priscilla, died of bone cancer on 8 April 1990 in a nursing home at Summerland, B.C., having suffered a stroke some years earlier. Her ashes were buried with her son, Greer, at Lakeview Cemetery.

Of his children, Theobald 'Paddy', who married Margaret Evangeline Mary 'Lally' Pease in 1944, left a legal practice to become a senior counsel in the criminal division with the attorney-general of British Columbia in 1959, and was appointed a judge of the provincial court at Nanaimo in 1972 until his retirement in 1984. He died at Ladysmith, Vancouver Island, in 1997.

Robert St John was a gold miner and trapper near the Yukon boundary and in 1936 he moved for a few years to Coolock Dairy Farm, Wakes Colne, Essex, England. There he married Honor, the second daughter of Colthurst's brother, Robbie, in 1937, but they later divorced. He was proprietor of the Franklin Motel, Kelowna, B.C., from 1955. He died in a health spa, having entered there with mental difficulties; his temperament was nervous and excitable, but very kind.

David, who married Edna Mary Wilkinson in 1940, was a commercial fisherman at Lakelse Lake, Terrace, B.C., established Waterlily Bay Resort in 1950 and died in 1992. He served during the Second World War as a flight sergeant in the Royal Canadian Air Force.

Dorinda, a teacher and a member of the Church Army, went to live in Bournemouth, England, in 1937 and never married. She served with the Women's Royal Naval Service during the war, then worked as a school matron and caregiver. She entered a nursing home in 2004 suffering from Alzheimer's disease and died in 2009.

Georgiana, a retired teacher, lives in Washington State. When I sent her an early draft of this book she responded:

> My dad said that he was the only one of us that was certified sane … I am impressed by your details. Reading it was like I was sitting on my father's knee listening to him … I thought you brought my father alive on the pages … I am not upset with the 1916 chapter – it was very good actually. I have lived with this all my life. I am just glad that the Irish aren't out to shoot me, so everything was great from then. My father said he was sorry every day. I knew him.[22]

Colthurst may well have been sorry but I feel that the consequences of his actions were regretted only in so far as they impacted on him; he was not preoccupied by the effect they had on others. He failed to face up to the truth and seems to have imagined, and eventually believed, a different version of the events that actually happened in France and in Dublin.

13

CONCLUSION

Since the horrific events of April 1916, John Bowen-Colthurst has been demonised for his actions, and the British government has been accused of a cover-up and letting a murderer use a plea of insanity to avoid the proper punishment for his actions. However, there has been little attempt made to actually understand the man behind these actions. The pertinent points of the story prove that this is a much more complex one than has previously been revealed. To sum up:

(1)   When one looks at Colthurst's actions in South Africa, Tidworth, France and Dublin, it is clear that he suffered mental stability problems when under pressure. He was in a volatile and frail mental state before the Rising, as shown by the medical reports and his own correspondence. He was posted to Dublin to train recruits and was deemed unsuitable for any further active service.

(2)   There is no hard evidence that any attempt was made by the authorities to cover up the murders. Certainly, there were understandable exercises in damage limitation and delays in taking appropriate action. However, allowance must be made for the chaos created by the Rising, when priority had to be given to dealing with the rebels and restoring order. These were not normal times, and normal procedures for dealing with the issue were not followed. Colthurst had already submitted a report in writing and

was ordered to remain in the barracks. His commanding officer passed the information up the chain of command. It is true that the authorities felt contempt for Francis Sheehy Skeffington and were not particularly perturbed by his death, but he was too well-known and politically connected for the matter to be hushed up. The rebellion had just ended when Francis Vane went to Lord Kitchener. While there are several aspects to the story where separate and distinct questions arise, they do not, in their entirety, amount to a conspiracy. It would be fair, to some extent, to think that incompetence was a contributory factor; many of those serving in the barracks were far from being of the best calibre.

Consider how a similar case progressed about the same time: Company Quartermaster Sergeant Robert Flood of the 5th Royal Dublin Fusiliers was a very experienced and reliable soldier who had enlisted in 1899 at the age of fourteen. On 28 April 1916 he was stationed in The Malthouse at the Guinness Brewery in Dublin, where he became confused, perhaps even paranoid, and temporarily lost his mental control. During the night he ordered the shooting of two British officers and two brewery employees. He was tried for murder but was found not guilty and returned to service. He was later killed in action with the 7th Royal Berkshire Regiment on 9 May 1917.[1]

(3)   Colonel Bird had no affection for Colthurst, considering him impulsive, eccentric and mentally unstable. Bird was harassed by the Colthurst family over the reports he made in 1914 and 1915, and then requested by them to testify his true opinion at the court martial. Clearly

no perjury was committed by Bird. The trial, though strictly controlled, was held in open court and there is no evidence that it was rigged, that a verdict was pre-arranged or that the other witnesses perjured themselves.

(4)   Colthurst was found guilty but insane. While he must bear primary responsibility, he acted on an irresistible compulsion even though he knew, almost immediately, that he ran a real risk of being hanged for the murders. It could be argued that Colthurst decided to execute Sheehy Skeffington because he had witnessed the murder of Coade and needed to be silenced. This, to me, does not seem to be the case, because there were other witnesses to that murder and Colthurst was not behaving rationally. A sane person would not have acted as he did. A psychopath may have done so but all the evidence indicates that Colthurst was not of such a disposition. Partial responsibility must rest with the Army for retaining him in the service, but they were not too particular as all available men, especially those with a wide amount of experience, were needed in a time of war. Perhaps he should have been more closely monitored, but Colthurst was found to be unsuited only for active service on a battlefield, with no indication that he was unsuitable for training troops or engaging in recruitment duties. Those responsible for his posting could not have anticipated the Rising.

(5)   The relegation to unemployment of Major Vane was a situation that existed long before the Rising and had no connection to his reporting the murders (see Appendix II). He was not the saint portrayed by some, and neither was Colthurst the devil incarnate.

(6)   Hanna Sheehy Skeffington's and Major Vane's accounts

are not entirely reliable and are, to some extent, exaggerated. Monk Gibbon was a disciple of Vane and never questioned his integrity in attempting to establish the facts.

(7)   Along with contemporary diagnoses, a modern psychiatric analysis of Colthurst's behaviour shows that while the man had mental and personality problems, he was not an evil person. He was human and, as such, imperfect. Probably more imperfect than most, yet still a man whom many loved and admired.

(8)   It should be remembered that a large proportion of the higher authority figures in Dublin, and of the troops on the ground, were Irish, and, as Tim Healy suggested, the Rising may be considered a predominantly Irish affair. Accordingly, if there was a cover-up, as some suggest, it could be considered an Irish rather than a British deception.

Perhaps now that a more accurate, detailed and comprehensive picture of the events has been presented here, a more understanding approach might be taken towards the life of John Bowen-Colthurst.

APPENDIX 1

BATTLE OF THE AISNE: SWORN STATEMENTS

C Company consisted of platoons 9 to 12. These are the sworn statements procured by Colthurst in defence of his actions at the Aisne in September 1914. They were taken at Portobello Barracks on 29 and 30 July 1915.

Sergeant Augustus Anderson was in No. 11 Platoon:

> Nos. 11 and 12 were left at the right corner of the wood while Nos. 9 and 10 advanced. We were there for a short time when we were joined by Major Spedding who gave us the order to 'fix swords' and advance out of the wood. We got out of the wood and found A Company on our right. As soon as we left the wood a very heavy shell fire and machine gun fire opened on us. We were going to open fire ourselves when Major Spedding stopped us telling us that those were our own people immediately in front. Major Spedding went back into the wood again and we then got the order to retire. It was then that most of our casualties occurred, mainly from shrapnel. We retired through the wood to our original position.

Sergeant William Flack was a corporal at the time of the attack:

> I was in No. 11 Platoon and in C Company. Our Platoon advanced through the wood until we got nearly out of it. Nos. 9 and 10 went out in front and Nos. 11 and 12 were ordered to wait in the wood. Major Spedding ordered us to 'fix swords and attack'. We all went on advancing about 150 or 200 yards in front of the wood. We were

ordered to lie down and not to fire on the men in front of us. We could see that these men were our own men. Fire was opened on us from our left rear. Major Spedding retired into the wood. Afterwards we were all ordered to retire into the wood. About six shells burst on us as we entered the wood. We made our way through the wood back to the rest of the Battalion.

Sergeant William Rainey:

Captain Colthurst marched us out in the morning from the position we were in into a wood, and our Platoon (No. 11) were told to remain there until we should get further orders. While we were waiting there I could distinctly hear Captain Durant (of A Company) give the command 'At the enemy retiring three rounds rapid fire'. Captain Durant was out in the open on our right front. When Captain Durant's left got up in line with our right, Major Spedding came into the wood and I heard him ask Sergeant Major Hart [sic] 'Whose men are these?' The Sergeant Major replied 'Nos. 11 and 12 Platoons of C Company'. Major Spedding then ordered us to fix bayonets and charge. We fixed our bayonets and made the charge. We had got about 100 yards out of the wood when fire was opened on us apparently from our left rear, from what I judged to be a machine gun. I saw about six men falling. Major Spedding then gave us the order to retire. When we started to retire shell fire came. I saw Captain Colthurst being carried in on a stretcher.

Sergeant John Baines:

I was Platoon Sergeant of No. 9 Platoon which was under the command of Lieutenant Peebles. We advanced to the edge of the wood on the German side and got behind a barrier of logs of timber. On each flank of our platoon we had a machine gun, one in charge of a Sergeant and the other of a Corporal. Our platoon and these guns were covering the advance of No. 10 Platoon which was under the immediate command of Captain Colthurst. No. 10 started to charge and we started firing. While No. 10 were charging Major Spedding came up on our right with a body of men. As soon as he got up to our position he shouted out 'Charge'. Most of the men in our platoon joined in the charge but Lieutenant Peebles directed me to keep as many men as possible in hand to cover the retirement. The men who had advanced with Major Spedding opened out and I got the order to cease fire. The Germans then opened fire from the rear on the men in advance of us and bullets were whizzing past our heads. Captain Colthurst then came back wounded and told Lieutenant Peebles to take command of the Company. All the men then started to retire through the wood and when the men had got past the barricade of logs Lieutenant Peebles told us to retire the best way we could.

Sergeant William Joseph Murphy:

I was a Section Commander in C Company, No. 10 Platoon. We were entrenched in the wood on the night of 14 September. Between 10 p.m. and 1 a.m. Sergeant Webb, the Platoon Sergeant of No. 10 and I were ordered by Lieutenant Magenis to be ready to attack at 4.15 in the morning. We made the attack early in the morning of the 15th. The whole Company advanced to the forward edge of the wood. Then Captain Colthurst ordered Nos. 9 and 10 Platoons to attack the German trenches under his command. We carried out the attack accordingly. When Nos. 9 and 10 got to the front of the wood I was ordered to take my Section forward to the attack. The attack was continued as the other Sections came up to our support. On the next advance of my Section Captain Colthurst was wounded and the attack was continued under 2nd Lieutenant Swaine until he was killed, shortly after our arrival at the German trenches. I was wounded myself soon afterwards. The total casualties on the advance appeared to me to be very slight, and could not have exceeded 15 in all. When I was wounded I lay on the field at the German Trenches.

After about five hours, two Double Companies of Germans came up and took over the trenches. I was taken prisoner but subsequently escaped. I could see from where I was lying wounded, that as the part of the Battalion that had advanced on my right retired through the wood they were being very heavily shelled.

Sergeant Major John Harte:

Captain Colthurst led our (the C) Company into the wood and we had advanced through it almost up to the edge furthest from our lines, when the scouts reported that the Germans were entrenched in front of the wood. Captain Colthurst ordered two men (picked shots) to fire on the Germans. Our Company consisted of Platoons 9, 10, 11 and 12. Captain Colthurst led out one (No. 10) Platoon to the left front, and No. 9 Platoon moved up to the front edge of the wood where there appeared to be some rough barricade or other slight cover. Captain Colthurst ordered me to remain behind in the wood with the half-Company consisting of Platoons 11 and 12. I was left in command of this half-Company. About 10 minutes after Captain Colthurst had left us Major Spedding came up and asked me what men we were. I told him that we were 'two Platoons of C Company'. Major Spedding ordered us to fix bayonets and to see the Germans off. We fixed bayonets and got out in the open in extended order about 200 yards beyond the wood towards the German Trenches. Captain Colthurst had then advanced somewhat on our left. Major Spedding then went back into the wood and came forward again. We then began to retire. Several men were killed and wounded during the retirement. We afterwards reformed at our side of the wood about 400 yards off where we had been attacked by the machine guns.[1]

APPENDIX 2

ALLEGATIONS AGAINST MAJOR SIR FRANCIS FLETCHER VANE, BT

Sir Francis Patrick Fletcher Vane was born in Dublin on 16 October 1861, the son of an English father and an Irish mother. He was appointed a military judge while serving in the Boer War, but was considered too pro-Boer: 'I knew my time was up so I resigned.' He succeeded his cousin, Sir Henry Ralph Fletcher Vane, as fifth baronet of Hutton in Cumberland in 1908. His first wife, Anna Oliphant da Costa Ricci, daughter of Baron Anselmo da Costa Ricci of Portugal, whom he married in 1888, died in 1922. Vane became a Knight Commander of the Order of Christ (Portugal) in 1889. He was a supporter of Home Rule, a socialist and, later, a peace agitator. He married his second wife, Kathleen Douglas-Crosbie, in 1927. He died in London on 10 June 1934, leaving an estate valued at £193.

The following extracts from Vane's military files show that he was not at all popular with his superior officers.[1]

> This Officer was formerly a Lieutenant in the Scots Guards and Captain in the 3rd (Militia) Battalion, Royal Lancaster Regiment. He was granted the Honorary Rank of Captain in the Army in 1903. On 8 September 1914 he was appointed recruiting Staff Officer at Leicester. On 3 October he was appointed temporary Major 9th (Service) Battalion, Royal Munster Fusiliers.
>
> On 17 September 1915 the General Officer Commanding, Aldershot Training Centre, forwarded an adverse report upon this Officer in which it was stated that Major Sir Fletcher Vane was devoid of any military knowledge, discipline or procedure, and was either incapable

of learning them or unwilling to do so; that he cavilled at and criticised, orders, instructions and memoranda issued for his guidance. It was said that he was fond of public speaking and of airing his extreme political views and the G.O.C. 16th Division [Parsons] had to issue a stringent order to him not to attend or speak at any public meeting. It was also stated that Major Sir Fletcher Vane writes long and very flippant or insubordinate official letters on every possible occasion; that his Commanding Officer – an Officer of great kindness and forbearance – having put up with Major Sir Fletcher Vane for twelve months, then reported to the General Officer Commanding the Division that Major Sir Fletcher Vane was making his command impossible.

The Divisional General stated that Major Sir Fletcher Vane was active, energetic and apparently took an interest in his Company but that he was such a 'crank' that his good qualities only made him more dangerous. Sir L. Parsons was quite convinced that it would be a crime to allow Major Sir Fletcher Vane to command men on active service and that he was so inordinately conceited that it was hopeless to improve him at his age (over 50). He suggested that he might be employed at recruiting in England but not in Ireland. The General Officer Commanding 48th Infantry Brigade concurred in the opinion of the Divisional General.

The letter was communicated to Major Sir Fletcher Vane who on 16 September made his remarks thereon, in which he asked for a Court of Inquiry to be held to inquire into the adverse report. A.G. 2B did not require his services as recruiting Officer. On 14 September Major Sir Fletcher Vane forwarded a long letter … in which he asks for a Court of Inquiry or Court Martial to inquire into his case. This the General Officer Commanding, Aldershot Training Centre, forwards without comment, although in his former letter he simply said that Major Sir Fletcher Vane was stated to be temperamentally unfitted for this position.

A.G.3., 29 September 1915.

Vane may also have had money problems. On being relieved of command of his company, and being placed on the non-effective list in October 1915, it was found that there was a deficiency of £62/11/11½ in the Company's accounts: 'The Cash Book of this company has not been kept for several months apparently.' Vane explained on 9 November that 'the money will be paid in at the earliest possible moment though I have not the least notion how the money has been expended – certainly not by me ... I have already written to obtain an advance to cover my liability'. In addition, a cheque he issued for £13 on 9 October 1915 to settle his mess bill was returned unpaid.

The result of these reports was that, on 15 October 1915, Major Vane was informed that there was no alternative but that he should relinquish his commission. Failure to do so would result in his being gazetted out of the Army. He appealed to King George V but this was unsuccessful, and he then threatened to raise the matter in parliament and in the press. The matter went all the way up to the secretary of state and all agreed that he should be gazetted out; this was done on 15 January 1916. However, at a meeting on 20 March 1916, Kitchener promised Lord Lieutenant Augustine Birrell and John Redmond, leader of the Irish Party, to provide an additional 100 recruiting officers in Ireland and the opportunity was taken, because of the lack of numbers, to employ Vane temporarily in that capacity.

On 26 March Vane wrote to the military secretary claiming that his old company, which he had trained for twelve months, was performing well at the Front and that many of the battalion's officers had written to him praising the way he had brought that company to a high standard of performance. He requested that an inquiry be instituted as to the truth of the matter and that he be allowed to rejoin his unit in the trenches.

He was appointed on 31 March to the Department of Recruiting under Lord Wimborne's scheme. Colonel H. V. Cowan, CB, CVO, AAG, Irish Command, in an undated memo from 1916, wrote:

> He was sent by the Department to Longford where a recruiting meeting was to be held, but his conduct was so extraordinary that he was recalled to Dublin. On 12 April he was granted a week's leave and left for

England. It was afterwards extended by the Department of Recruiting as they no longer desired to employ him.

On the outbreak of the rebellion he reported himself to the O.C. 3rd Royal Irish Rifles at Portobello and was employed on various duties by that Officer. No authority for his employment was given by or asked for from Headquarters, Irish Command, nor by the O.C. Troops, Dublin. A considerable number of Officers on leave from other stations reported themselves in the same way and were employed.

Among other duties he was ordered by the O.C. 3rd Royal Irish Rifles to take a party to clear a road for some wagons which were being fired at from the South Dublin Union. He reported that he had attacked the Union and had lost some 6 men killed and 14 wounded. His conduct was favourably reported upon by Brigadier-General Maconchy and he felt aggrieved that he had not been mentioned in the despatch of the Commander-in-Chief, and has written a series of letters on the subject, some before the despatch was published.

He states that he reported the fact of the shooting of the prisoners at Portobello Barracks to me on 1 May. I have no recollection of such a report. On several occasions, when he had previously come to my Office, I had found his statements unreliable, and had doubts as to whether his eccentricities were natural, or due to being under the influence of drink.

A letter from Vane to H. J. Tennant, under-secretary of state for war, on 12 May 1916, stated:

> I told you then it was the act of a madman – that I could prove that he was mad – as I told Lord Kitchener and Mr Walter Long – and I said that it was the only thing to do, to admit the grave mistake, and to plead madness – or else infinite harm will accrue in my country.

In an additional letter to Tennant on 12 June, Vane outlined how he had been instrumental in assuring opinion in Ireland that the army was not to blame for Colthurst's actions. He had visited Hanna Sheehy Skeffington and explained the whole situation to her. He therefore told Tennant that the government owed him the Order of Saint Patrick and that he at least deserved a staff post.

On 13 August D. S. Hammond at the Curragh replied to Cowan's earlier memo:

> I am only able to give same from memory, and in a very general way. He was a source of worry and annoyance to his CO and his Brigadier, and was constantly being reported to the GOC [General Officer Commanding] of the Division, who made several attempts to get rid of him. Sir F. Vane had no sense of discipline, affected a sort of contempt for all the ordinary rules, regulations and customs of the service, and wasted everyone's time by sending in (often direct to Divisional Headquarters) long reports on all sorts of ridiculous subjects and imaginary grievances of his own. In my opinion he is most eccentric, and is eaten up with personal vanity, which was largely the cause of making himself the nuisance he always was in the Division.
>
> The circumstances under which he was eventually got rid of were that his CO (Lieutenant-Colonel H. F. Williams, 9th Royal Munster Fusiliers) reported to the GOC, in October last, that things had come to a climax, and that he could not possibly put up with Sir F. Vane any longer. He reported that Sir F. Vane was practically undermining his authority in the Battalion, and was generally doing great harm. He said that he had frequent trouble with him over money matters, and that a cheque, which he had lately given in payment of his Mess Bill, had been returned dishonoured.
>
> Colonel Williams also showed the GOC a pile of insubordinate letters that Vane had written to him personally, and gave evidence of various acts of insubordination, the exact facts of which I cannot now remember. Sir L. Parsons then wrote another strong recommendation that Major Sir F. Vane should be removed, which was backed up by General Sir A. Hunter, Commanding Aldershot Training Area, and I remember Sir A. Hunter stated that Vane's own letters and appeals themselves showed his unfitness to be retained in the Battalion. I presume all the correspondence is still at the War Office.

From Captain R. H. Fowler, 14 August:

> I attach herewith a confidential statement from Captain Kelly outlining the circumstances under which Major Sir Francis Vane was recalled

from duty with the Recruiting Canvas at Longford. This officer was ordered to proceed to Longford on 4 April 1916 and was instructed by telegram on 10 April to report at this office for instructions which he acknowledged by telegram. He presented himself at this office on 11 April and was granted a week's leave from 12 April and, as the Department of Recruiting would not employ him any more, his leave was further extended until such time as his case was decided upon.

The report from Captain R. C. Kelly, late chief organiser to the Department of Recruiting, stated:

On the evening of the day on which this Officer commenced duty in Longford I received a telephone message from the Chairman of the Longford Committee, T. W. Delany, informing me that a deputation was coming up on the following morning on urgent business. The Deputation arrived: Mr Delany, Mr T. P. Wall, BL, and two other gentlemen whose names I do not remember. Mr Delany informed me that unless the above Officer was recalled from Longford, it was felt that the local recruiting helpers could not proceed with the work, and that they would therefore feel bound to resign. They informed me in confidence of certain peculiarities of conduct on the part of the above Officer which had forced them to this conclusion.

Vane was relegated to unemployment on 30 June 1916, his services being no longer required. Further complaints about his finances arose. Messrs P. Lyons & Sons, Main Street, Charleville, County Cork, issued an invoice to Vane for £1/10/– in respect of a 'Motor to Ballyvonare Camp then to Mallow and back to camp' on 2 March 1915. On 8 January 1916 they stated that, 'Having applied several times for payment of this a/c and getting no reply from Major Sir F. Vane I have been advised to apply to the Army Pay Department of the War Office.' They replied that because 'this Officer having severed his connection with the Army, no assistance can be rendered in this matter'. By 23 August 1916 his mess bill of £6/4/6, due to the 3rd

Royal Irish Rifles, remained unpaid and 'repeated applications have failed to obtain payment'.

There is no doubt that Vane did the honourable thing in bringing the murders to light, but that is not the reason his career was ended, as has been alleged. He wrote to the prime minister, 6 October 1916, seeking an appointment as organiser of a new recruitment drive in Ireland:

> I have acquired considerable popularity among the Irish people. They declare every day through innumerable letters and in the Irish press that their gratitude to me is sincere ... In recruiting I have always had success and much experience ... I suggest to you, Sir, that you will utilise my popularity in Ireland and my experience in recruiting generally by appointing me to the work of organising this new effort to obtain recruits in that country.

Having failed to obtain another position in the Army, he then attempted to undermine it. Below are two samples of his letters that were intercepted and copied by MI5. The first was to Tom Quelch, secretary of the Workers' and Soldiers' Council, London, 19 July 1917:

> I shall be very glad to attend the Conference on the 28th instant but I do not quite see how it will be possible for me to represent one of the bodies enumerated. It is true that I am the initiator of the World Order of Socialists but owing to its constitution I am afraid I could not represent it. I have urged that it should, at this juncture, take a different stand on the proclamations of the Russian Government, but at present without result. And of course among Democratic bodies it would be no use my pretending to represent the National Liberal Club.
>
> I suggest and I beg you to transmit this to Mr P. Snowden [Philip Snowden, MP] and other members of the Council, that to represent in the Army men who are likely to join, in the first instance a few officers like myself, who are pledged to Socialism, or even those who are strongly democratic in views, shall be appointed temporarily to advise on military questions touching the Organisation. Afterwards they can easily become representative through appeal to the Military members.

I am sure that you will recognise my point in this. At the present moment it is unlikely that many men accustomed to organisation and administration will be found qualified to represent any of the mentioned organisations, and therefore you will be depriving yourselves of some of the most useful and enthusiastic members, and whose participation in the work will be an encouragement to other soldiers. I shall be glad to hear what decision is come to about this as I have a number of brother officers all clamouring to join in the movement.

To Edmund D. Morel, Union of Democratic Control, 12 August 1917:

Thank you for the literature and especially your book … Now as to work. I will write to Major Maitland Hardiman at once. I too have been anxious to form among soldiers a propagandist body. In fact for the three months before the War broke out I had been engaged with the late Baroness Von Suttner, in trying to get together officers of various nations, who had seen war, with the object of making its futility, brutality and stupidity known.[2] Indeed when she died I was under a pledge to go to Vienna to pay her a visit and to arrange this with her. But do not misunderstand my position. As a retired officer I came into this war voluntarily, indeed was the first British officer to report himself at the Front in uniform (14 August 1914, to General Pau at Belfort). I did this deliberately after having published a pamphlet (the proofs of which were read by Norman Angell and approved) called *The Other Illusions*. My reasons being, as stated at the time in the *Clarion*, because it was a fight for a small nation, and being so it was pledging the predatory powers in a course of moral action, and because I saw a chance through this war of making it thoroughly hateful to the people, while it had the effect of training the proletariat in arms, and thereby transferring the physical force from the exploiters to the exploited. Therefore *au fond* I am not a peace man. I was trained a soldier, but I am opposed to racial and capitalist wars, and prefer to reserve our strength to fight the powers of evil.

I am against this war now because its aims have been changed from idealistic ones to realistic, from defence to conquest. As most people know, my last fight was in Dublin, where I fought my own fellow citizens, and was specially recommended for so doing, but I fought fair.

When officers under me started murdering, I refused to condone murder for 'reasons of State' and reported the murders to Lord Kitchener. I also opposed the hysteria of revenge which the Government and Sir J. Maxwell initiated, which has now made Ireland antagonistic to England, when at the beginning of the War she was more in sympathy with England than she has ever been since 1798.

Now what can we do? I can bring in a certain number of officers. Lieutenant Gibbon, Army Service Corps, c/o F.P.O. 93, B.E.F., a very gallant young officer and an extremely able writer, who fought well under me in Dublin, has become a Conscientious Objector at the Front. He wishes to be in danger but absolutely refuses now to kill. I think it would be well for you to write to him mentioning my name and letting him have some of the papers. Through Mr Snowden and others I am doing my best to save him from the wrath of ignorant Generals, and have written about him to Sir D. Haig pointing out his course and his sincerity.

Captain Craig Jennings, late 5th Lancers, is the officer who refused to 'mutiny' at the Curragh. He for this acquired the enmity of General Gough, he was persecuted and finally got rid of in the meanest and most inexcusable manner at the Front. His address is Brooklawn, Athlone.

Colonel J. Whyte, Senior United Services Club, should have the papers. A very able officer for years in the political service in Persia. These will help others to form a nucleus. They are men who know all about the atrocious tyranny, as brutal as stupid, of the Army Council, and if anywhere Democratic Control is necessary it certainly is in the War Office. For myself my case is so flagrant that even the War Office is squirming; Mr G. M. Robertson is dealing with it. Within six weeks of being recommended for valuable service in the field, and for promotion, I was relegated to unemployment. I was I believe the only Field Officer specially recommended for service in the Rebellion. So much for personal.

Now I have rather an interesting series of letters – 'The Letters of a German Princess'. This lady is a friend of mine and we have corresponded from 1913 up to February 1917. She is a cultured woman and was pro-English, and she writes her thoughts about the War and I write mine, from my national point of view. They are quite genuine letters, they are letters (this is confidential) from Princess Marie Zur Lippe – but of course her name will not appear. She is a cousin of the Kaiser.

Now I thought these would be good propaganda because at this time it is of the utmost importance for our people to understand, whether they agree or not, the opinions of unprejudiced Germans. That she is unprejudiced is shown by the fact that she has corresponded with me throughout the War. I have not settled with any publisher yet though I have two nibbling, but if you think they are valuable you can have them. Perhaps I had better see you on Thursday next about this, when I shall be in Town.

Again, if you care for a pamphlet on *Ireland and the War* I can let you have it. I have been for long in correspondence with the leading Sinn Féiners, with a view to causing them (which they have now done) to adopt our attitude in respect to effecting a permanent Peace.

In the interim, 20 July 1917, he wrote to the prime minister seeking a court of inquiry and giving a false account of his relegation to unemployment:

I think I may ask you … to assist me to clear myself of libellous persecution. The facts are these, and they can be proved. Directly after I had reported to Lord Kitchener … my enemies in Dublin and elsewhere spread reports of the most villainous kind affecting my personal character. I have no doubt that these were invented to weaken me as a witness or possibly to injure my career as a soldier. At any rate they did – and I can show that these were secretly put into motion by responsible officials, possibly by those who were directly or indirectly implicated in the shootings.

Vane's book, *Agin the Governments*, gives his own version of events, some of which can be seen to be untrue from the available evidence. *The Irish Times*, 24 April 2000, carried an article by Pádraig Ó Cuanacháin about his case:

Sir Francis Fletcher Vane suffered as a result of his action. He was dismissed from the Army, or – as a recently released document from the Public Records Office nicely puts it – 'this officer was relegated to unemployment owing to his action in the Skeffington murder case in the Sinn Féin rebellion'. For a number of years he waged a campaign for reinstatement, appealing even to the King, but failed in his efforts. Apart from his career, Vane was a most interesting man. He was widely travelled, acted as a war correspondent, founded the boy scouts in Italy, was an underwriter at Lloyds, and wrote books including *Principles of Military Art* ... He was even an unsuccessful Liberal candidate in the 1906 election. He died in 1934, no doubt sadly disillusioned with the Empire he had once served loyally ... Vane deserves to be honoured ... and is there not a moral duty on the Irish Government to raise the matter officially? Surely there is some process whereby the British establishment could review the case, reinstate his name on the roll of officers and offer an apology to his descendants. It would be the just and proper thing to do.[3]

The issue of the reason for his removal from the active Army list has been raised several times in the media, calling for Vane's character to be cleared and his unfair dismissal acknowledged. However, the above quote is selective, disingenuous and taken completely out of context. It is contained at the end of one of his two large files in an inconsequential folder titled 'For refund of cost of passage from Italy' in WO339/13389. In March 1919 Vane made an application to the War Office for a gratuity to cover expenditure incurred in returning from Italy at the start of the war in 1914 and for arrears of pay. Numerous memos were circulated within the War Office in order to decide if he was entitled to these reimbursements. In the very early stages of this process an anonymous clerk made the incorrect statement as to how Vane's career was ended. His note continued: 'The files on which action was taken are on the Search list. You have, no doubt, a record of the circumstances of the case.' This was what he thought had happened, but many of those involved had no idea who Vane was or what he was supposed to have done. His file could not be located at the time. 'We are sorry that we have no record of the case. This being so, we think that the question of his gratuity must be considered de novo, and the circumstances of the relinquishment by this officer gone into.' The next reply stated: 'I quite agree. Can you from your records find out the circumstances of his relinquishment? So far as I remember the case was a notorious one at the time.' Enquiries were made of General Sir Francis Davies, KVCO, KCMG, KCB, who was known to be familiar with the matter. His reply, on 5 June 1919, corrected the misunderstanding about Vane, recording 'that it was owing to representations he made to Lord Kitchener that the murder of Skeffington came to light'. He went on to say that Vane was later reported to be no longer required for recruiting duty by the commander-in-chief of Ireland and was placed on the unemployed list. 'I feel sure that nothing was said about inefficiency though I have no doubt they were glad to be rid of him. Under the circumstances I confirm that he is entitled to gratuity.' This resulted in the expenses being reimbursed but the pay arrears being refused because of the lapse of time.

Hansard, 1 August 1916: Henry W. Forster, financial secretary to the War Office, in reply to Thomas O'Donnell: 'On the general question of the further employment of Sir Francis Vane, I can only say a report has been received from … Sir J. Maxwell that this officer's services are no longer required for recruiting duties, and as there is no other employment for which he is required he is now unemployed. He was adversely reported upon as a regimental officer and cannot be employed in this capacity again.'

So a simple clerical error had led to yet another conspiracy theory because of a failure to read all the available documentation. There are two sides to every story!

BIOGRAPHIES OF CHARACTERS IN THIS NARRATIVE

Below are additional details that arose during the course of my research for some of the characters in this narrative. It is not exhaustive by any means, but may be of interest. For Monk Gibbon, Francis Vane and Francis and Hanna Sheehy Skeffington, please refer to the bibliography.

Aldridge, 15582 Sergeant John William, was born in Cheltenham, Gloucestershire in 1866, the son of John David and Charlotte Caroline Aldridge *née* Jenkins. His father was an umbrella maker. The 1871 Census shows the family at 2 Hereford Court, Cheltenham. By 1881 John was an errand boy. He enlisted as number 2203 Private in the 2nd Gloucestershire Regiment, 13 July 1887, understating his age as eighteen years and three months. He married Elizabeth Tancred of County Kildare at the Church of Our Lady of Refuge, Rathmines, Dublin, on 1 January 1891. They had ten children. He served in India from January 1891 to November 1894. Posted to the Army Reserve in December 1894, he rejoined the 2nd Gloucestershire Regiment on 1 December 1899. He served in the Boer War from January 1900 to July 1902 and was awarded the Queen's South Africa Medal with clasps for Paardeberg, Driefontein, and the Relief of Kimberley. Posted to the Army Reserve on 13 March 1903, he was discharged on 12 July 1903. By 1911 he was a gardener and domestic servant at Killadreenan, Newcastle Lower, County Wicklow. He trained the local group of Irish National Volunteers, and on his resignation was given a medal that read: 'Presented to Instructor J. W. Aldridge by Newcastle Corps I.N.V. as a token of esteem in which he was held by the members, October 1914'. He enlisted in the 8th Royal Dublin Fusiliers on 6 October 1914 and was posted to the 9th Battalion as a corporal. He understated his age as forty. He may have had defective eyesight, as a medical note on his file stated: 'Fit for the Army as an Instructor on the barracks square but not on the Range. He would be dangerous with a rifle.' He was posted to the 3rd Royal Dublin Fusiliers on 1 April 1915 and to the 10th Royal Dublin Fusiliers on 29 November 1915. Promoted to sergeant on 3 January 1916, he was a colour-sergeant at the Royal Barracks in Dublin. He reported to Portobello Barracks at the start of the rebellion and was in charge of the guardroom when the murders took place. He later served with the 11th Royal Dublin Fusiliers and was discharged as being no longer physically fit for war service on 11 March 1918, and granted the Silver War Badge. Aldridge appears to have died in Gloucestershire in 1931.[1]

Allatt, Colonel Henry Thomas Ward, was born in Boulogne, France on 18 February 1847, the son of Dr Christopher John Robert Allatt, a physician, and Mary Elizabeth Allatt *née* Buckle. He was commissioned as an officer in the 46th (South Devonshire) Regiment of Foot. He married Constance Margaret McTiernan at Chertsey in 1888 and they had four children. By 1891 he was a major, commanding the depot of the Duke of Cornwall's Light Infantry at Bodmin, Cornwall. The 1901 Census shows him as a lieutenant colonel and living at 12 Alexander Road, Farnborough, Hampshire. By 1911 he was retired and living at Thumblands, Runfold, Farnham, Surrey. During the war he was employed on the Special List as a draft-conducting officer and made his first journey to France on 3 August 1915. Gibbon (1968, pp. 62–3) described him as: 'An elderly white-haired Colonel … a little plump man … With his drooping white moustache, he was the typical "dug-out", but he was not a fire-eater or a jingoist. Rather he seemed to take a boy scout's delight in being able to make himself useful.' He died at 23 Royal Avenue, Belfast, of cardiac failure on 8 May 1916. His Medal Roll listing states 'Died of heart failure caused through the Dublin Riots.' *The Irish Times* of 11 May 1916 reported: 'When the outbreak occurred he was in England but he managed to reach Dublin a few days later, and he did effective work in improvising an armoured car out of an ordinary motor lorry and an old boiler. He carried supplies to the troops and in various other ways performed valuable work … The remains were removed from Belfast last night *en route* for Farnham, Surrey.' The *British Medical Journal* of 20 May 1916 reported: 'died suddenly … of heart failure following his exertions in Dublin during the rebellion. He had served in South Africa and held the Queen's medal with four clasps. He had retired from the Army for some years, but rejoined when the war broke out, and was attached to the Royal Irish Rifles. He was on duty in Dublin in charge of an armoured car.' Hanna Sheehy Skeffington later inferred that he had committed suicide: 'Colonel Allatt had died mysteriously in the interval, according to some he committed suicide in Belfast when Colthurst was condemned, saying, "The game is up".'

Balck, Charles Augustus John Albert, MB, was born in Rostock, Germany in 1874, the son of Reverend Georg Christian August (1801–81) and Lucy Elizabeth Balck *née* Foote (1844–1929) of Rostock, Mecklenburg, Germany. His mother was from Kew Green, London, and married his father in 1873. His name at birth was Carl August Johannes Albrecht Balck. In 1899 he gained his MB, Bachelor of Surgery, at Edinburgh University. He served as a civil surgeon in the Boer War and was awarded the Queen's South Africa Medal with clasps for Cape Colony, South Africa 1901 and 1902. A German subject, he applied for a UK Certificate of Naturalisation on 14 July 1902, while living at 78 Sterndale Road, Hammersmith, London. He was commissioned as a lieutenant in the Royal Army Medical Corps on 1 September 1902 and promoted to captain in

1906. He was awarded the Frontier of India Medal with clasp in 1908. By March 1914 he was a major. Employed in Ireland at the start of the war, he was wounded during the rebellion. He is named incorrectly in the 1916 proceedings as Balch. On 11 July 1916 he was posted to Sierra Leone. By 1923 he had married Frances 'Eileen' Boyd and was living at Roseland. He retired as Lieutenant Colonel C. A. J. A. Balck-Foote, MB, in 1929. He changed his name by Deed Poll to John Albert Foote BM, BS, in 1938. At that time his address was White Lodge, Andover, Hampshire. His son John died of wounds suffered in battle in Italy on 16 September 1944, while serving with the 2/4th Hampshire Regiment. Balck-Foote died at Aldershot on 7 January 1959. At that time his address was 14 Victoria Road, Fleet, Hampshire.

Beatty, Second Lieutenant Joseph Harold, was born at 1 Waterloo Place, Donnybrook, Dublin, on 6 June 1894, the son of Christopher and Ellie Beatty *née* Corr. His father was a commission agent. By 1911 the family was living at 6 Sandford Terrace, Ranelagh, Dublin. His brothers John and Walter both became solicitors, practising as Vincent & Beatty at 62–63 Dame Street, Dublin. Joseph was a dentist's apprentice, having been educated at St Mary's College, Rathmines. He enlisted as 7/2719 Cadet in the 7th Leinster Regiment on 8 April 1915. He was at that time a clerk employed by his father at Beatty & Sons, wholesale merchants, 3 Cope Street, Dublin. Roman Catholic. Appointed a lance corporal and granted a commission in the 3rd Royal Munster Fusiliers on 24 September 1915, he was posted to No. 3 (Junior) Command Company, Irish Command School of Instruction, at Moore Park, Kilworth, County Cork. The officer commanding, Major Edward W. P. Newman, reported that Beatty 'took no interest whatsoever in his military training and that he showed no capacity for commanding men' and 'in my opinion, never likely to make an efficient officer'. He served with the 3rd Royal Munster Fusiliers at Aghada Camp, Cork Harbour. 'I was laid up as the result of a blow from a rifle while on duty, for two months.' He was at home on sick leave when he reported to Portobello Barracks on 25 April 1916. His surname was recorded in the barrack register as Beattie. The adjutant of 3rd Royal Irish Rifles gave Beatty a certificate on 3 May 1916 stating that he had 'done very good work in Portobello Barracks and in the streets during the recent Sinn Féin rising'. He was a patient at Richmond Hospital, Dublin, from 1 September 1916. Beatty was requested on 18 September 1916 to resign his commission on the grounds of his inefficiency. He appealed to the Army Council, citing his injury as the reason he had failed to pass an exam. A representation on his behalf made by Captain D. D. Sheehan, MP, was unsuccessful and Beatty resigned on 29 October 1916. He was then employed as a superintendent in a munitions factory. On 5 February 1917 he enlisted as 11/29298 Private in the 11th Royal Dublin Fusiliers. He went to France on 23 April 1917 and was posted to C Company, 9th Royal Dublin Fusiliers. Owing to various minor ailments he did not actually join his unit until 18 August and was appointed lance corporal the following week. He transferred as 18239 Private to the 6th Connaught Rangers on 15 March 1918. He was wounded and taken prisoner on 21 March 1918. Repatriated on 2 December 1918, he was posted to the Army Reserve on 29 March 1919. His character was rated as very good. His address at that time was 6 Waterloo Road, Ballsbridge, Dublin. He married Gladys N. E. Budge at Islington in 1923. In 1939 he was a retired builder residing at 274 Worple Road, Wimbledon, London SW20, when he applied for a Short Service commission in the Royal Artillery. At an interview held on 9 August 1939 he was rated at the lowest grade then in existence. His file noted, considering his previous military history, that the grading 'is no doubt confirmatory of the fact that there has been no outstanding improvement since and we do not think that he should be enrolled – at any rate so long as there is no shortage of officers'. Also taken into account was the fact that he only rose to the rank of lance corporal before he was taken prisoner in 1918. Beatty died in Surrey in 1964.[2]

Bird, Major General Sir Wilkinson Dent, KBE, CB, CMG, DSO, was born in Campbellpore, India, in 1869, the only child of Captain John Dent Bird, 20th Hussars, and Katherine Shortt. His widowed father was murdered by one of his troops in Aldershot in 1874. He was initially under the guardianship of his grandfather John Bird, and then, from 1884, his aunt Miss Ann Charlotte Bird, in Brighton, England. Educated at Wellington College and Sandhurst, he was commissioned in The Queen's Royal (West Surrey) Regiment in 1888. Promoted to lieutenant in 1890. He served under the Niger Company in the Niger Expedition, 1897, taking part in the expeditions to Egbon, Bida and Ilorin, and was mentioned in dispatches. He was promoted to captain and given the brevet of major. He took part with 1st The Queen's in operations on the north-west frontier of India in 1897–8 and served in South Africa in 1899–1900 with the Rhodesian Regiment. At the Relief of Mafeking he was severely wounded, losing the use of an arm. Mentioned in dispatches and created a Companion of the Distinguished Service Order in 1901. He married Winifred Editha, daughter of Major J. B. Barker, in 1902, and had two daughters. He was employed at the War Office from 1902 and was chief instructor and staff officer at the School of Musketry, Hythe, Kent in 1903. In 1905 he was a professor at the staff college in India, was made a brevet lieutenant colonel in 1909 and general staff officer, second grade, at the War Office in 1910. He was posted to the 2nd Royal Irish Rifles on 24 September 1913 and served with the British Expeditionary Force. He was severely wounded, losing a leg on 19 September 1914 and was mentioned in dispatches. In 1915 he was appointed ADC to the King. Other appointments included general staff officer, first grade, at the War Office, 1915; temporary brigadier general, 1916; lieutenant governor and secretary, Royal Hospital, Chelsea, 1918; and temporary major general. He was created a CB in 1916 and a CMG in 1918. He was an Officer of the French Legion of Honour and awarded a French Croix de Guerre. He retired from the army and was made a KBE in 1923. He was colonel of The Queen's Royal Regiment from 1929 to 1939. Bird lived at Glenturf, Middleton Road, Camberley and died at Frimley and Camberley District Hospital, Frimley, Surrey, in 1943.

Bowen-Colthurst, Robert (Robbie) MacGregor, married Winifred Susan Bartholomew West, daughter of the late Reverend Charles F. C. West, vicar of Charlbury, Oxford, on 5 December 1907, at Bilton, Warwickshire. They lived at Coolnegera, Macroom, County Cork, and at Brookville, Raheny, Co. Dublin. The marriage produced four children: Peggy Winifred Ishbel 'Biddy' (1909), Honor Georgina Beatrice (1911), Charles Patrick Russell 'Paddy' (1913) and Maureen Elizabeth Hope (1914). John's only brother, he was on the staff of the lord lieutenant of Ireland as vice-chamberlain from 1908. In 1912 he began working with the Irish Department of Agriculture, engaged in the protection of Irish produce, and later succeeded the Earl of Carrick as inspector for Irish agricultural interests in Britain. He left for France on 5 March 1915 and was killed in action on 15 March.[3]

Coade, James Joseph 'J. J.', was born in Dublin in early 1897, the son of John Joseph and Mary Jane Coade. Roman Catholic. The 1901 Census shows the family at St Joseph's Place, Inn's Quay, Dublin. His father was at that time a hall porter. By 1911 the Coades were living at 28 Upper Mount Pleasant Avenue, Dublin with their nine children. Mr Coade was working in the Weights and Measures Office of Dublin Corporation. J. J. was six feet tall and in 1916 was a bicycle mechanic. Fr O'Loughlin stated that Coade was a well-conducted youth and that he died in hospital at the barracks during the night. When Fr O'Loughlin saw him, there appeared to be no sign of a broken jaw or any other marks on his face. On removing a bandage from her son's body, Mrs Coade saw a bruised wound to the left side of his head that was consistent with a blow from a rifle butt.[4] He was buried in Glasnevin Cemetery, Dublin.

Dickson, Thomas, was born in Glasgow in 1884, the son of Samuel and Annie Dickson. Both parents were Irish. Roman Catholic. His father was a plumber and gas fitter with Glasgow Corporation. The 1901 Census shows the family living at 28 Glebe Street, Glasgow. Thomas was an advertising agent. Mountjoy Prison General Register states that on 13 May 1910 he was committed for trial having 'embezzled and converted to his own use money, to wit £24/18/10 and £36/3/1'. He was discharged on 19 May 1910. At that time he was a grocer and provisions dealer, residing at 31 Bolton Street, Dublin. On 20 March 1912 he was sentenced to nine months' hard labour in Mountjoy for obtaining the sum of 13 shillings by false pretences. By that time a commission agent living at 85 Lower Camden Street, Dublin, he was described as 4 foot 7¼ inches in height, 103 pounds, 'both legs deformed', brown eyes, dark brown hair, with a fresh complexion. Bombardier McCaughey, a member of the firing squad, described him to the Royal Commission of Inquiry as 'very knock-kneed and small and he wore his hat in a curious way on the back of his head'.[5] His effects were collected from the 3rd Royal Irish Rifles, Victoria Barracks, Belfast, on 22 May 1916 by his mother and brother Samuel, who both lived in Glasgow. Thomas lived at 12 Harrington Street, Dublin. The *Weekly Irish Times* (1917, p. 264) stated: 'During Dickson's business career some of his undertakings had involved himself and other persons in very unfortunate consequences.' He was engaged to a Dublin lady at the time of his death and had just finished arranging for a special printing of his paper to include the Martial Law Proclamation. His parents only learned of their son's death through a statement made in parliament by the prime minister. Two brothers came over from Glasgow to claim his body. He was buried in Glasnevin Cemetery, Dublin, on 19 May 1916.

Dobbin, Lieutenant William Leonard Price, MC, was born in Maldon, Victoria, Australia, in 1897, the only son of William Wood Dobbin, MBE, and Emily Josephine Dobbin *née* Cuzens. He had a sister, Eileen Emily, born in 1889. When his mother died in 1900 the family returned to Ireland. His father married Catherine Shaw McLaughlin in Belfast in late 1901. The 1911 Census shows his father as governor of HM Prison, Waterford. William was gazetted a second lieutenant in the 3rd Royal Irish Rifles on 26 June 1915. Gibbon (1968) said he was 'tall, slight, fresh complexioned ... friendly, gentle, gracious'. He joined the 2nd Royal Irish Rifles on 25 June 1916. He was recalled from France in August 1916 to give evidence before the Royal Commission of Inquiry, the sittings of which were postponed until his return on 31 August. He returned to his unit on 4 September 1916 and moved to the 74th Infantry Brigade HQ on 5 February 1917. He was awarded the Military Cross on 1 January 1918 for gallantry and devotion to duty. He rejoined the 2nd Royal Irish Rifles on 27 January 1918 and was posted to D Company and promoted to lieutenant on 7 February. Witherow (1920) said: 'Then there was a young Sandhurst Lieutenant called Dobbin who was rather famous as being in charge of the firing party that shot Sheehy Skeffington during the Dublin Rebellion. He was a very nice fellow indeed and we got on well together.' Dobbin was killed by shellfire on 21 March 1918, aged twenty.

Kelly, Alderman James Joseph, was born in Dublin in 1860. He married in 1893 and his wife, Julia Agnes, was born in County Wicklow. They had no children. He was a moderate nationalist. He was not present at the time of the raid on his shop, but was arrested later and sent to Richmond Barracks, Dublin. His sister gave evidence to the Royal Commission of

Inquiry stating that the soldiers wrecked the shop, then bombed it with hand grenades. Kelly spent 26 April to 8 May 1916 in Richmond Barracks and was then deported to Wandsworth Prison in London. He was released on 12 May having been roughly treated during his detention. He ran as an independent nationalist candidate in the 1918 general election against the Irish Party candidate William Field and the Sinn Féin candidate Countess Markievicz, who won. His wife died in 1922 and he remarried in 1923. His children included Marie, Maeve and Patricia. A granddaughter posted the following on www.Boards.ie on 25 June 2014: 'He went bankrupt in 1939 … Mr Kelly passed away in 1954.'

Maxwell, 7149 Sergeant John Arthur, was born at Cloneygowan, Portarlington, King's County (Offaly), on 3 May 1887, the son of David Maxwell. In 1893 his father was a constable in the RIC at Upper Philipstown, King's County. The 1901 Census shows John (13), with his siblings Elsie (12) and David (10) living at Clonmore RIC Barracks, King's County, where their father was sergeant. By 1911 his widowed father was a pensioner living at Charleville Demesne, Tullamore, King's County, with his daughter Caroline Constance. At that time John was serving as a corporal with the 1st Royal Irish Rifles in Burma, aged twenty-five. He was a member of their hockey team. As was quite common, he overstated his age on enlistment. He served in the army for eight years and two months and then served as a constable in the RIC for one year and ten months. He joined Leeds City Police as constable number 683 on 27 March 1914. Mobilised on 4 August 1914, he went to France with the 2nd Royal Irish Rifles on 14 August 1914. He was regimental provost sergeant of the 3rd Royal Irish Rifles at Portobello Barracks during the Rising and witnessed the murders there. He also served with the 7th Royal Irish Rifles. Commissioned second lieutenant in the Reserve of Officers, 11 April 1918, he joined the 1st Royal Irish Rifles on 3 October 1918. He was wounded on 15 October 1918. Posted to the 3rd Royal Irish Rifles, he retired on 2 December 1919. He rejoined Leeds City Police on 19 December 1919 and was posted to E Division (CID) on 7 September 1925. He was promoted to sergeant on 12 August 1927. On 5 February 1943 he retired from the police as unfit because of conjunctivitis. He appears to have died in Leeds in 1970.

McIntyre, Patrick James, was born at Ballyconlone in County Wexford on 14 June 1877, the son of James and Bridget McIntyre *née* Fitzpatrick, of Killowen Lower, Gorey, County Wexford. Roman Catholic. The 1901 Census shows that his father was a herdsman. The Kilmainham Prison General Register shows that on 28 February 1901 Patrick was in court on a charge of loitering and was sentenced to two days in prison. Height 5 foot 5¼ inches; red hair and blue eyes. He was then living at Werburgh Street, Dublin, and was described as a hotel porter. The 1911 Census shows his brother Herbert as a pupil at Artane Industrial

School in Dublin. Patrick was then a barman and a visitor at the home of Mrs Marion MacPherson, 6 Swifts Alley, Dublin. In 1916 he was at 12 Fownes Street, Dublin. The Royal Commission of Inquiry was told that his 'loyalty was notorious because his newspaper was founded on that basis – it was the employers' paper he was editor of.'[6] He was a teetotaller. McIntyre is buried in Dean's Grange Cemetery, Dublin.

Morgan, Captain Samuel Valentine, was born on 5 June 1880 at Church Street, Newtownards, County Down, the son of John and Elizabeth Morgan *née* Calwell. Roman Catholic. His father, a shoemaker, was later sergeant instructor of musketry in the 3rd and 4th Royal Irish Rifles. The oldest of eight children, Morgan enlisted on 28 January 1896 as Boy No. 4717 at Newtownards and was posted to the 3rd Royal Irish Rifles as a bugler. He was re-posted as details bugler in the 2nd Royal Irish Rifles and appointed lance corporal on 1 June 1901. On 1 October 1901 he was promoted to corporal and then lance sergeant on 23 September 1902. Posted to the depot and promoted to sergeant on 4 January 1903, he served as orderly room sergeant with the Louth Rifles (6th Royal Irish Rifles Militia) from 1903 to 1908. Lieutenant Colonel A. R. Cole-Hamilton's farewell message of 1908 recalled: 'Sergeant S. V. Morgan, whose never-failing hard work, good temper, zeal, and tact have contributed so much to the excellent state of the battalion.' Posted to the 3rd Royal Irish Rifles on 28 June 1908, he was appointed orderly room sergeant, and promoted to colour-sergeant, then, on 28 June 1911, to quartermaster sergeant. The 1911 Census shows him living with his widowed mother at Conway Square, Newtownards. He married Rose Gertrude Marquess of North Street, Newtownards, a teacher and daughter of John Marquess, a farmer, on 21 August 1911. They lived at Victoria Bar, Belfast and their son John Leo was born on 6 August 1912.

 The Irish Times of 11 February 1915 reported that 'On parade yesterday of all officers, non-commissioned officers and men of the 3rd (Reserve) Battalion, Royal Irish Rifles, at Wellington Barracks, Dublin, under the command of Major F. M. G. McFerran, Brigadier General F. E. Hill, CB, DSO, Commanding 31st Infantry Brigade and Dublin Garrison, presented Lieutenant and Adjutant S. V. Morgan with the Long Service and Good Conduct Medal … In making the presentation General Hill said it was unique for a combatant officer to receive this distinction which was usually awarded to NCOs and men after eighteen years' service whose character was irreproachable. He further said that any soldier might earn the VC for an act of bravery committed on the spur of the moment, but it took a soldier 18 years to earn the Good Conduct Medal. Lieutenant and Adjutant Morgan was awarded the medal on 1 October 1914 on which date he was also gazetted to commissioned rank from the rank of Quartermaster Sergeant. General Hill quotes this officer to the rank and file as an example of how any soldier might rise from the ranks.'

Soon after the Rising Samuel was ordered to the Front but had been ill with tonsillitis. A medical board at Belfast on 23 December 1916 recorded that he had been under treatment and was considerably debilitated. He applied for a posting to a school of instruction. A medical board at King George V Hospital, Dublin, on 28 March 1917 found he was suffering from a deflected septum of the nose. He recovered and was recommended for fourteen days' leave and then was ordered to rejoin his unit. He did so on 1 May 1917 and was posted to the 2nd Royal Irish Rifles. Appointed acting captain of D Company on 1 August 1917, he was killed in action on 10 August.[7]

Morris, Lieutenant Max Cyril, MBE, was born on 16 January 1880 at Liscard, Cheshire, the son of John and Elizabeth Morris. His mother's father, Tim Kinsella, was Irish and worked as a customs officer in Liverpool. The 1881 Census for Wither's Lane, Liscard, shows that Max's father was a ship owner. By 1891 the family was living at 2 Quarry Bank, Liscard, where his father was a coal agent. Max was then a boarder at Seafield School, Victoria Road, Liscard. He later attended Sidcup College. He married Pauline Mortimer Hunt at Epping on 5 February 1900, and lived at Foots Cray, London, working as a traveller for patent medicines. The 1911 Census shows him living at 48 Adamstown Road, Plumstead, with the occupation of telephone engineer, head of the employment department. He was then employed as shipping and transport manager to the Western Electric Co. Ltd, North Woolwich, where he had a staff of fifty men reporting to him, including some clerical workers. He applied for a commission on 18 January 1915: 'The applicant has considerable experience in the handling of transport and has held for some years the position of shipping manager in a firm exporting some thousands of tons of heavy cable and electrical goods annually.' He added: 'This work calls for careful organisation and prompt decisions … It may be useful to mention that I have an expert knowledge of motor cycle engines.' Commissioned as a temporary lieutenant in the Army Service Corps on 31 March 1915, he was posted to the Army Service Corps, Labour Company, at Aldershot. His wife was then living at Belmont Cottage, The Green, Sidcup. Posted to France on 12 April 1915, he was employed at the Labour Depot in Le Havre. On 25 August 1915 he returned to England on transfer to the 11th East Surrey Regiment. He was employed as an instructor with the Young Officers' Company at Moore Park, Kilworth, County Cork. He reported for duty at Portobello Barracks, Dublin on 24 April 1916 and arrested Francis Sheehy Skeffington the next day. He was also involved in the raid on the home of Thomas Dickson on the afternoon of 26 April, as part of a group of two officers and twenty-five men under the command of Captain Murphy, 1st Royal Irish Fusiliers. He left for France to join the 9th East Surrey Regiment in June 1916. Reporting sick on 30 July 1916, he was admitted to the 8th General Hospital, Rouen, then entered the hospital at Osborne, Isle of Wight on 7 August 1916. A medical board held on 11 August 1916 stated: 'Contracted influenza from which he has recovered but looks pale and rather debilitated', so he was sent on sick leave. Ordered to report to Irish Command on 19 August 1916 to give evidence to the Royal Commission of Inquiry, he caught a further chill and was granted further sick leave. He joined the 3rd East Surrey Regiment at Dover on 26 November 1916 and the 12th East Surrey Regiment in France on 1 January 1917, as pioneer officer. He left his unit two weeks later and was admitted to hospital with trench nephritis and influenza. He returned to England on 30 January 1917. 'Anaemic and run down. He sleeps badly. There is a neurasthenic tendency.' He was then employed as deputy assistant, controller of timber supplies, at the Board of Trade, Caxton House, Tothill Street, Westminster. His address in 1919 was 6 Hume Street, Dublin. The *London Gazette* supplement of 30 March 1920 records the fact that he had been awarded an MBE. He relinquished his commission in 1921, with an address at that time of 70 Victoria Street, London SW1. Morris invented new and useful improvements in carburettors for internal combustion engines, US patent number 62,415 in 1926. It was called the RAG carburettor and manufactured at Tooting. RAG may refer to an Irish woman, R. A. Garston, who is thought to have financed the project. Later he had various civilian occupations, including working with motor racing teams. He died at Willesden, London, in 1954, while employed by de Havilland.[8]

O'Carroll, Councillor Richard Patrick, was born in Dublin in 1886. Roman Catholic. Married Annie Esther Power in 1902. In the 1911 Census he was living at 49 Cuffe Street with his six children. He was quartermaster of the 3rd Battalion, C Company, Irish Volunteers. A conflicting account of events during the Rising by Irish Volunteer Seumas Grace stated that O'Carroll had joined him at Earlsfort Terrace. He arrived on his motorbike and sidecar combination in which he had Mauser ammunition that he distributed to the members of the company. He was captured on the return journey, when he was pulled off his bike in Camden Street by Bowen-Colthurst and shot. 'This was a serious blow to us; as a result of it our right flank was left open. O'Carroll had been detailed with four men to hold Parson's shop at the corner of Haddington Road and Baggot Street Bridge'.[9] He died in hospital at Portobello Barracks on 5 May 1916 and is buried in Glasnevin Cemetery, Dublin.[10]

Rosborough, Major James, was born in Ferry Quay Street, Londonderry, on 26 March 1870, the son of Andrew and Jane Rosborough *née* Babington. Presbyterian. His father was a grocer. The 1901 Census shows his parents at Ballycallaghan, Bonds Glen, Londonderry. The 1911 Census records his father as a farmer who had five children living. James was educated at Foyle College, and at Trinity College, Dublin, where he gained his BA in 1894. He also did a 'one year's law course'. Commissioned in the

3rd Royal Irish Rifles Militia in 1893, he was promoted to lieutenant in 1895. Posted to the 6th Royal Irish Rifles (Louth Rifles) Militia in 1896, he was mobilised during the South African War and spent nine months' home service at Sheffield and Aldershot in 1899–1900. On 18 October 1900 he was made an honorary captain. In 1901 he was in West Africa and Gambia with the 2nd Battalion Central Africa Regiment and took part in an expedition against Fodi Kabba, for which he was awarded a medal and clasp. He was also in East Africa and Somaliland in 1902–4 with the 1st King's African Rifles and was company commander with this regiment at Nairobi and Nandi, East Africa, in 1905–6. He was mentioned in dispatches on 18 September 1906. He was seconded to the Louth Rifles 1906–8 and served in Zanzibar and Nyasaland until 1910. On 21 January 1914 he married Erdie Agnes McKinstry. Mobilised at Holywood on 5 August 1914, he was appointed second-in-command of the 3rd Royal Irish Rifles and was promoted to major on 12 September.

General Maxwell felt that Rosborough should resign his commission because of his performance during the Rising. A file cover note dated 6 July 1916 stated: 'This is not a case for disciplinary action. Will you please deal with it?' A letter to Lord Crewe from Reverend Joseph McKinstry (Rosborough's father-in-law and a Presbyterian minister at Randalstown) of 11 July, pleaded the case. The War Office insisted that Rosborough must resign his commission. Rosborough's resignation was dated 28 July. His wife petitioned HM the Queen on her husband's behalf. Reverend McKinstry wrote to Andrew Bonar Law, MP, on 11 August, referring to a meeting they had had the previous day and again pleaded the case. Bonar Law sent the letter to Lloyd George, adding, 'Carson is also interested in the case'. Bonar Law proposed that no action be taken until the special commission in Ireland had reported. A memo dated 11 September advised that the Royal Commission of Inquiry had completely cleared Rosborough's character regarding the affair and enquired whether any military employment had yet been found for him. On 6 November the order to resign was cancelled. Posted to France, he joined the 2nd Royal Irish Rifles on 24 December 1916. He assumed the duties of town major at Bully-Grenay on 26 March 1917. He returned to England on 23 October 1917. Posted to the 30th Liverpool Regiment at Rugby on 1 March 1919, he went with them to France on 19 August 1919, returning to England on 27 January 1920. He was appointed education officer/instructor with the 10th Hussars on 23 October 1920. His father-in-law wrote to Sir Edward Carson, KC, MP, thanking him for arranging this position. Applications by Rosborough for a permanent position as an education officer were rejected. Lieutenant Colonel Seymour of the 10th Hussars stated that, in his opinion, Rosborough was not up to the job: NCOs had been leaving his classes and going to an army schoolmaster. Rosborough wrote to the War Office applying for a position as courts martial officer, but was advised that there were no positions of any sort available for him.

Rosborough was discharged from the Royal Ulster Rifles on 20 April 1921. He lived from 1931 to 1949 at Dunrandal, 2 Norman Road, Kingsway, Hove, Sussex. About 1950 he emigrated to Australia and lived at 25 Billyard Avenue, Elizabeth Bay, Sydney, New South Wales. He died at the War Veterans Home, Narrabeen, NSW, on 30 July 1957.[11]

Tooley, Lieutenant Fred Simmons, MC, was born in Eaton Bray, Dunstable, Bedfordshire on 6 March 1896, the son of Frederick Arthur Hubert and Maria Tooley. His father was a flour miller. The 1901 Census shows Fred living with his grandfather Joseph Pratt, a farmer, at Leighton Road, Buckinghamshire. His parents were at Eaton Bray with his siblings Doris (3) and Marjorie (1). He attended Ashton Grammar School, Dunstable, from 1908 to 1912, after which he began working in the family business. He was gazetted a second lieutenant in the Royal Irish Rifles on 24 August 1915. The Royal Commission of Inquiry noted that he attended and was available as a witness, but was in a delicate state, having returned home on sick leave from the Front with shell-shock. *The London Gazette* of 26 November 1917 recorded that he had been awarded the Military Cross: 'For conspicuous gallantry and devotion to duty. When the enemy had seized a village, the officer organised and led a counter-attack. After driving the enemy out, although he had only ten men left, he held the place against two attacks, only withdrawing when driven out by large forces of the enemy.' Tooley married Dorothy Clara Weitzel at St Michael's Parish Church, Golders Green, Middlesex on 13 April 1918. At that time he was an acting captain in the Royal Irish Rifles. He transferred to the Royal Air Force in 1918. His address in 1920 was Clackaway House, Les Hubitts, Guernsey, Channel Islands. Enlisted as 133881 Lance Corporal in the Royal Artillery, Territorial Army in 1934. He was commissioned a lieutenant in The Queen's Regiment on 15 June 1940 and later promoted to captain. Tooley died in Surrey in 1964.[12]

Wilson, Second Lieutenant Alexander Stewart, was born in Glasgow on 29 January 1897, the son of John Rorison Young and Isabella Wilson *née* Boa. Presbyterian. They moved to Ireland about 1902. The 1911 Census shows the family living at 11 St Columba's Road, Drumcondra, Dublin. His father was an ironfounder's agent. The family later moved to 62 Frankfort Avenue, Rathgar, Dublin. Alexander attended St Andrew's College, Dublin. From January 1915 he was a member of a Voluntary Training Corps in which he was a section commander. He applied for a commission, preferably in a Scottish regiment, on 24 August 1915. He enlisted as 3800 Private in the 6th Black Watch (Royal Highlanders) Territorial Force at Perth, Scotland, on 14 September 1915. Commissioned to the 7th Royal Dublin Fusiliers, 5 October 1915, he was posted to the Irish Command School of Instruction at Moore Park, Fermoy, County Cork. While on leave he reported to Portobello Barracks for duty on 25 April 1916. Wilson was killed in action with the 10th Royal Dublin Fusiliers on 20 April 1917. The *Waterford News* of 4 May 1917 reported that he was the nephew of Robert Costelloe of Tramore, County Waterford. His brother John served in the Second World War as an officer with the East Yorkshire Regiment.[13]

Wilson, Second Lieutenant Leslie, was born at Frizinghall, Yorkshire on 30 September 1895, the only child of Sam Thornton and Ada Wilson. The 1901 Census shows the family living at 76 Beamsley Road, Shipley, Yorkshire. His father was a stuff merchant's manager. By 1911 his father was a dress stuff merchant living at Spring House, Sandy Lane, Allerton, Bradford, Yorkshire. Wilson had a public school education and was an undergraduate divinity student at Trinity College, Dublin when he applied for a commission on 24 August 1915. He was a cadet in the Officers' Training Corps there. Gazetted a second lieutenant in the 6th Royal Irish Fusiliers on 5 October 1915, he was attached to the 4th Battalion. Because of exposure on the rifle range he became ill with pneumonia and was on sick leave from 31 January 1916 at 80 South Circular Road, Portobello, Dublin. A medical board on 27 March 1916 stated that 'although improving, he is still unfit for duty'. Though in poor health, he reported for duty at Portobello Barracks when the rebellion broke out. By 8 May 1916 he was found to be sufficiently recovered for Home Service only and posted back to the 4th Royal Irish Fusiliers. On 9 August 1916 his commanding officer, Lieutenant Colonel J. H. Patterson, sent a confidential memo to the medical board at King George V Hospital, Dublin, stating 'he has been continually on the sick list and when he is at duty he is quite useless and is never likely to become a useful officer. The boy has no vices and would make a good curate – a calling which I understand he desires to adopt.' On that day the board recommended that he should resign his commission and stated 'he is still debilitated and unfit for any but light duty. Being a delicate lad, with a weak constitution, he is considered quite unfit – permanently – for the Service and in this opinion he quite concurs himself.' At the end of August 1916 he stated at the Royal Commission of Inquiry that he was taking Holy Orders. He relinquished his commission on 14 September 1916, and was granted the honorary rank of second lieutenant and a Silver War Badge, being no longer fit for war service. His address was given as The Homestead, Menston-in-Wharfedale. He studied at The London College of Divinity. He returned to 80 South Circular Road in Dublin for the summer of 1917. A medical board on 18 August 1917 found him fit for service and he was ordered to report to the 3rd Royal Irish Fusiliers at Glenfield Camp, Clonmany, County Donegal. He was posted to C Company, 1st Royal Irish Fusiliers, which he joined on 27 April 1918. He was soon found to be inefficient and was sent to II Corps Infantry School for further training from 23 May to 21 June 1918. On completion, the course commander reported that 'this officer lacks power of command, is very poor at drill and is weak in most subjects. He tried hard to improve himself and took an interest in the course.' Having returned to his unit, his company commander, Captain T. S. Jenkinson, reported on 2 July that, owing to Wilson's inefficiency as a platoon commander, 'I cannot venture to take him into action with the Company and have therefore relieved him of his command.' Having 'had every opportunity to perform his duties' the battalion commanding officer decided to get rid of him and passed this wish up through the chain of command. Brigadier General E. Vaughan, 108th Brigade, commented on 12 July 1918: 'I consider him quite unsuitable as an officer and unfit to lead men in the field. He is lacking in military spirit and I do not consider that he should ever have been given a commission and I recommend that his services be dispensed with.' Lieutenant General R. B. Stephens, Commander of X Corps, stated on 23 July 1918: 'It is evident that ... Wilson is of no use as a combatant officer but he appears to be well-intentioned.' Wilson was ordered back to England and arrived on 12 August 1918. He pleaded his case, claiming that he had been sent to the Front without much training. Of particular concern to him was that if he had to resign 'this matter would prevent any Bishop from wanting me at any future time and would therefore ruin my career'. In an interview at the War Office he 'expressed a wish that, if called upon to resign his commission, he might not be noted as eligible to be called up in the ranks, as the Bishop had said he would ordain him'. He resigned his commission on 5 November 1918. The 1939 Register shows him as a vicar at Rowley Regis, Staffordshire, with his wife, Mabel Beatrice. Reverend Wilson died at Burton Road Hospital, Rowley Regis, on 31 May 1965. His estate was valued at £24,745.[14]

ENDNOTES

Introduction
1   Available at: https://en.wikipedia.org/wiki/Francis_Sheehy-Skeffington.
2   Letter from Georgiana Sutherlin (GS) to me dated 21 March 2005, author's (JWT) papers.
3   Letter from Dr Francis Sheehy Skeffington to me dated 29 February 2012, JWT papers.

1   The Background and Early Life of John Bowen-Colthurst
1   *Penticton Herald*, 26 September 1959.

2   War in South Africa
1   Christiaan Rudolf De Wet, *Three Years' War* (Charles Scribner's Sons, New York, 1902), p. 74.
2   Lieutenant Colonel George Brenton Laurie, *History of the Royal Irish Rifles* (Gale & Polden, London, 1914), pp. 379–80.
3   These figures include some men of the 2nd Northumberland Fusiliers who were with the Irish Rifles: two officers killed, twelve men killed or wounded, seventy taken prisoner. Laurie (1914), p. 380.
4   Anon, 'The Last Cartridge: An Incident at Reddersburg', *Black & White Budget*, Vol. 3, No. 28, London, 21 April 1900.
5   De Wet (1902), p. 76. A Burgher was an enfranchised citizen of the South African Republic (Transvaal) during the years of its existence, 1857 to 1900.
6   *Daily Mail*: 'My private diary of the war. A prisoner en route to Pretoria', by the Earl of Rosslyn. Newspaper cutting in the Boer War scrapbook of John Bowen-Colthurst (JBC), Royal Ulster Rifles (RUR) Museum, Belfast.
7   JBC to Georgina Bowen-Colthurst (GBC), letter dated 1 July 1900, RUR Museum.
8   *Ibid.* The Captain Spencer mentioned was Archibald C. D. Spencer. For his Boer War service, Colthurst was awarded the Queen's South Africa Medal with four clasps: Transvaal, Orange Free State, Cape Colony and South Africa 1902.

3   Service in Tibet
1   JBC to Pixie Bowen-Colthurst (PBC), letter dated 6 April 1904, JWT papers. Lieutenant Bertram A. Forbes was a son of the Earl of Granard.
2   JBC to PBC, letter dated 31 May 1904, GS papers.
3   In Tibet, La means a crossing point over a mountain or river. A jong, or dzong, is a fort.

4   Laurie (1914), pp. 335–7.
5   *Ibid.*
6   Tibet scrapbook of JBC, RUR Museum.
7   Tibet diary of JBC, RUR Museum.
8   *Ibid.*
9   JBC to PBC, letter dated 7 August 1904, GS papers.
10 JBC to Eliza Bowen, letter dated 20 August 1904, Tibet scrapbook of JBC, RUR Museum. 34° Fahrenheit is approximately 1°C.
11 JBC to GBC, letter dated 26 August 1904, RUR Museum.
12 Tibet diary of JBC, RUR Museum.
13 Tibet scrapbook of JBC, RUR Museum.
14 *Ibid.*

4   Home Service

1   GS papers.
2   *The Irish Times*, 2 September 1907.
3   Note with JBC's photographs, JWT papers.
4   Sheehy Skeffington papers, MS33,625(5), National Library of Ireland. Court martial transcript.
5   This story was recounted during the section 'Orange Songs' by Kevin Casey on *Sunday Miscellany*, RTÉ Radio 1, on 11 July 2004.
6   Letter from Doug Sutherlin (DS) to me dated 17 January 2012, JWT papers.
7   Fred Crawford (FC) papers. Letter to Lieutenant Colonel William A. G. Saunders-Knox-Gore dated 18 March 1910, Public Record Office of Northern Ireland (PRONI), D/1700/10/1/769–770.
8   Cian O'Carroll, *Knappogue: The Story of an Irish Castle* (Mercier Press for Shannon Heritage, Cork, 2002), p. 50.
9   FC papers, PRONI: D/1700/10/1/922.
10 John Bowen-Colthurst, military file, WO374/14934. JBC to the Military Secretary, 31 January 1940. National Archives, Kew (NAK).
11 A Brahmin is from the highest of the main Hindu castes, whereas a Pathan is of a lesser ethnic group in the area of Pakistan and Afghanistan.
12 John Bowen-Colthurst, Home Office file, HO144/21349, NAK.
13 Comments by Dr Paul Miller to me, 16 May 2008, JWT papers.
14 Sheehy Skeffington personal papers, MS33,625(5), National Library of Ireland.

5   The Great War

1   Captain Gerald Lowry, *From Mons to 1933* (Simkin Marshall, London, 1933), pp. 8–9.
2   War Diary of the 2nd Battalion The Royal Irish Rifles (2RIR), WO95/1415, NAK.
3   Joseph Goss, 'Narrative on the Battle of Le Cateau', *Quis Separabit*, Regimental Journal of the Royal Ulster Rifles, Summer 1961.

4   John F. Lucy, *There's a Devil in the Drum* (Faber, London, 1938), pp. 150–1.
5   Sheehy Skeffington personal papers, MS33,625(5), National Library of Ireland.
6   Lowry (1933), p. 14.
7   *Ibid.*
8   Lucy (1938), pp. 170–1.
9   Lowry (1933), p. 15.
10   War Diary, 2RIR, WO95/1415, NAK.
11   War Diary of the 3rd Division, WO95/1375, NAK.
12   Lowry (1933), pp. 15–16.
13   War Diary, 2RIR, WO95/1415, NAK. I have corrected this extract for the purposes of clarity. Bird erroneously attributed C Company's action to D Company in the original text.
14   Lucy (1938), p. 176.
15   Letter from Dr Paul Miller to me dated 20 September 2012, JWT papers.
16   JBC to Linda Bowen-Colthurst (LBC), letter dated 22 November 1914, JWT papers. Captain R. Wade Thompson of Clonskeagh Castle was deputy lieutenant for the County of Dublin.
17   Comments by Dr Paul Miller to me, 16 May 2008, JWT papers.
18   John Bowen-Colthurst, military file, WO374/14934, NAK. King George V Hospital was later renamed St Bricin's Military Hospital.
19   JBC to LBC, letter dated 22 December 1914, JWT papers.
20   John Bowen-Colthurst, military file, WO374/14934, NAK.
21   Comments by Dr Paul Miller to me, 16 May 2008, JWT papers.

6   A Career Ruined

1   John Bowen-Colthurst, military file, WO374/14934, NAK.
2   Comments by Dr Paul Miller to me, 16 May 2008, JWT papers.
3   John Bowen-Colthurst, military file, WO374/14934, NAK.
4   *Ibid.*
5   *Ibid.*
6   Georgina Bowen-Colthurst (1916), 'Career of Captain J. C. Bowen-Colthurst', unpublished typescript, JWT papers.
7   Comdt Patrick D. O'Donnell, 'A Short History of Portobello Barracks', *An Cosantóir*, Journal of the Irish Defence Forces, February 1969.
8   Letter from Dr Francis Sheehy Skeffington to me dated 16 August 2012, JWT papers.
9   Joost Augusteijn (ed.), *The Memoirs of John M. Regan, a Catholic Officer in the RIC and RUC, 1909–48* (Four Courts Press, Dublin, 2007), pp. 87–9. Regan was a member of the Court of Inquiry held in Belfast on 10 May 1916.
10   Sheehy Skeffington papers, MS41,209/5.
11   Dublin Castle Special Branch Files, Francis Sheehy Skeffington, CO 904/215/408, NAK.

12 Royal Commission of Inquiry as detailed in *Weekly Irish Times*, 'Sinn Fein Rebellion Handbook, Easter 1916' (Dublin, 1917), p. 222.

13 Sheehy Skeffington papers, MS40,473/3, referring to the 1798 Rebellion. James Robert 'Jack' White, DSO, the son of Field Marshal Sir George Stuart White, VC, GCB, OM, GCSI, GCMG, GCIE, GCVO, County Antrim.

14 Bureau of Military History (BMH), Irish Military Archives, Cathal Brugha Barracks, Dublin. Witness Statement (WS) 1769 by Patrick J. Little.

7 The 1916 Rising

1 *Weekly Irish Times*, 2 September 1916.

2 Witness Statement by Mrs Julia Hughes, BMH WS 880. The house has since been re-numbered as 21 Grosvenor Place.

3 Enquiry into the death of the late Sheehy Skeffington, WO35/67, NAK.

4 *Weekly Irish Times* (1917), p. 224. The venue was the Women's Franchise Rooms in the building.

5 Sir Francis Fletcher Vane, *Agin the Governments* (Sampson Low, Marston and Co. Ltd, London, 1928), p. 263.

6 Sheehy Skeffington papers, MS33,625(5). Witness Statement by Andrew McDonnell, Irish Volunteer Officer, BMH WS 1769: 'Jim Coade, a neighbour ... had no connection with the Volunteers whatever.' Laurence Byrne lived at 7 Upper Mount Pleasant Avenue. He stated at the inquiry that Coade was smoking a cigarette and Colthurst told him to take that 'damned' cigarette out of his mouth. Coade threw it to the ground. Father Joseph O'Toole cuttings, BMH, p. 90. See the short biographies in this book for more information on Coade (p. 254), Wilson (p. 262) and Aldridge (p. 250).

7 Sheehy Skeffington papers, MS33,625(5).

8 *Ibid.*, MS33,605(8). Farrell had written to Hanna Sheehy Skeffington (HSS) on 24 December 1916.

9 Séamus O'Farrell, BMH WS 193.

10 Michael Noyk, BMH WS 707, p. 8.

11 The *Weekly Irish Times*, 2 September 1916, gave details of a Melbourne newspaper article from early July that was presented to the Simon Commission on 28 August: 'The communication professed to be a record of the experiences of an Australian officer who was present. It contained this statement: "They called for bombers and I was turned over to a captain, an enormous man of about 6 foot 4 inches. At 10.30 we went and attacked a shop ... near the barracks we saw three men. The captain wanted to know their business and one answered back, and so the captain just knocked him insensible with the butt of his rifle."'

12 *Weekly Irish Times* (1917), p. 209. Sir John Simon, chair of the Royal Commission of Inquiry, stated that Sheehy Skeffington, being of a superior social position, was put into a separate cell and made as comfortable as possible. Enquiry into the death of the late Sheehy Skeffington, WO95/67, NAK. The guardroom register for 25 April 1916

shows that Sheehy Skeffington was detained at 8 p.m. and the other two journalists were detained at midnight.

13   Comments by Dr Paul Miller to me, 16 May 2008: 'The understanding that Colthurst took from the passage sounds very much like an autochthonous (primary) delusion, but in this case it does not fit with a diagnosis of schizophrenia, rather it fits with the functioning of a mind under extreme stress.' JWT papers.

14   Monk Gibbon, *Inglorious Soldier* (Hutchinson, London, 1968), p. 43. This book gives a detailed account of what happened in the barracks but contains some errors, especially when it comes to personalities. Gibbon (1896–1987) was the son of a Church of Ireland clergyman. He went on to become a conscientious objector and respected writer. He was in close contact with Major Vane during and after the rebellion, admiring and unquestioningly believing his version of events. Vane also supported him in his later difficulties with the army, which influenced his interpretation and reporting of the situation. See Appendix II.

15   Gibbon (1968), pp. 44–5.

16   Statement of Michael Ireland, Court of Inquiry at Belfast, 10 May 1916, WO35/67, NAK. There are conflicting accounts that seven armed men were brought out to the yard to form the firing party. It seems that Rifleman Ireland was incorrectly counted among them.

17   *Weekly Irish Times* (1917), p. 224.

18   Sheehy Skeffington papers, MS33,625(5).

19   GBC (1916), JWT papers.

20   Hanna Sheehy Skeffington, *British Militarism as I Have Known It* (The Donnelly Press, New York, 1917). There must be a suspicion that the quote, 'he'll die later', may be an embellishment adopted from Major Goodman's recollection of the dog-shooting incident in India.

21   Sheehy Skeffington papers, MS33,625(6).

22   John J. (Seán) Murphy, BMH WS 204, and Thomas Slater, BMH WS 263.

23   Military Service Pensions Collection (MSP) for Patrick Nolan, Irish Military Archives, MSP33, Ref: 21180.

24   Letter to Monk Gibbon cited in O'Donnell (1969).

25   Major James Rosborough, military file, WO339/27301, NAK. From a statement he made on 22 July 1924.

26   Enquiry into the death of the late Sheehy Skeffington, WO35/67, NAK. Company Sergeant Major James Lyle had been part of the detachment Colthurst led in Tibet. A Belfast man, he enlisted in 1894 and was discharged from the army on 11 June 1916, aged forty-two, on completion of his service.

27   Gibbon (1968), p. 62.

28   Letter from Dr Paul Miller to me dated 11 January 2015, JWT papers.

29   *Ibid.*

30   *Weekly Irish Times* (1917), p. 106.

31   See Appendix II.

32   Captain E. Gerrard, BMH WS 348.

33   Gibbon (1968), p. 48.

34   Sheehy Skeffington papers, MS33,605(8). Farrell subsequently deserted and fled to the USA. He was writing from 146 Washington Street, Waterbury, Connecticut.

35   *Weekly Irish Times* (1917), p. 22. Father O'Loughlin was born in Australia in 1868.

36   *Ibid.*, p. 213.

37   *Ibid.*

38   Enquiry into the death of the late Sheehy Skeffington, WO35/67, NAK.

39   An interview from RTÉ Archives as broadcast on *Bowman*, RTÉ Radio 1, 16 August 2015. A report in both *The Times* and *The Manchester Guardian* of 25 August 1916 stated that 'Sir John Simon had visited the house and some bullet marks were there. Mr Healy replied that a mason and labourer were employed to deface [*sic*] the marks that were made by the fusillade'. Cooney and Colley viewed the house before Sir John's reported visit.

40   Enquiry into the death of the late Sheehy Skeffington, WO35/67, NAK.

41   *Weekly Irish Times* (1917), p. 219.

42   Major James Rosborough, military file, WO339/27301, NAK.

43   *Hansard*, 31 December 1916, Sir James MacPherson's reply to Laurence Ginnell.

44   Major Vane, military files, WO339/13888, NAK. See Appendix II.

45   Vane (1928), p. 268.

46   Enquiry into the death of the late Sheehy Skeffington, WO35/67, NAK.

47   *Ibid.* Major William S. B. Leatham was a district inspector with the RIC who had been seconded for military service during the war.

48   Enquiry into the death of the late Sheehy Skeffington, WO35/67, NAK.

49   Vane (1928), p. 269.

8   Consequences

1   'Confidential report by F. H. Boland', Alfred Bucknill, BMH WS 1019, p. 2.

2   *Ibid.*

3   *Ibid.*, p. 1.

4   John Bowen-Colthurst, military file WO374/14934, NAK.

5   Enquiry into the death of the late Sheehy Skeffington, WO35/67, NAK.

6   John Bowen-Colthurst, military file, WO374/14934, NAK.

7   *Ibid.*

8   *Ibid.* The Irish attorney-general then decided that the amendment was unnecessary and that a general court martial could proceed under the Army Act.

9   Sheehy Skeffington papers, MS33,605(4).

10   *Ibid.*

11   Sheehy Skeffington papers, MS33,608(1).

12   GBC to JBC, letter dated 5 June 1916, quoting from Phil. 4:6–7, JWT papers.

13   Richard M. Fox, *Louie Bennett: Her Life and Times* (Talbot Press, Dublin, 1958), pp. 59–60.

14   United Press Association, London, 6 June 1916, per the National Library of New Zealand.

15   A transcript of the evidence is contained in the Sheehy Skeffington papers, MS33,625(5), and is the source of all the witness quotes from the trial.

16   John Bowen-Colthurst, military file, WO374/14934, NAK.

17   Letter from Dr Francis Sheehy Skeffington to me dated 16 August 2012, JWT papers.

18   Fox (1958), p. 61.

19   Timothy M. Healy, *Letters and Leaders of My Day*, Vol. 2 (Thornton Butterworth, London, 1928), pp. 562–3. Details of a 'wild life' are not provided in the available court transcript but it is the case that Colthurst had a penchant for womanising.

20   Sheehy Skeffington papers, MS33,605(5).

21   Weir to JBC, letter dated 5 June 1916, JWT papers.

22   John Bowen-Colthurst, military file, WO374/14934, NAK.

23   Thompson to JBC, letter dated 2 July 1916, JWT papers.

24   John Bowen-Colthurst, Home Office file, HO144/21349, NAK. I have no information regarding an insane cousin.

25   Major James Rosborough, military file, WO339/27301, NAK.

9   Broadmoor

1   John Bowen-Colthurst, Home Office file, HO144/21349, NAK. Colthurst was Broadmoor inmate number 316/018.

2   Holden to JBC, letter dated 3 August 1916. Holden, an evangelical Christian, was then vicar at St Paul's Church, Portman Square, London. JWT papers.

3   JBC personal papers, RUR Museum.

4   *Weekly Irish Times*, 2 September 1916.

5   *Weekly Irish Times* (1917), p. 216.

6   Father Joseph O'Toole, 1916 press cuttings from the *Irish Independent*, p. 96, Military Archives, Dublin, 227/39.

7   *Weekly Irish Times*, 2 September 1916.

8   *Ibid.*, 21 October 1916.

9   Trinity College, Dublin, Manuscript Department, MS2074, 'Ireland in 1916'. Quoted in 'Called to Arms: Australian Soldiers in the Easter Rising 1916' by Jeff Kildea in the online *Journal of the Australian War Memorial*.

10   JBC papers, RUR Museum.

11   Hunt to JBC, letter dated 15 October 1916, JWT papers.

12   John Bowen-Colthurst, Home Office file, HO144/21349, NAK.

13   *Ibid.*

14   *Manual of Military Law* (War Office, HMSO, London, 1914), p. 5.

15   John Bowen-Colthurst, military file, WO374/14934, NAK.

16 John Bowen-Colthurst, Home Office file, HO144/21349, NAK.

17 *Morning Post*, 26 June 1917.

18 John Bowen-Colthurst, Home Office file, HO144/21349, NAK.

19 *Ibid.*

20 *Ibid.*

21 *Ibid.* The Notts and Derby boys were the Sherwood Foresters killed in the action at Mount Street Bridge.

22 JBC personal papers, RUR Museum.

23 John Bowen-Colthurst, Home Office file, HO144/21349, NAK. Reverend Colthurst had been chaplain of the Royal Hibernian Military School until 1903.

24 *Ibid.*

25 JBC papers, RUR Museum.

26 *Ibid.*

27 John Bowen-Colthurst, Home Office file, HO144/21349, NAK. Carson, a cabinet minister without portfolio, had led the UVF in opposition to Home Rule for Ireland.

28 Milner to LBC, letter dated 19 October 1917, JWT papers.

29 JBC personal papers, RUR Museum.

30 *Ibid.*

31 *Ibid.*

32 John Bowen-Colthurst, Home Office file, HO144/21349, NAK. Archer-Shee's half-brother was George Archer-Shee, whose expulsion from Osborne Naval College inspired the play *The Winslow Boy*.

33 *Ibid.*

34 Craig to LBC, letter dated 28 December 1917, JWT papers. Craig, later 1st Viscount Craigavon, had mobilised the pre-war unionist resistance to Home Rule and helped to organise the UVF. He became the first premier of Northern Ireland.

35 JBC personal papers, RUR Museum.

36 *Ibid.*

37 *Ibid.*

38 *Ibid.*

39 *Ibid.*

10 Towards Freedom

1 FC papers, PRONI, D/1700/5/13/21.

2 John Bowen-Colthurst, Ministry of Pensions file, PIN26/21245, NAK.

3 John Bowen-Colthurst, Home Office file, HO144/21349, NAK.

4 *Ibid.*

5 *Ibid.*

6 *Ibid.*

7 JBC personal papers, RUR Museum.

8 Dr Thomas W. Lumsden had arranged a scheme whereby shell-shocked soldiers in England were allowed to work and recover in participating country estates.

9   John Bowen-Colthurst, Ministry of Pensions file, PIN26/21245, NAK.
10   John Bowen-Colthurst, Home Office file, HO144/21349, NAK.
11   *Ibid.*
12   GBC to JBC, letter dated 13 August 1918, JWT papers.
13   John Bowen-Colthurst, Home Office file, HO144/21349, NAK.
14   *Ibid.*
15   John Bowen-Colthurst, Ministry of Pensions file, PIN26/21245, NAK.
16   *Ibid.*
17   JBC personal papers, RUR Museum.
18   Hornby to JBC, letter dated 3 December 1918, JWT papers.
19   John Bowen-Colthurst, Home Office file, HO144/21349, NAK.
20   *Ibid.* Psychasthenia was considered to be an obsessive-compulsive disorder whereby a person lacked the capacity to resolve doubts and uncertainties or to resist obsessions that are known to be irrational.
21   *Ibid.*
22   JBC personal papers, RUR Museum.
23   *Ibid.*
24   Anonymous leaflet, undated, JWT papers.
25   Witness Statement by Michael O'Sullivan, BMH WS 793.
26   John Bowen-Colthurst, military file, WO374/14934, NAK.
27   John Bowen-Colthurst, Home Office file, HO144/21349, NAK.
28   *Ibid.*
29   Letter from Royds to HSS dated 18 January 1921, Sheehy Skeffington papers, MS24,14.
30   Mrs Peggy Bowen-Colthurst Scott (1938), reminiscences held by Georgiana Sutherlin (GS papers). Georgina actually died in Cork, not London.
31   Edward Neville, BMH WS 1665, p. 3.
32   Jeremiah Murphy, BMH WS 772, pp. 5–6.
33   Statement by Captain Séamas Moran, Irish Military Archives, MSP34, Ref: 10227.
34   This address led to the incorrect assumption that he became a bank manager, as stated in *Church and State in Modern Ireland, 1923–1979* (Dublin, 1984) by Professor John H. Whyte, and has been repeated in many publications.
35   LBC to JBC, telegram dated 26 April 1921, JWT papers.
36   Michael Mullane, BMH WS 1689.
37   *The Irish Times,* 2 December 1921. Georgina's English estate held assets valued at £4,516/15/–.
38   Peter Hart, *The I.R.A. at War 1916–1923* (OUP, Oxford, 2003), p. 205.
39   LBC to JBC, letter dated 25 May 1921, JWT papers.

11 Canada

1   Nadine Asante, *The History of Terrace* (Terrace Public Library Association, British Columbia, 1972), p. 105. Marianne Holtham (1869–1956) went to Canada with Linda Bowen-Colthurst as governess to the children and seems to have returned to England in 1925.

2   Tim Sheerin, *Lady Hostage* (privately printed, Dripsey, County Cork, 1990), p. 194.

3   Mrs Peggy Bowen-Colthurst Scott (1938), reminiscences held by Georgiana Sutherlin (GS papers).

4   Information provided by Lord Dunboyne, letter dated 29 March 2006, JWT papers.

5   Patrick Hegarty, BMH WS 1606, pp. 27–8.

6   John Bowen-Colthurst, Home Office file, HO144/21349, NAK.

7   *Ibid.*

8   *Ibid.*

9   Letter from GS to me dated 15 August 2005, JWT papers.

10 John Bowen-Colthurst, Home Office file, HO144/21349, NAK.

11 *Ibid.*

12 *Ibid.*

13 John Francis Bosher, *Vancouver Island in the Empire* (Llumina Press, Plantation, Florida, 2012), eBook version.

14 *The Daily Colonist*, 6 March 1934.

15 John Bowen-Colthurst, Home Office file, HO144/21349, NAK.

16 *The Daily Colonist*, 1 May 1940.

17 John Bowen-Colthurst, Home Office file, HO144/21349, NAK.

18 *Ibid.*

19 *Ibid.*

20 John Bowen-Colthurst, military file, WO374/14934, NAK.

21 John Bowen-Colthurst, Home Office file, HO144/21349, NAK.

22 Sheehy Skeffington papers, MS41,178/97. Matier, a clerk with the Liquor Control Board, originally came from Kilkeel, County Down.

23 GS papers.

24 Sheehy Skeffington papers, MS41,178/97, signature illegible.

25 *Ibid.*

26 Yates to JBC, letter dated 5 February 1938, JWT papers. The exact cause for this is not known.

27 Letter from Gillett-Gatty to Hanna Sheehy Skeffington dated 14 June 1939. Sheehy Skeffington papers, MS 177/17.

28 *Ibid.*

29 *Ibid.*

30 *Ibid.*

31 *Ibid.*

32 *Ibid.*

33 *Ibid.*

34 *Ibid.*

35 John Bowen-Colthurst, military file, WO374/14934, NAK.

36 Priscilla Bowen-Colthurst (1989), 'My Life', memoirs held by Georgiana Sutherlin (GS papers).

37 John Bowen-Colthurst, Home Office file, HO144/21349, NAK. The *Hie Maru*, previously *Hiye Maru*, had been renamed in 1938.

38 *Ibid.*

39 John Bowen-Colthurst, military file, WO374/14934, NAK.
40 John Bowen-Colthurst, Home Office file, HO144/21349, NAK.
41 *Ibid.*
42 *Ibid*
43 *Ibid.*
44 *Ibid.*
45 John Bowen-Colthurst, military file, WO374/14934, NAK. Tophet was a place near Jerusalem where Canaanites sacrificed children to their god, and Pertinax was a Roman Emperor.
46 *Ibid.*

12 Final Years

1   Priscilla Bowen-Colthurst (1989), GS papers.
2   Elizabeth Bowen, *Bowen's Court* (Little Brown, New York, 1942), p. 438.
3   JBC to Elizabeth Bowen, letter dated 19 June 1943, GS papers.
4   Colthurst spoke English, French, German and Spanish fluently, and Persian, Urdu, Pashto, Hindi, Dutch and Japanese with varying degrees of proficiency.
5   JBC to Elizabeth Bowen, letter dated 22 February 1946, GS papers.
6   Priscilla Bowen-Colthurst (1989), GS papers.
7   GS papers.
8   Letter from GS to me dated 11 March 2004, JWT papers.
9   Letter from GS to me dated 2 May 2005, JWT papers. The British-Israel-World Federation believes that the Ten Lost Tribes of the Northern House of Israel's descendants are to be found in the Anglo-Saxon-Celtic and kindred peoples of today. It also believes the Covenants made between God and Abraham, Isaac and Jacob are everlasting, and that the British nation plays an important part in God's plan.
10 *Penticton Herald*, 26 September 1959. Interview with reporter Bill Stavdal.
11 Priscilla Bowen-Colthurst (1989), GS papers.
12 Doug Sutherlin (DS) letter to me dated 16 January 2012, JWT papers.
13 DS letter to me dated 17 January 2012, JWT papers.
14 Letter from GS to me dated 18 October 2005, JWT papers.
15 JBC to Elizabeth Bowen, letter dated 3 August 1963, GS papers.
16 DS letter to me dated 25 January 2012, JWT papers.
17 DS letter to me dated 16 January 2012, JWT papers.
18 Priscilla Bowen-Colthurst (1989), GS papers.
19 Letter dated January 1966, GS papers.
20 Memorial leaflet for JBC, JWT papers.
21 Letter from GS to me dated 5 March 2004, JWT papers.
22 Letter from GS to me dated 16 November 2006, JWT papers.

13 Conclusion

1   *Weekly Irish Times* (1917), pp. 116–21; Tom Tulloch-Marshall, 'CQMS Robert Flood and His Part in the Tragedy at the Guinness Brewery,

Dublin, April 28th 1916', *The Armourer*, issue 43 (Beaumont Publishing Ltd, Cheshire, 2001), pp. 29–32.

Appendix 1 Battle of the Aisne: Sworn statements
1   John Bowen-Colthurst, military file, WO374/14934, NAK.

Appendix 2 Allegations against Major Sir Francis Fletcher Vane, Bt
1   Extracts are taken from his military files, WO339/13388 and 13389, NAK.
2   Bertha von Suttner was awarded the 1905 Nobel Peace Prize.
3   This was reiterated in another inaccurate account of events in *The Irish Times* on 26 August 2006 by Dara Redmond, a grandson of Thomas MacDonagh, who was one of the executed rebel leaders: 'it was Sir Francis … who won our respect'.

Biographies of Characters in this Narrative
1   Pension file, WO364/26, NAK. Additional details supplied by Liam Dodd.
2   Military file, WO339/42322, NAK.
3   Military file, WO339/26595, NAK.
4   Father Joseph O'Toole cuttings, BMH, p. 94.
5   Father Joseph O'Toole cutting from the *Irish Independent*, BMH.
6   Father Joseph O'Toole cuttings, BMH, p. 97.
7   Military file, WO339/21471, NAK. Additional details supplied by his grandson, Hugh Pitfield. In a letter dated 9 May 1916 to General Maxwell, Mr Skeffington, Frank's father, stated 'I may add that Lieutenant Morgan (a friend of my son's) deplored this miscarriage of justice, but only knew of the affair when all was over'.
8   Military file, WO339/27109, NAK. Additional details supplied by his grandson, Martin Hugh Morris.
9   Seumas Grace, BMH WS 310, pp. 4–5.
10   Military Archives, WID237.
11   Military file, WO339/27301, NAK.
12   Royal Air Force Officers' service records, AIR76/510/50, NAK.
13   Military file, WO339/43896, NAK.
14   Military file, WO339/43897, NAK.

BIBLIOGRAPHY

Unpublished Sources

Author's (JWT) papers

Taylor, James W. (JWT), collection of letters, papers and photographs; in the possession of the author in Wexford, Ireland

Bowen-Colthurst, Georgina (1916), 'Career of Captain J. C. Bowen-Colthurst', unpublished typescript held by JWT

Bowen-Colthurst, John (JBC), personal papers held by JWT

Bowen-Colthurst, Pixie (PBC), letter dated 6 April 1904 held by JWT

Bowen-Colthurst, Rosalinda (Linda) (LBC), letters held by JWT

Georgiana Sutherlin (GS) papers

Sutherlin, Georgiana (GS), private family papers; in the possession of GS in Spokane, Washington State, USA

Bowen-Colthurst, Priscilla (1989), 'My Life', memoirs held by GS

Scott, Mrs Peggy Bowen-Colthurst (1938), reminiscences held by GS

Other

Bowen-Colthurst, Georgina (GBC), papers held in JWT papers or Royal Ulster Rifles (RUR) Museum, Belfast

Bowen-Colthurst, John (JBC), personal papers, including his Boer War scrapbook and Tibet diary and scrapbook, held by the RUR Museum, Belfast

Bowen-Colthurst, John, military file, WO374/14934; Home Office file, HO144/21349; Ministry of Pensions file, PIN26/21245, National Archives, Kew

Bowen-Colthurst, Robert MacGregor, military file, WO339/26595, National Archives, Kew

Bureau of Military History (BMH), witness statements, Irish Military Archives, Cathal Brugha Barracks, Dublin

Crawford, Fred (FC), personal papers held at the Public Record Office of Northern Ireland (PRONI), manuscript files D/1700/10/1/847, 895, 922, 935–6, 960

Dublin Castle Special Branch Files, Francis Sheehy Skeffington, CO 904/215/408, National Archives, Kew

'Enquiry into the death of the late Sheehy Skeffington', WO35/67 and WO95/67, National Archives, Kew

Hansard

Kilmainham Prison General Registers, National Archives, Dublin
Military Service Pensions Collection (MSP), Military Archives, Dublin
Mountjoy Prison General Registers, National Archives, Dublin
O'Toole, Father Joseph, 1916 press cuttings, Military Archives, Dublin, 227/39
Sheehy Skeffington, Francis and Hanna, personal papers held at the National Library of Ireland, manuscript files
Trinity College, Dublin, Manuscript Department, 'Ireland in 1916', MS 2074
Vane, Sir Francis Fletcher, military files, WO339/13388 and 13389, National Archives, Kew
War Diary of the 2nd Battalion, the Royal Irish Rifles, WO95/1415, National Archives, Kew
War Diary of the 3rd Division, WO95/1375, National Archives, Kew
Witherow, Thomas Hastings, 'Personal recollections of the Great War' (1920), Liddle Collection, Leeds University

Printed Sources

Allen, Charles, *Duel in the Snows: The True Story of the Younghusband Mission to Lhasa* (John Murray, London, 2004)
Anon, 'The Last Cartridge: An Incident at Reddersburg', *Black & White Budget*, Vol. 3, No. 28, 21 April 1900 (London)
Asante, Nadine, *The History of Terrace* (Terrace Public Library Association, British Columbia, 1972)
Augusteijn, Joost (ed.), *The Memoirs of John M. Regan, a Catholic Officer in the RIC and RUC, 1909–48* (Four Courts Press, Dublin, 2007)
Berne, Eric, M.D., *Games People Play: The Psychology of Human Relationships* (Ballantine Books, New York, 1964)
Bosher, John Francis, *Vancouver Island in the Empire* (Llumina Press, Plantation, Florida, 2012)
Bowen, Elizabeth, *Bowen's Court* (Little, Brown, New York, 1942)
Caulfield, Max, *The Easter Rebellion* (Gill & Macmillan, Dublin, 1963)
Clutterbuck, Colonel Lewis A. in association with Colonel William T. Dooner and Commander the Hon. Conyngham A. Denison (eds), *The Bond of Sacrifice* (Anglo-African Publishing Contractors, London, 1916)
Cody, Séamus, John O'Dowd and Peter Rigney, *The Parliament of Labour: 100 Years of the Dublin Council of Trade Unions* (Dublin Council of Trade Unions, Dublin, 1986)
de Rosa, Peter, *Rebels: The Irish Rising of 1916* (Bantam Press, London, 1990)
De Wet, Christiaan Rudolf, *Three Years' War* (Charles Scribner's Sons, New York, 1902)

Doherty, Gabriel and Dermot Keogh (eds), *1916: The Long Revolution* (Mercier Press, Cork, 2007)

Downer, Martyn, *The Sultan of Zanzibar: The Bizarre World and Spectacular Hoaxes of Horace de Vere Cole* (Black Spring Press, London, 2010)

Falls, Cyril, *The History of the First Seven Battalions: The Royal Irish Rifles in the Great War* (Gale and Polden, Aldershot, 1925)

Fleming, Peter, *Bayonets to Lhasa* (Rupert Hart-Davis, London, 1961)

Fox, Richard M., *Louie Bennett: Her Life and Times* (Talbot Press, Dublin, 1958)

Foy, Michael and Brian Barton, *The Easter Rising* (The History Press, Stroud, Gloucestershire, 1999)

Gibbon, Monk, *Inglorious Soldier* (Hutchinson, London, 1968)

Goss, Joseph, 'Narrative on the Battle of Le Cateau', *Quis Separabit*, Regimental Journal of the Royal Ulster Rifles, Summer 1961

Graves, C. Desmond, *The Irish Transport and General Workers' Union* (Gill & Macmillan, Dublin, 1982)

Hart, Peter, *The I.R.A. at War 1916–1923* (OUP, Oxford, 2003)

Healy, Timothy M., *Letters and Leaders of My Day*, Vol. 2 (Thornton Butterworth, London, 1928)

Hegarty, Shane and Fintan O'Toole, *The Irish Times Book of the 1916 Irish Rising* (Gill & Macmillan, Dublin, 2006)

Howard, Joseph Jackson, LL.D., and Frederick Arthur Crisp (eds), *Visitation of Ireland* (privately printed, 1897)

Kildea, Jeff, 'Called to Arms: Australian Soldiers in the Easter Rising 1916', *Journal of the Australian War Memorial*, https://www.awm.gov.au/journal/j39/kildea/

Laurie, Lieutenant Colonel George Brenton, *History of the Royal Irish Rifles* (Gale & Polden, London, 1914)

Levenson, Leah, *With Wooden Sword: A Portrait of Francis Sheehy Skeffington, Militant Pacifist* (Gill & Macmillan, Dublin, 1983)

Lewis, Samuel, *A Topographical Dictionary of Ireland* (S. Lewis and Co., London, 1837)

Lowry, Captain Gerald, *From Mons to 1933* (Simkin Marshall, London, 1933)

Lucy, John F., *There's a Devil in the Drum* (Faber, London, 1938)

O'Carroll, Cian, *Knappogue: The Story of an Irish Castle* (Mercier Press for Shannon Heritage, Cork, 2002)

O'Donnell, Comdt Patrick D., 'A Short History of Portobello Barracks', *An Cosantóir*, Journal of the Irish Defence Forces, February 1969

Peake, William (compiler), *A Collection of Orange and Protestant Songs* (published under the authority of the Grand Lodge of Ireland and the Grand Black Chapter of Ireland, Belfast, 1907)

Rosslyn, Earl of, *Twice Captured: A Record of Adventure during the Boer War* (W. Blackwood, Edinburgh, 1900)

Sheehy Skeffington, Hanna, *British Militarism as I Have Known It* (The Donnelly Press, New York, 1917)

Sheerin, Tim, *Lady Hostage* (privately printed, Dripsey, County Cork, 1990)

Taylor, James W., *The 2nd Royal Irish Rifles in the Great War* (Four Courts Press, Dublin, 2005)

Thom's Official Directory, 1912 (Alex Thom and Co., Dublin, 1912)

Tulloch-Marshall, Tom, 'CQMS Robert Flood and His Part in the Tragedy at the Guinness Brewery, Dublin, April 28th 1916', *The Armourer*, issue 43 (Beaumont Publishing, Cheshire, 2001)

Vane, Sir Francis Fletcher, Bt, *Agin the Governments* (Sampson Low, Marston and Co. Ltd, London, 1928)

Ward, Margaret, *Hanna Sheehy Skeffington: A Life* (Attic Press, Cork, 1997)

War Office, *Manual of Military Law* (HMSO, London, 1914)

Weekly Irish Times, 'Sinn Fein Rebellion Handbook, Easter 1916' (Dublin, 1917)

Who Was Who 1897–1990 (A. & C. Black, London, 1991)

Whyte, Prof. John H., *Church and State in Modern Ireland, 1923–1979* (Dublin, 1984)

Wilson, Herbert W., *With the Flag to Pretoria* (Harmsworth Brothers, London, 1901)

World Health Organization (WHO), *The International Statistical Classification of Disease and Related Health Problems,* 10th Revision (ICD–10) (WHO, Geneva, 2007)

Yeates, Padraig, *Lockout: Dublin 1913* (Gill & Macmillan, Dublin, 2000)

INDEX

280